Van Heflin

Van Heflin, MGM publicity still for *East Side, West Side* in 1949.

Van Heflin
A Life in Film

DEREK SCULTHORPE

McFarland & Company, Inc., Publishers
Jefferson, North Carolina

ISBN (print) 978-0-7864-9686-0
ISBN (ebook) 978-1-4766-2303-0

LIBRARY OF CONGRESS CATALOGUING DATA ARE AVAILABLE

BRITISH LIBRARY CATALOGUING DATA ARE AVAILABLE

Printed in the United States of America

*McFarland & Company, Inc., Publishers
Box 611, Jefferson, North Carolina 28640
www.mcfarlandpub.com*

To my dear aunt Audrey
who never forgot *Green Dolphin Street*

Table of Contents

Acknowledgments

I wish to thank my researcher at Norman, Oklahoma, Julie Moring; also Jim Kyle, editor of *The New Classen Life*; and Elizabeth Windes and Ron Stewart in Oklahoma. I would especially like to thank Elizabeth McCall in New York and Suzanne Noruschat, archivist Yale University Library for taking so much time on my behalf. I would like to thank Guy Budziak for his invaluable help and Adolfo Fernandez-Punsola for his great support and encouragement. I also wish to thank Ron Stevenson for his helpful input; and the wonderful Lizabeth Scott for her kind response to my inquiries. Thanks also to Kristina L. Southwell, Archivist of The Western History Collection at the University of Oklahoma Library for her assistance, and Joe L. Smith, Nicole Holford Lockney, Arthur Grant and Bob DiMucci. Finally I wish to thank my parents, my sister Janie, brother-in-law Gerhard and my aunt Audrey for their encouragement.

Preface

"You always sat tall in the saddle for me as a kid growing up. You were a strong male figure in my life.... Thank you for what you did for the kid sitting in the darkness before the big silver screen..."—Patrick Gooden, November 26, 2013[1]

The above quote is one of more than 1500 tributes to Van Heflin on a website called Find a Grave which is devoted to the final resting places of famous and ordinary people alike. There is no physical memorial for Heflin; his ashes were scattered in the Pacific Ocean in accordance with his wishes, for it may be truly said of him that his heart never left the sea. But film stars need no tombstone; their legacy never leaves us. It influences us ever after, often in the subtlest of ways. Patrick Gooden's words are heartfelt and sincere; they speak for generations for whom *Shane* is not just a Western but perhaps one of the most moving allegories of the human condition committed to celluloid. The decent virtues which Heflin's character Joe Starrett embodies are hardly likely to perish while men continue to strive to improve their lot. Heflin is not the lead and his character might appear dull and resolutely ordinary; but in this actor's hands, Starrett lives for all time and his quiet heroism is never forgotten.

This is the first full-length book about Van Heflin, who for me is the most overlooked actor of his generation. He brought such truth to every role and made even weak films appear far better than they really were. Although not often the lead, he was more than capable of carrying any movie given the chance, and it was truthfully said of him that he never gave a bad performance. I was surprised to find so little about him; such an outstanding Oscar-winning actor working during the heyday of the studios surely deserves to be put on the map and given his due. After all, he was a leading player in some of the most interesting classic films of the era: *Possessed, The Prowler, Shane* and *3:10 to Yuma,* to name just a few.

He had such a range; he impressed in Westerns, melodramas, comedies, swashbucklers, film noirs, war movies, even musicals. In short there was nothing he could not do as an actor, for he had a fundamental integrity that lent credence to everything in which he appeared. His early years, spent roaming the seas, and his long apprenticeship on stage imbued all his film roles with a sense of reality and sure technique, but he had something more besides. He was, in a word, unique. Often compared to Spencer Tracy, arguably the finest actor of his time, Heflin was very highly regarded among his acting colleagues. As the great Lionel Barrymore of the famous acting dynasty said of him, "He is one of the most capable natural actors I've seen."[2]

Like many others, I first became aware of Heflin through *Shane* and I too was impressed by his character and the way in which he made the normally drab (in filmic terms) virtues of honesty and integrity could appear so appealing. While everyone remembers Alan Ladd as Shane and Jack Palance as the black-clad gunman Wilson, none of the action would have any resonance were it not for the strong sense of community among the homesteaders symbolized by Joe Starrett and his absolute certainty of right. Few other actors had that combination of ability to handle action scenes and philosophical questions with such ease. This was reflected in all of Heflin's work. Whether he was a rugged star of Westerns or a bookish police scientist, he had an essential ring of truth.

Heflin was a quiet but noticeable presence in films; even in the war movie *Battle Cry* he gives a convincing portrayal of the problems of leadership with seemingly few brush strokes. His Major Sam "High Pockets" Huxley sometimes appears hard as nails to his men, at one stage driving them almost beyond endurance on a tough, sustained march; at the same time he worries incessantly over them like a mother hen. Heflin reached inside himself so much so that he got to the emotional core of his characters. We understand his deeply flawed but human Frank Enley in *Act of Violence*, a man haunted by his past as much as his nemesis Joe Parkson; and his Sam Masterson seems almost the only sane character in *The Strange Love of Martha Ivers*. He was able to portray all the human frailties; he could convincingly be noble or mean, strong or weak, sly or honest as the day is long and never seem to be acting. He also had one of the best and most distinctive voices. His husky, throaty delivery and "lived in" tones gave his acting both reality and conviction. His eyes were invariably expressive and his acting technique subtle and all the more effective. Even when playing characters on the verge of hysteria, he was the most modern of actors.

For some reason he was not often considered a natural leading man, and he never forgot Louis B. Mayer's assertion that he would never "get the girl at the end of the picture."[3] However, over the years his leading ladies included Judy Garland, Gene Tierney, Ruth Roman, Marsha Hunt, Evelyn Keyes, Susan Hayward, Patricia Neal and Julie Adams to name just a few. In *East Side, West Side* Cyd Charisse fell hopelessly in love with him; in *Possessed* Joan Crawford would have done anything for him but he rejected her; and in *The Strange Love of Martha Ivers* he had the choice of Barbara Stanwyck and Lizabeth Scott and when he went for Scott, Stanwyck found life unbearable without him. The tall, broad-shouldered Heflin had many female admirers who praised his rugged good looks. As Mike McCrann observed in his perceptive tribute on his "Vintage Hunk" page, Heflin was "sexy in a buttoned-down way."[4] In the late 1940s Hedda Hopper got "letters by the batches asking [her] to get on the bandbox" for him[5] at a time when he was described as "hotter than a ten cent firecracker" and the "idol of many bobbysoxers and others too."[6] Dorothy Manners outlined his special appeal: "He is one of those attractive homely men many women go for more than the curly-haired muscle boys.... He has red-blond kinky hair, gray eyes and the 6' 160 pound physique of an underfed college professor."[7]

In this book I aim to cover Heflin's life and discuss his film, theater, radio and television work, talking in depth about his most notable performances in several key films with a discussion of his acting technique. Where possible I use Heflin's own words to describe the events of his life. I sought out every interview I could find and watched all his films, which took a long time to track down. I employed researchers, scoured newspaper reports and journals; I watched all relevant interviews with his co-stars. In Oklahoma I pursued a number of leads and one of my researchers consulted his archive at the University. My researcher in New York tried valiantly to get around the 100-year rule which applies to all divorce cases in the city and prevents any disclosure about the split from his first wife until 2036. I read extensively and also contacted many of his fellow actors to little avail. I wrote to his son and contacted his daughters and his niece but unfortunately received no responses.

My hope with this book is to lay down a marker so that everyone, film buffs and the uninitiated alike, will come to appreciate the vital but underrated contribution of one of the finest actors of his generation.

One

The Call of the Sea
(1908–32)

Oklahoma to California

"My father was a drunk, although he was a fabulous character and he and my mother always loved each other even when they were separated." [1]

The windswept town of Walters, Oklahoma (motto: "Small town, big heart"), was not long established when the Heflin family arrived some time towards the fall of 1907. Only six years earlier the town did not exist and the state itself was still known as Indian Territory, part of a vast area that was home to the Chickasaw Nation. It was a quiet settlement in what later became known as Cotton County. The family did not stay long, moving to bustling Oklahoma City, some ninety miles to the southwest, shortly after the birth of their second son, named for his father Emmett Evan, on December 13, 1908. [2]

Emmett Heflin Sr. had lived in the state since at least 1900, when he was staying with his sister Salie and brother-in-law Aron Adams. [3] He was not a native, having been born in Lawrence, Alabama, in 1879, the son of Alexander Heflin and Mary Murfee (sometimes Murphie). The Heflin family, of French-Irish descent, went way back in the history of Alabama. With the coming of the Civil War, Van's grandfather Alexander was about 15 when he enlisted in the Confederate Army, joining his elder brothers James, William, Hugh and Thomas. They were part of Colonel (later General) Philip Dale Roddey's Escort in the 4th Alabama Cavalry. This was formed in 1862 at Tuscumbia and was "once publicly recommended for its good discipline and order." [4] Alexander was born in November 1849 and died in May 1940 at Carter, Oklahoma, in his 91st year. [5] He fought in the Civil War and his son Emmett saw action in the First World War (1917–18). Alexander lived to see the beginning of the Second World War in which his grandson Van would later serve with distinction.

Emmett, a dentist, was 27 when he married 18-year-old Fanny Bleeker Shippey on May 9, 1906, in Los Angeles. The Shippeys were a socially prominent family from Long Beach, California.[6] Their eldest son Martin was born the following year in the same place. Young Evan called his father "The Doctor." There was also mention of a farm; the family spent a long time in court trying to establish whether it belonged to Texas or Oklahoma because oil was discovered nearby and both states were angling for the taxes.[7]

"The Doctor" first set up practice in Tishomingo where he shared an office with Bill Murray, who was later governor of Oklahoma.[8] After a brief stay in Walters, he was based in Oklahoma City from 1909, and remained there. During the 1920s the doctor was in partnership with a Mr. Price at Huckins Estate Building at 104 ½ West Main; the family lived at 1611 North McKinley. If the teenage Evan happened to be home from the sea in later years, he was sometimes required to assist in the surgery. As a former patient, who was a fearful 17-year-old at the time, once recalled, "I was afraid of Dr. Heflin and he said he had to drill my teeth.... He called in his son Van to hold me down."[9]

Evan lived his formative and school years in Oklahoma City where he attended grade school, then Classen High School. He seldom mentioned his childhood in later years. In one of his few anecdotes, he related how he was given an allowance of a penny a day and rather than buying penny candy, he would save up until he had 10 cents for a better candy bar he liked. Ever afterwards, whenever he was tempted to gamble, he thought of those candy bars and how long it had taken for him to save up.[10] His determination and self-discipline were obviously already present.

The seeds of his ability to express emotion through his acting appear to have been sown early in childhood. When his father bought a shiny new car, Evan immediately rounded up his friends and gloated about it. The next day his dad sent the car back; Evan's friends needled him mercilessly, but he assumed a supreme nonchalance and shrugged it off successfully. On the few times his father hit him he never cried out. Instead he would go to the attic and sulk "quietly and effectively" for hours.[11]

When he was around twelve, the family moved to Long Beach, California, to stay with his mother's parents and Evan got his first view of the sea. His grandparents, Martin and Caroline Shippey (née Willard), had both been born in Illinois and moved to Long Beach in the early 1900s.[12]

They had four children, Roderick, Eveanna, Hugh and Heflin's mother Frances. By the time young Evan was foisted on them, his uncles and aunt had all left home. For the remainder of his life, he thought of California as his home despite the fact that he had been born and spent his formative years in Oklahoma. "When I retire ... it will be right there in Southern California," he said in 1961. "A man must have roots. And mine are right there."[13]

He went to the Polytechnic High School at 1600 Atlantic Avenue, Long Beach. Many famous people passed through there; the bandleader Spike Jones was a friend, and his contemporaries included John Wayne. The school has always been noted for academics and athletics; Heflin "studied hard" and was naturally academic, but not distinguished on the athletic field. He had one unsuccessful tryout for the lightweight football team. The team and coach watched his efforts—and then elected him manager.[14] He soon found an aptitude for debating and drama encouraged by the drama coach Miss L. V. Breed. He said she was the first to set his mind on the theater and taught him a great deal.[15]

Although his parents separated, they were nonetheless always listed together on the census, and in 1921 his sister Frances was born. It would appear that his parents lived separate lives but they never actually divorced.

The Sea, the Sea

> "I must go down to the seas again, to the lonely sea and the sky, and all I ask is a tall ship and a star to steer her by."—From "Sea Fever" by John Masefield

After growing up in the vast farmlands of Oklahoma, young Evan's first sight of the Pacific Ocean had a profound and lasting effect. He was mesmerized by the sea, and never forgot his first glimpse of what looked like freedom. There was a fissure in his parents' marriage which left him confused and he was very unhappy at that time; a friend described his life then as "hard and miserable."[16] But there was consolation in the sea with its eternal promise of escape from whatever troubles might come his way throughout life.

He was always an avid reader and as a child devoured tales of pirate ships and adventure on the high seas. Among his favorites were *Robinson Crusoe, Treasure Island, Moby Dick* and the stories of Jack London. He lost himself too in the cinema, where he was captivated by adventure serials.[17] As he got older, the power of the sea began to cast a spell over him. During all the years at school, then later at university, he felt his thoughts returning to its untold possibilities. He loved to learn even when he was young; he had a thirst for knowledge and above all a desire to understand. The writer to whose world he was most drawn was Joseph Conrad. The combination of adventurer and philosopher appealed to him strongly and seemed to mirror much of the restlessness in his own soul.

His grandmother Caroline was the one adult in his early life who had a profound effect on him; she has been described as "a colorful woman, highly imaginative, with salt in her veins." Her next door neighbor was head of the Seaman's Employment Bureau and young Evan spent his Saturdays there amid the seasoned mariners soaking up the atmosphere and listening to their yarns. Among them he seemed to find the warmth, connection and sense of family missing in his home at Oklahoma.

It came as no surprise when, during his first vacation from high school, fourteen-year old Evan hopped onto a fishing schooner bound for Mexico.[18] His grandmother was delighted; she had always wished to travel but never had the chance and took the keenest interest in all his voyages. She was forever consulting her *National Geographic,* marking off the places where he was going and making him find out all about them. He always took his camera along and loved to take snapshots. On his return he related to her all he had seen.[19]

In 1924 when Evan was 15, the man next door hired him to join the crew of a liner, the *City of Los Angeles,* which sailed from San Pedro, California, to Honolulu.[20] He made four round trips in all but it was not quite the adventurous or glamorous life he had imagined and he discovered little about handling ships; he was merely an assistant laundryman operating mangles.

Undeterred, he signed on as a seaman's rating on an oil tanker the following year. To South America he sailed on the *S.S. West Cactus* for the McCormick Steamship Company on the Pacific Argentine Line.[21] He made several trips around the coast of Brazil and saw the River Plate in Argentina. In 1926 he graduated from high school and signed for yet another stint; this time on an oil tanker, the *F.H. Hillman.* The route took him from the U.S. West Coast through the Panama Canal and on to England. On the long voyage they encountered a hurricane and some of the most treacherous weather ever recalled. During this trip he almost lost his life. As he described in vivid detail, the hurricane struck in the Caribbean soon after the ship left Cristobal; he had just been relieved as lookout on the forecastle and made his way up to the wheel when it hit.

The ship was enveloped by massive waves. With no chance of any relief reaching them, he and the skipper took turns at the wheel until he thought his arms would fall off. At times he held onto the wheel to keep from collapsing from sheer exhaustion. For three days the ship stood up to the storm. According to Van, "Our decks were saturated, all lifeboats were swept away and three members of our crew went over the side in the rush of the waters. One of these was my partner who had relieved me as lookout. He was lost from the station which I'd left just before the storm broke."[22]

In England, Van had only a brief time to visit London and see all the items on his extensive itinerary. He became so fascinated by Westminster Abbey that he quite forgot the time and spent the whole day there, even returning the following day just before the ship sailed.

His was a rough and ready existence. He had a quick temper and fights were a regular occurrence onboard; but he was just as ready to shake hands and forget all about it. He grew up fast and was popular with the men, who soon shortened Evan to Van, which stuck. As a teenager he enjoyed the roustabout life; he relished the freedom, the constant adventure, the drinking bouts and the camaraderie. And all the time he was learning about other lands and ways of life. This undoubtedly had an effect on his later sense of perspective. Although a patriotic American, he had a distinct world view and always enjoyed travel. As an actor he had a major appeal to a European and worldwide audience, for he had seen beyond the horizon.

The work itself was physically demanding—conditions onboard small frigates and schooners were poor—but he never minded the many hardships. Besides that, it gave him his famous "ruggedness" on which he would later trade. Nevertheless he realized that the life of a sailor he had imagined was not as idyllic as it seemed. "It's like Hawaii," he once remarked. "You dream you can pick mangoes or beautiful babes out of the trees. You find it's just another place."[23]

University 1926–28

When Van returned to Long Beach that fall, he discovered that his family had moved back to Oklahoma. While he visited them, his mother persuaded him to continue his education. He enrolled at the University of Oklahoma at Norman. His parents thought he should settle down for a while.[24] He studied diligently for the next two years. He was a Phi Delt at University, but only through the influence of his much more confident elder brother Marty. Years later Van was asked by an interviewer about his college days and whether he was the "house official actor who, during rushing, would tap on his water glass at the festive board and declaim that flaming bit from *Henry V* about 'God for Harry, England and St. George!'" He replied, "Hell, no, the University and the Phi Delts shared a common admiration for athletes and joint disinterest in Shakespeare, who didn't play football."[25]

Many years later he wrote the lead article for the fraternity's national monthly publication *Scroll*.[26] At the university one of his tutors was Josh Lee, head of the Public Speaking Department from 1919 until he left to run for Congress in 1934. Once described as "a slick-tongued, silver-haired Demosthenes," he was considered one of the best public speakers in the country. Heflin recalled wryly that it was the only class he ever flunked.[27]

He gravitated to the drama class because he had fallen for a girl in the group, so he said. But if truth be told, he had harbored acting ambitions since childhood. Here he came under the great influence of assistant head of drama Miss Ida Z. Kirk and tentatively began to find his calling.

Kirk immediately saw the latent talent of the restless Evan, her most outstanding pupil. He would accept any part he was given and often two or three more. He was no angel and could be willful but she was more than a match for him. Heflin welcomed the discipline and admitted that no one had ever talked to him the way she did—not even his grandmother. Nor did he forget her; years later when he was a successful movie star, he made several return trips to his old alma mater to see Miss Kirk and visited her when she was in a hospital in 1948 shortly before she died. He remembered her advice "along with her patience and genuine talent imparting the principles of drama.... She worked hard with me and was generous in her encouragement. Finally she said, 'I think you should go on the stage.'"[28]

Broadway Beckons

Heflin was undecided on his direction, and during another vacation he drifted back to the sea. In reality he had no sense of urgency to complete his studies and little appetite for law. "I got the urge to travel again," he said, "so I lit out for California." There was a ship sailing for New York, a city he had always wanted to see, and while there he decided to look up his cousin.[29]

There are several versions of his first meeting with Broadway producer Richard Boleslawski and how he got his big break; like a mariner's yarn, it changed in the telling every time. His earliest account is the most prosaic, and seems the most likely: He telephoned his cousin who said she was giving a cocktail party and asked him to come right up. When he got there, he realized she had stage ambitions and that some of the guests were actors. He was dressed somewhat outlandishly: his sailor's cap, a silk shirt he had bought in Panama, a pair of faded dungarees and cowboy boots that were too big to fit in his kit bag. He thought he must have looked a sight and described himself as "just a hick, but not awed by anything." He imagined the assembled crowd had fun at his expense. But before long, one of the men, an actor, approached him and asked how long he would be in New York. Van replied that he wanted to stay and get a job. The actor was giving up his part in *Mr. Moneypenny* and suggested that Van see Channing Pollack, the play's author and producer. "You could do it," he said, "it's the part of a fresh young kid." In Van's later version of the story, he recounted the scene differently and seemed to view the offer as some form of criticism; he saw it as a challenge. The over-sensitive adolescent was actually being given a great opportunity.[30]

The next morning at six a.m. he went to see Pollack and waited in his office until noon. Van had been given a long list of plays to say he had appeared in, most of which Pollack had directed; this amused the renowned writer. Pollack gave him a letter of introduction to Boleslawski, the play's director. Boleslawski read the letter, which had the desired effect: Van got the part. Boleslawski told him his salary would be $100 which Van assumed was per month because he had been getting around $40 a month at sea. He was ecstatic when he realized it was per week.[31]

Heflin became fascinated by the world that Boleslawski represented and the possibilities of a life on stage. "Boley" professed himself intrigued by the "strange mixture of college-bred gentleman and two-fisted sailor" that he recognized in Heflin. The erstwhile director was a pivotal influence on him and more instrumental than anyone in his later decision to cast his lot with acting.[32]

Boleslawski was almost forty at the time they met; he had studied acting under the great Stanislavsky. During the First World War he had been a cavalry officer with the Tsarist army but left his native land after the fall of Russia to the Bolsheviks in 1917. He migrated to the United States and enjoyed a highly successful stage and later film career as director and producer; his movies include *Rasputin and the Empress* (1932) and *The Garden of Allah* (1936). While making the latter he drank some un-boiled water on set, complained of feeling unwell and died not long afterwards of a suspected heart attack at age 47. It was a sad loss. He was a true artist and could recognize talent; John Carradine described him as "a big, lovable bear of a man ... a great director and everybody loved him."[33]

Both producer and director having taken a liking to Van, the 19-year-old sailor was handed the part of Junior Jones in the three-act comedy which opened at the Liberty Theater in October 1928. As the son of the epigrammatic John Jones (played by the popular Scottish character actor Donald Meek), he had a mostly subordinate role and little chance to shine. However, he did display a gift for comic timing. *Mr. Moneypenny* was a satire of consumerism; its central character, a bored bank clerk, dreams of having great wealth. As William Grange described the scenario, suddenly Mr. Moneypenny appears and transforms the clerk into a Wall Street financier complete with "a Park Avenue apartment, important friends, night clubs, fancy restaurants, and brokerage houses—all displayed in a series of raucous, hallucinatory images. In the end, the clerk realizes he is not content with this new life, for the qualities of sincerity, genuineness, and plain common sense seem to have no place in the materialist world." He drops out of the mad race for the dollar when he comes to understand that these people who strive for it have "everything but an appreciation of beauty, simplicity, ideals, courtesy, and God."[34]

Pollack's plays have been called well-structured and quixotic in nature; he utilized much from German Expressionism. Dubbed by *Variety* as an "expressionistic moral fable," *Mr. Moneypenny* ran for only six weeks and a total of sixty-two performances.[35] The New York critics were always dismissive of Pollack's work, and especially so of *Mr. Moneypenny*, a satire on materialism and sophistication which they seemed to take personally. This over-ambitious production employed 112 actors and cost over $100,000 but soon ran into financial difficulty. By keeping the cost of tickets low to encourage the non-theatergoing public, Pollack did not help his own cause even though houses were at around 96 percent capacity. The critics were the chief problem; Dorothy Parker, Robert Benchley, Brooks Atkinson et al. ensured that *Mr. Moneypenny* had a very short run. Pollack grew tired of dealing with "theater habitués and the sons of habitués" and eventually the critics saw him off from Broadway altogether; he never wrote another play after 1931, arguably ensuring that the stage hereafter remained little more than "an elitist exercise" in the minds of most ordinary people.[36]

Among the cast, Heflin was not singled out for praise or blame. But the realities and insecurity of theater soon came home to him and the constant criticism of the venture left him disillusioned. He seemed to take the failure personally. Long before the play's run ended in December 1928 he had already decided to return to his first love. As he said, "[B]y the time the play folded.... I had had enough of the stage. It wasn't anything like what I thought it would be. So I said the hell with it, and went back to sea."[37] The show closed on a Saturday night and on Sunday morning he caught the first tramp steamer out. He was on his way to South Africa perhaps before the scenery was being dismantled.

Back to Sea

"You learn every emotion at sea."

Van's education was on hold; his stage career had stalled at the first hurdle; the sea beckoned once more. This time he was in earnest, determined to start the new year of 1929 as he meant to continue. During the next two and a half years he traversed the globe. He made three trips to the west coast of South America, then travelled to the Orient; he saw China, the Philippines, Bali; the torrid islands in the Pacific and Indian Oceans and up to Alaska. He applied to be a rating and eventually reached the rank of third mate on a merchant ship. He had numerous adventures which he sometimes recounted in his inimitable style. One time he bought a set of six marmosets from a peddler in Brazil for the equivalent of $5 American. One escaped and frightened the life out of a fireman called Fred who was rather too fond of alcohol and often suffered hallucinations. Fred went into the fire room for a rag when one of the "rags" came to life and the monkey jumped on his head, then disappeared. He came out screaming about a devil jumping him and was tied down in his bunk for his own wellbeing—with Van assisting and not daring to mention his escaped monkey.[38]

His years spent roaming the oceans of the world taught him all about life. They also gave him a unique insight into human nature and motivations which he undoubtedly drew on in his acting. Living in close quarters with others for long periods, he gained a real understanding of psychology. "You learn every emotion at sea," he once remarked.[39] He was observant, intelligent and ever open to new lands, cultures and ideas. These were some of the wellsprings that gave him his professional impetus. He also learned many practical things, such as the value of money, which also stayed with him. A journeyman sailor would never be rich and there was always someone else willing to spend all he earned, be it girls, shipmates or fair-weather friends in port. Hence his later financial caution; he invested all the money he ever made as a highly successful actor with an honest broker and was never in debt.

He did not forget his education and took a number of books along with him such as the LaSalle Extension Course, figuring at one stage that he might make a good maritime lawyer. His interest in practicing law waned and ultimately lost out to his love of the sea when he reached Sydney, Australia, after a long Pacific voyage. Everyone else was going ashore and he couldn't bear to "sweat out the layover" in his bunk with his law books so he acted like a true sailor and went ashore.[40] His time in port was never wasted, and wherever the boat would dock he would go to libraries, study native periodicals, visit points of interest and above all talk to people.[41]

By the beginning of 1931 he was 22 and confirmed in his life as a sailor bold with his kitbag over his shoulder, winking at the girls and whistling on his way. His next goal might be second mate, then first mate, then who knows? Perhaps in time he would make captain and have a vessel of his own. The future course of his life seemed fully mapped out. But appearances can be deceptive, and seeds sown in his mind by Miss Breed at high school, by Miss Kirk at University and during his abortive Broadway run by the ever-supportive Richard Boleslawski began to germinate. Eventually the realization dawned on him that the road less travelled might be the one for him.

Two

The Lure of the Stage
(1931–41)

"One morning I woke up in San Francisco broke. I had been rolled the night before, and couldn't even remember where I'd been. I decided I'd be a bum all my life if I stayed at sea."[1]

The restlessness Heflin felt was not sated by his many years at sea; whatever he was searching for, the peripatetic life of a sailor provided no permanent answer. He realized many things during the three years since his Broadway "flop" *Mr. Moneypenny* and one thing was certain: The life of an actor must surely be far less hard work than that of a seaman, and the pay far better too. All the time he was at sea he kept in touch with Richard Boleslawski, who had written in his last letter to him some words which seemed to strike home: "Stay at sea until you can't help coming back to the stage. Then you won't have any illusions. The stage will be bigger than you are and you'll be glad to be a part of it. Now you want the stage to be part of you. Stay until you are sure."[2]

Epiphanies come in strange guises; some in a flash of light, some with a full orchestra and chorus. Heflin's came in a cheap rooming house off the Embarcadero in San Francisco amid the wail of ferryboats across the bay. Two days earlier he had been paid $200 off the boat from Shanghai, China. He had been rolled the night before by a couple of seamen he met in a bar; now he was clean broke. He took a good long look at himself and knew he had to turn his life around; Boleslawski's words came back to him: "Stay until you are sure." Now he was sure.

Once his mind was set on something, there was no compromise. "There can't be," he once remarked. "It would be the end of me to myself."[3]

In 1931 he returned to Oklahoma University and managed to eke out enough credits for a degree the following spring, finishing his last two years of college in one year, although he had long since abandoned any notion of actually practicing law.[4] He said he wished to pursue a career as a drama teacher and get a Master's degree. His real ambition was to become an actor. Indeed, his classmates long afterwards recalled his single-minded dedication to his art.[5]

His first leading role for the Mummers group at the University was as Hilary Fairfield in Clemence Dane's *A Bill of Divorcement*. For his final role in *Berkeley Square* (December 1931) he received a glowing review in the student newspaper *The Oklahoma Daily*: "Heflin ... fired the imagination of an audience of 40 Friday night.... Speaking with an authority which told of months of training on the stage in New York City [he] held the attention of the audience from his first entrance to his final curtain."[6]

He made several influential contacts at the University; he met the part–Cherokee writer Lynn Riggs, a fellow Oklahoman, then later he met Jasper Deeter, who invited him to join the Hedgerow Players based at Rose Valley near Philadelphia. Founded by Deeter nine years previously, the Hedgerow company soon established itself as America's outstanding repertory theater. This became the training ground for generations of actors including contemporaries Ann Harding and later famous stars such as Richard Basehart and Keanu Reeves. Repertory theater was derived from the British stage and introduced into America by Frank Conroy and others. The idea was that a roster of different types of plays would be produced, Shakespeare, Shaw, Ibsen, Restoration comedies and contemporary works, and so players would gain wide practical experience and knowledge of stage craft in a relatively short space of time. It meant memorizing a great many plays and understanding the different requirements of each. He spent six months trouping with the Hedgerow Players and learned a lot about acting and the mechanics of theater. He then had a season at Cape Cod, Maine, and decided to study at Yale University.[7]

He enrolled on a course at Yale Dramatic School in 1932 and during the next two years learned all about the art and craft of acting.[8] (According to the archives at Yale, Heflin was a non-graduate in fine arts in 1935.) Here he studied for some time under Professor George Pierce Baker, a legendary name in the theatrical world. After a lifetime connected to the stage, he had been instrumental in founding the School of Drama at Yale and taught the history and theory of drama there from 1925. Over the years his students included Eugene O'Neill, Philip Barry, S.N. Behrman and Tom Wolfe, among others. Baker set up 47 Workshop, a prestigious company which produced many and varied plays and was effectively an academy for actors, writers and directors. Heflin directed in 47 Workshop and also at the Community Theater in South Carolina. He later said that his famous teacher "was nearing the end and had only occasional flashes of inspiration," and that he learned most by "acting in stock at Denver and talking with theater people."[9]

He studied the Delsarte system of acting technique under Frances Robinson Duff, who had earlier taught Katharine Hepburn and later Jennifer Jones.[10] This system was first developed by the nineteenth century French musician and teacher Francois Delsarte, who sought to show how the emotions could be expressed through a specific range of voice and gestures. The technique caught on and was especially popular in the United States from the 1870s onward. In later years it became somewhat mannered and merely degenerated into stereotyped and melodramatic gesticulations devoid of the very heart that Delsarte sought to restore. Heflin utilized the principle of this system in its true original form which was based on Delsarte's close observations of people. However, the actor developed an "easy naturalism" which took him very far in his own direction, based on many of his own wide observations.

One of the Yale productions in which he appeared was *The King's Coat* in January 1933. Written by student Fred Kleibacker, this told the story of General Benedict Arnold during the Revolutionary War; Heflin appeared as Major Andre, "the officer with whom Arnold plotted and who finally won Arnold over to the British side."[11] The author sought to present the notorious traitor in three dimensions, and the result was judged "intensely interesting" and the final scene in particular "deeply affecting." However, the same critic was less enthusiastic about the acting, which he deemed "adequate." Directed by George Pierce Baker, the single performance at the University Theater was seen by representatives of the Theater Guild and the Group Theater, perhaps including Katharine Hepburn.

Heflin had some small successes in the provinces in a range of dramas; he appeared in such classics as William Congreve's Restoration comedy *Love for Love*, Shakespeare's *Much Ado About Nothing* and Aristophanes' *Birds* starring Beatrice Lillie with a Gershwin score.

He accompanied Alexander Dean, director of the Yale Dramatic Association, to Dennis, Massachusetts, for a season in summer theater. During his time there, Kenyon Nicholson and Charles Robinson staged *Sailor Beware* with Van cast in the starring role of Herb Marley, a rumbustious sailor on shore leave. At last he had another chance on Broadway and the play was due to open at the Lyceum in September 1933. Producer Courtney Burr had attempted to get a dozen different stars for the lead roles but was dissatisfied with their attitude (and the salaries they demanded) and so decided to audition unknowns instead.[12] After six rehearsals, Van was summarily dismissed with the deeply ironic note (considering his almost seven years at sea) "Not the type." He was kept on as an understudy.[13]

The easy life of an actor was proving far harder than he had envisioned. "I hated the stage at first.... I feel as an actor I was a good sailor," he once said, reflecting on this period.[14] He fell on hard times again, did numerous odd jobs and made half-hearted attempts to return to his former life; he earned a pittance cleaning fish and scrubbing decks on a barge.[15]

Around this time he was living with 21-year-old actress Esther Scherr at 60 West 8th Avenue; they married on July 20, 1934, at the Municipal Building in Manhattan.[16] Esther was born in the Bronx although both her parents hailed from Austria.[17] She often modeled for artist Raphael Soyer, who was best man at their wedding. The couple separated after about six months and she filed for divorce in 1936. Heflin maintained that they parted friends.[18] In 1941, while Heflin was making *Johnny Eager* for director Mervyn LeRoy, he was invited to his home. "On the walls he saw nothing but portraits of his ex-wife, portraits by Soyer, whose work LeRoy was collecting.... When Heflin went home he brooded about it, and stared at his own two Soyer portraits of his ex-wife. Heflin gave them to LeRoy the next day, 'to make [his] collection complete.'"[19]

In 1934 he may have had a relationship with 18-year-old dancer Eleanor Segal, who had a son, David, in September 1935. When David Siff reached the age of forty she told him that his father was Van Heflin. Around the time of his birth, Eleanor was living "with her parents and two sisters in a comfortable but cramped apartment on the Grand Concourse in the Bronx, near 163rd Street." Although they were undoubtedly in the same city, if not in the immediate vicinity at the same time, the evidence is circumstantial which Siff fully acknowledges in his honest and discursive memoir.[20]

On occasion Heflin acted in plays that had short runs. One was Otto Indiq's Hungarian-set comedy *The Bride of Torozco* at the Henry Miller Theater during September 1934. Invited by the play's director, Herman Shumlin, Van played Andreas, whose bride-to-be Klari (Jean Arthur) discovers she is Jewish, which puts the wedding on hold until it is revealed that this too was a clerical error and she was actually Protestant. Hopes were high for the first night, attended by Dashiell Hammett and Ira Gershwin amongst others.[21] The play was poorly received despite the "compelling" Jean Arthur and the always valued presence of Sam Jaffe. According to one critic, it was "too slowly paced, too talky and too wearisome," and it closed after less than two weeks.[22] The famous *New York Herald-Tribune* critic Percy Hammond wrote, "Mr. Van Heflin is an unreasonably bad actor." Heflin ever afterwards saved this cutting in his wallet. "Whenever I get a little cocky," he later said, "I pull out that review and read it again. It's the kind of thing that keeps you on your toes."[23] He commented, "I was nicely panned. The less said about it the better. At that stage I decided I couldn't quit as a failure, I'd get success and then quit."[24]

In Martha Madison's mystery melodrama *The Night Remembers* at the Playhouse, Heflin played a "bored, gullible young man" lured to a weird old house by a beautiful femme fatale, hypnotized by her father and left alone in a candle-lit room surrounded by corpses. The next day he tries to find the girl and the house without success and has to conclude that the whole thing may have been a dream. This too did not come alive for audiences and closed after 23 nights just before Christmas 1934.[25]

For most of 1935 he did more odd jobs and some stock work in provincial theaters; was constantly employed on radio; and again toyed with the idea of returning to sea. He appeared in a number of plays including Robert Hare Powel's satiric farce *Beware of the Bull.* Toward the end of the year he was offered the role of Tooteboy Zinnheiser in James Hagan's farming saga *Mid-West* which opened at the Booth Theater in January 1936. Although this too had a disappointingly short run (despite some promising notices), it led directly to his next assignment in S.N. Behrman's "captivating gem" *End of Summer,* starring opposite Ina Claire.[26] This was his first association with the Theater Guild on Broadway; his first, *Races,* never made it from Philadelphia. At last he had the good fortune to essay a prominent role that played to his strengths in a well-received production that enjoyed a decent run.

He originally rehearsed for the part of Will the juvenile lead, and then two days before the show opened was devastated to be told he was not wanted. He was about to walk away dejectedly when they called him back and asked him to play Dennis instead. He was elated but also admitted to being "scared to death" having never played comedy before. He acknowledged how much Ina Claire helped him; he had great fun working with her and "getting the thrill of hearing an audience actually enjoy a show."[27]

Behrman's play appeared to be a light comedy, but had prescient things to say about the darkening international situation and particularly the rise of fascism. The original ending was quite somber, suggesting a fascist future. But in all the try-out cities this did not go down well, so the author shifted the balance slightly and the part of Dennis McCarthy the communist anarchist was "recast with the dynamic, sexually attractive Van Heflin,"[28] who provided all the "lusty laughs" of the piece.[29] The writer later said that this was his favorite of all his plays. This production also marked a real turning point for its star. After seeing Heflin in *End of Summer*, Katharine Hepburn suggested he should try his luck in Hollywood. She was subsequently instrumental in securing him a film contract with RKO, which kept him away from the stage for most of 1937.

End of Summer was directed by Phillip Moeller, a true craftsman and a great influence on the young star. Despite being thrown in at the deep end, he seemed unfazed during rehearsals by all accounts.[30]

His next was a melodrama set at the time of the Indian Wars. But Richard Carlson's *Western Waters* at the Hudson lasted a mere six nights (December 1937 into January 1938). The critics were not impressed: "overwritten, over-produced and leaves a feeling of utter unreality," said one. But Heflin "won critical cheers for his performance as the rip-roaring river man.... [He] struggles manfully with the leading role of Kaintuck and does manage to give it moments now and then that makes it seem almost real."[31]

Robert Ardrey's *Casey Jones* at the Fulton, directed by a young Elia Kazan, was a critical success but a financial failure. This was an expertly realized reconstruction of the life of the legendary railroad man complete with an elaborate set incorporating a replica locomotive. Casey (Charles Bickford) is at the end of his career; his eyes are bad and his employers want to take him off the Express and put him on hauling freights. In the end he decides to retire on a pension rather than become a has-been. Heflin played young railroad engineer Jed Sherman, friend of the title character, among a cast which included Peggy Conklin as Casey's daughter Portsmouth and Howard da Silva. A contemporary report showed just how relaxed the youngest cast member was during rehearsals:

Van takes time out to balance a pool cue on his chin. There is a pool game scene in the play and he likes the feel of that cue. "Kaz" speaks up. "If you handle all your cues as you do that one, we'll have a hit."

There were some tensions between the director and the leading man, the moody, ever-suspicious Charles Bickford. Bickford got along well with Heflin, who later described Bickford as his "closest friend."[32] *Variety* lauded the romantic Van as "the most likable character.... [He] makes love to Peggy Conklin on the stage of the Fulton every night, [and] continues with Susan Fox after the curtain rings down."[33]

Casey Jones was Kazan's second Theater Guild production and he put a great deal of time and effort into it. He was a meticulous director who kept a stack of notes about a foot high which he made while watching countless rehearsals. He went over every flaw and alteration with each cast member individually and listened patiently to all their suggestions. Despite all their painstaking efforts, this promising production soon ran into financial difficulties, lost money and closed after less than a month in March 1938.[34]

Away from Broadway, Heflin made an impression in a variety of roles. He was effective in Sidney Howard's comedy *Ned McCobb's Daughter* at the County Playhouse (June 1938) starring Mildred Natwick in the title role. Although the play was built around Natwick, Heflin as brother-in-law Babe Callahan attracted the attention. His character is described as a "rough, tough, belligerent, braggadocio ... an opportunist to a certain degree, but as clever as he is, is no proof for Connie's shrewdness." The same reviewer remarked, "Heflin plays a difficult role with marked ability, and he is such a good 'no good' that he wins a great deal of admiration for his part."[35] The Company also played Sing Sing Prison Theater to an audience of 1,500 using "lifers" as stagehands.[36]

Heflin often told stories about this time in his life when he was struggling. Although the yarns are humorous, they give an insight into the precarious existence of all young actors. One time "The Doctor" wrote to tell him about local boy Sherman Billingsley, who made good and was starting a saloon called the Stork Club. He asked Heflin to drop in to see him because he was an old friend and might throw some business his way. So one evening he went to the Club and walked straight up to the velvet rope in his slacks to see Sherman. The doorman took one look and told him to get out, which hurt his feelings. The following year, after Heflin got the part in *The Philadelphia Story*, Sherman sent him a radio on opening night, as was his way. Thinking that he remembered him after all, Heflin went along after the show and barged through the crowd up to the velvet rope again. The same doorman informed him that he never forgot a face and told him to scram. This time his feelings were really wounded and he told a New York columnist about it. He in turn told Sherman. The next night Heflin received a big bottle of champagne and a personal invitation to dinner. This time when he walked up to the velvet rope he was wearing the tuxedo he had worn in the play. The doorman took one look at him and told him he "didn't look any better in a tux." He was about to tell him to scram but then asked him his name. "When I told him," said Van, "he almost fainted [and said] 'I've been looking for you for three years.'"[37]

For most of 1938 Heflin's main girlfriend was actress Susan Fox; the following year he was, according to the gossip columnists, going steady with Katharine Hepburn, who he once described as "just about the best friend a guy could have."[38] In early 1940 he was pursued by petite nightclub chanteuse Mae Bertelle of the Diamond Horseshoe.[39] Later that year he was secretly engaged to 16-year-old heiress Gloria Vanderbilt. The episode is described in *Double Exposure,* a twin autobiography she wrote with her mother Thelma Lady Furness. Gloria's first love was one Geoffrey Jones, whom she planned to marry. Her mother explained, "Then one night Gloria came into my room and announced that she wanted to get into bed with me.... In my bed in the dark she said, 'Mummy, I'm not in love with Geoffrey any more—I'm in love with Van Heflin and I'm going to marry him.'"

A month later she introduced her mother to her new beau: Howard Hughes. "She was in love with him and going to marry him."[40]

His next venture marked the turning point: He was cast as reporter Macaulay Connor in *The Philadelphia Story*, his most notable role to date and a part "which Philip Barry had supposedly written for him."[41] However when he joined this production the omens were not good. The Theater Guild was on the verge of bankruptcy and Barry had not had a hit for a long time. But the combination of the play's wit and the talent of a great ensemble cast including Joseph Cotten and Shirley Booth meant this was a real winner and sold out for most of its 417 performances. During his first rehearsal Van "quit because he didn't like the way he was treated in the third act." Barry made a "couple of concessions" and placated his temperamental discovery.[42]

Sardonic, left-wing *Spy* reporter Macaulay is invited to cover the forthcoming society wedding of Tracy Lord (Hepburn) to a suitable candidate from her same social set, George Kittredge (Frank Fenton). Things do not go according to plan and after several misadventures on the morning of the wedding, the groom is replaced by C. Dexter Gordon (Cotten), from whom she had just gone through a long divorce. This sophisticated high comedy was Katharine Hepburn's project from start to finish; she chose the cast herself (even persuading the reluctant Cotten to appear) and bought the rights to it. Later she was given a present of the film rights by Howard Hughes and sold them to MGM's Louis B. Mayer for $250,000.[43] In the process she lost a certain degree of artistic control over cast, director and producer. Hepburn wanted Spencer Tracy and Clark Gable for the main roles; she got Cary Grant and James Stewart, which most believe to have been a stroke of genius. The film was a hit and became a classic of its era.

Heflin's personal notices were excellent. "It would be hard to improve upon Van Heflin's honest and solid description of a tough-minded writer," wrote *New York Times* critic Brooks Atkinson. This remarkably successful play opened at the Schubert Theater on March 28, 1939; it closed a year later almost to the day and toured for nearly another year. By then Heflin had turned thirty-one and his movie career was beginning to gather momentum after a faltering start.

Heflin was extremely busy at this time. There were eight performances weekly of *The Philadelphia Story* and he featured on radio six times a week. Once the Broadway run ended, the company embarked on a long tour of the country. Beginning at the end of September 1940 at the Forrest Theater in Philadelphia, they played 47 dates in total, moving from Rochester, New York, then up to the Royal Alexander Theater in Toronto, Canada, a country which had already been at war for a year. The itinerary took in many towns and cities in Ohio including Toledo, Dayton, Cleveland and Cincinnati. They moved on to St. Louis, Missouri; Detroit, Michigan; Milwaukee and Madison, Wisconsin; reached Indiana in December, and spent the pre–Christmas days in Cedar Rapids, Des Moines and Sioux City, Iowa. After a few days off for the festive season, the tour resumed in Kansas City, Missouri; and spent New Year's Day 1941 at the Shrine Theater in Van's home town of Oklahoma City for a matinee and evening performance. The remainder of the tour passed through Fort Worth, Waco, Austin, San Antonio and Houston, Texas; then via New Orleans through Mississippi, Tennessee and Alabama. It finally ended on January 30 at the Erlinger Theater in Atlanta, Georgia.[44]

Despite the hectic schedule and constant travelling, Van enjoyed the rough-and-ready life touring (even the "punk hotels") and noted all the different reactions to lines in audiences across the country.[45] He also came to realize the power of movies and their relation to the theater after the film version of *The Philadelphia Story* was cast with James Stewart playing his role. Stewart, he observed, "could be seen by as many people in two days as had seen me in two years of the play's run. And he could get an Academy Award for doing it."[46] It must have been galling for Van to lose out on the movie part because he was not considered "box office" and even more so to be billed in the trailer as "the man who played Jimmy Stewart's part in the stage version."[47] It was some time before he could even bring himself to watch the movie. When he did, he finally decided that he should cast his lot with Hollywood.[48]

Ironically, after his greatest success it would be another twelve years before he returned to the stage. But his heart really never left it. He learned his craft there and always stressed the importance of theater to any aspiring actor—or even the biggest stars. He felt actors should escape from the cocoon of Hollywood and return to the stage as often as possible. "Those who do," he reflected, "will find it will help them and also the profession of which they are a part."[49] He had lived a life before his acting career so was always able to keep everything in true perspective. He remained a grounded personality who kept in touch with the real world which gave him the acute sense of reality he brought to every role he essayed.

Three

Hollywood Awaits
(1936–41)

A False Start at RKO

"I'd rather not talk about it. I made three awful pictures and I thought I was through with movies forever."
—Heflin on his RKO contract[1]

The 1930s was the beginning of a golden age of film although few may have realized it at the time. The coming of sound had moved things on apace and despite the apparent staginess of many productions, the best of them have stood the test of time. The films Heflin made at this stage of his career were not the best of their time and display many of the faults and only some of the virtues of the decade. Clearly he was not impressed with them but they nevertheless have some merit if only to show his development as an actor.

Few young actors received the roles they deserved when just starting out; there was intense competition and the studio system was in full swing. Until an audience was established for a particular star, he or she was not in a position to pick and choose. Within the constraints of working in Hollywood, Heflin gave his best. The fact that he managed to make an impression at all given his material and limited scope speaks volumes for his skill, determination and promise in the profession.

Once Katharine Hepburn had helped secure his contract with RKO via her friend Howard Hughes, Heflin did a screen test and he signed up in New York. Studio bosses were satisfied with his test, but he was not a known quantity for them; they "wanted to be sure he would 'go' with the public." RKO executives were doubtful because he wasn't in their view handsome; "[H]e had few of the conventional assets, his appeal to women

25

After seeing Heflin in *End of Summer*, Katharine Hepburn helped him secure his first movie contract with RKO through her friend Howard Hughes. His first film was a stolid period drama, *A Woman Rebels* (1936), which was a box office failure. "I always start with stinkers," he quipped. He later enjoyed great success on stage in *The Philadelphia Story* alongside Kate.

was questionable, he was too quiet-mannered and didn't excel at wearing clothes." However, they did agree that he could act.[2]

Leading lady and friend Hepburn also knew he could act and asked for him to be cast opposite her in *A Woman Rebels* (1936). Set in Victorian England and based on the novel *Portrait of a Rebel* by Netta Syrett, this was ultimately less a feminist rallying call than a stolid period drama. Heflin, playing a lord, was required to age twenty years. Hence his character acting credentials were already established at the age of twenty-seven.

Pamela (Hepburn) and her sister Flora (Elizabeth Allan) are living under the strict regimen of Paterfamilias Byron Thistlewaite (Donald Crisp), a judge. Flora marries a dashing soldier, Lieutenant Alan Freeland. Pamela is lonely and begins an affair with Hon. Gerald Waring Gaythorne (Heflin), whom she often meets in the Left Wing of Madame Tussaud's in front of the *Romeo and Juliet* display. Alan and Flora move to Italy. Pamela visits them and meets a diplomat, Thomas Lane (Herbert Marshall). Flora is expecting a child and Pamela confesses that she too is pregnant. Lane proposes to Pamela but she turns him down, fearing that if the scandal came out it would ruin his career. News arrives of the death of Alan in an explosion. On hearing this, Flora collapses on the stone steps and hurts her head. She loses the child and hovers between life and death. She makes Pamela promise that when her child is born, she will raise it as her niece.

Daughter Flora is born and calls her mother Auntie Pam. Pamela embarks on a career of her own, initially working for Mr. White, editor of a woman's magazine. At first she follows his conservative editorial stance but an encounter with an unmarried mother who commits suicide arouses her to rebellion. She is very successful in fighting for the cause of women's rights and in time begins her own periodical.

Years pass and the adult Flora is courted by young Gerald Waring, son of her old paramour. Pamela forbids Flora to see Gerald again and, fearing the truth coming to light, goes to Waring's house to plead with him not to say anything. He agrees, but two servants see her leaving his quarters at two o'clock in the morning and she is cited in the divorce case which Waring's wife has been seeking for years.

This was Hepburn's picture from start to finish and she made the best of her role as a fiery eccentric. But this was precisely the kind of persona audiences were beginning to find tiresome. She herself considered the material "mediocre" and had to be persuaded to take the role by producer Pandro S. Berman, who believed it would restore her popularity after the disappointing *Mary of Scotland* lost the studio a great deal of money.

The weak screenplay tiptoed around its own subject matter; it seemed barely able to bring itself to mention pregnancy, and it felt as though the mere mention of the word *bastard* might have brought the scenery crashing down. Pamela's affair with Gerald consists mostly of assignations in the gazebo and especially in the Left Wing of Madame Tussaud's where standing in front of the *Romeo and Juliet* display under an inconstant moon seems to lead to more than a girl ever bargained for. *A Woman Rebels* would hardly have frightened the horses in 1836 let alone 1936. Any sense of real rebellion was thoroughly diluted and the result was judged "remote and insubstantial" at best and "lamentable" at worst. Suffice to say it did not do well at the box office.[3]

Heflin was not required to contribute substantially. He is introduced at a dance; looking very young, he is soft-spoken, courtly in manner, with a charming smile. He seems light on his feet and admits to being the black sheep of his family; he is quite obviously a cad. The young actor tries to inject as much life as possible into the turgid script, but little can be done. He seems a tender lover with an appealing personality; however his scenes are fairly brief and once the affair with Pamela ends, he is not seen again until much later, when he is twenty years older. He plays these scenes well and here at last the dramatic situation might have appealed to him. The older Gerald is bitter and has had an unhappy life; his son hates him and the only satisfaction he has is in not granting his wife a divorce and therefore depriving her of his fortune. As he says pointedly, "Two people can be bound together as much by hate as they can by love." Far more time could have been given to the character of Gerald Waring and his later life, if perhaps all the chief characters had been developed simultaneously and more of his home life had been shown. But the witless screenplay ensured that the film had the appearance of disparate scenes which seemed not to hang together.

This was not a personal disaster for Heflin, by no means a failure, but it was not an auspicious start to his movie career. The director Mark Sandrich, who had recently scored with *Top Hat*, seemed uninterested and the screenwriters Anthony Veiller and Ernest Vadja hardly warmed to their task. Some reviews were positive; Frank Nugent (*The New York Times*) commented, "Delving into the fascinating ugliness of Victorian England, RKO Radio [has] found material that is picturesque, humorous and tragic."[4]

A Woman Rebels did little to enhance anyone's reputation and unsurprisingly lost the studio $222,000 in the process.[5] "My first picture was awful," Heflin later commented. "I always start with stinkers—it's the story of my life."[6] But it did at least lead to a long-term radio contract.[7]

His second venture sounded more promising: *The Outcasts of Poker*

Flat (1937) was based on two stories by popular Western writer Bret Harte (the other was *Luck of Roaring Camp*). It's set in one of the many gold mining camps of California in the 1850s, where John Oakhurst (Preston Foster) runs the saloon and gambling house. A child is born; the father is unknown and the mother dies; Oakhurst becomes the child's foster father and names the girl Luck. Eight years later, Luck is an expert card player and the town is more lawless. The Reverend Sam Woods (Heflin) and school-teacher Helen Corby (Jean Muir) are invited to the town by its law-abiding residents. Oakhurst immediately falls for Helen and forces Luck to go to school. Before long there are shootings at Oakhurst's place and the righteous citizens demand that Woods run the gambler and his associates out of town, which he is unwilling to do. Things come to a head when a man is killed and Oakhurst kills another man in revenge. Made to leave, he heads out with his friends including the Duchess and Kentuck. Helen Corby joins them on the outskirts of town as the snow begins to fall.

What could have been an entertaining human drama became little more than a stagey second feature which never seems to rouse from its stupor. Screenwriter John Twist failed to bring the enterprise to life. Harte's characters and situations were always larger than life, full of robust humor and pathos. This proved to be an opportunity missed, a poor adaptation of the author's warm and rousing stories which lost most of his innate "feeling and appreciation for character" and suffered under Christy Cabanne's leaden direction. The result was "just another routine western."[8]

Heflin's character the Reverend Sam Woods was a composite personality who appeared in neither of the original stories.[9] Heflin gave the role the stamp of authenticity and authority required despite the poorly realized screenplay. His all too apparent youth, his curly hair and ready smile belied the ability he already displayed to inhabit a character. Woods appears mild-mannered and may wear the collar but he is determined. His flashes of temper show he is not a man to trifle with and he will do anything to see fairness prevail.

Heflin was so good, he put most of the other actors to shame. Preston Foster was a decent but rather deadpan lead. Jean Muir was merely weak; she played the schoolmistress in an over-pious manner and her later switch to bitchy repartee with the Duchess did not convince. Some of the characters seemed worthy of Harte—for example, Kentuck and the bartender (a lively vignette by Billy Gilbert)—but even they were not allowed to develop beyond two dimensions.

Despite the apparent failure of *The Outcasts of Poker Flat*, Heflin emerged with credit. As he intones with his customary sincerity the words

of eulogy for John Oakhurst, gambler, in the final scene, comforting a tear-
ful Luck, he gives a glimpse of what might have been a much more engaging human drama. *Variety* praised his showing and noted that he "proves
he is deserving of further consideration."[10]

His third entry for RKO was *Flight from Glory* adapted by David Sil-
verstein and John Twist from Robert D. Andrews' story. An unscrupulous
villain Ellis (Onslow Stevens) recruits maverick and down-on-their-luck
pilots to fly run-down planes over the Andes. He keeps them in debt by
over-charging for food and liquor. Into this community of outcasts comes
disgraced flyer Wilson (Heflin), who has had his license revoked in the
States. His wife Lee (Whitney Bourne) promptly falls in love with the chief
pilot Smith (Chester Morris). Wilson has a drinking problem and when
he sees another pilot crash he resorts to drink once again. Hilton offers
Wilson and his wife enough money to return to the United States, but
they refuse. Soon Wilson is too intoxicated to fly so Hilton takes his flight
and crashes. Realizing the harm he has done, Wilson is filled with shame
and guilt. Ellis asks him to take a flight out and he agrees; Ellis accompanies
him as co-pilot. As they fly "high over the mountains [Wilson] hands the
controls over to … Ellis … and jumps to his death."[11] Ellis cannot control
the plane and crashes spectacularly. Wilson's widow finds happiness with
Smith and the two go back to the States to start anew.

Featuring some remarkable aerial photography for its time, *Flight
from Glory* showed "an unusual cross-section of life among exiled men
who daily flirt with death and who are unable to forsake their dangerous
occupation."[12] Set in a bleak South American air base, this was a tense and
exciting story "intensified by the brooding spirit of the lonely little community and its people and of the vast peaks that tower above them."[13] Wilson is a weak character, totally reliant on drink; his one act of redemption
is his suicide at the end. His death leads to that of the chief villain of the
piece, Ellis, who has a mortgage on the lives of all who work for him. The
isolation of the air base and the shame of the characters' past misde-
meanors crowds in on them all under the terrible pressure of their dangerous missions in ramshackle airplanes. Wilson is a prototype for a
number of Heflin's characterizations: a weak but believable personality,
not essentially bad but lacking any kind of resolve and ultimately unable
to live with himself or his own sense of failure.

Few of the actors were praised individually; this was an ensemble
piece which presented a "striking series of portrayals" and all the participants gave "outstanding characterizations." Some critics did single out
Heflin who showed "splendid acting ability."[14]

Heflin (center) made a good impression as the love rival to James Ellison for the affections of Marsha Hunt in RKO's *Annapolis Salute* (1937), a romantic yarn set at the U.S. Naval Academy in Maryland.

Annapolis Salute (also known as *Salute to Romance*) was described at the time as a "thrilling and vivid romance" about rivalries among midshipmen at a Naval college.[15] Long-serving non-combatant Petty Officer Chief Martin (Harry Carey) longs to see his son Bill (James Ellison) become an officer and vicariously fulfill his own thwarted ambition. Bill falls for Julia Clemons (Marsha Hunt) who is also being courted by Clay V. Parker (Heflin), a "spoiled socialite who [only] enters the Academy to gratify a wealthy relative" (his millionaire grandfather). Bill wishes to marry but Navy regulations forbid this until after graduation; he is prepared to resign in order to wed. He later faces expulsion after an incident in which he is accused of running away from an accident without reporting it to the authorities; this could mean the end of his Navy career before it has begun. In the end, all turns out happily: The two feuding midshipmen become lasting friends, Bill gets the girl, and his father achieves his long-held ambition when he sees his son graduate in a rousing and patriotic finale.

Filmed mostly on location at the U.S. Naval Academy at Annapolis, Maryland, during the summer of 1937, this movie showed many scenes of college life such as "drills and parades, class-room work, social life, including a spring dance at the armory, small-boat drill, crew racing and other phases of a midshipman's existence..."[16]

Partly written by its director Christy Cabanne, himself a former Academy cadet, this predictable "adolescent lesson in love and loyalty" nonetheless did good business at theaters where service yarns always proved popular.[17] The Navy gave its full cooperation and were immensely satisfied with the result. With its upbeat tone and stirring patriotic climax, this was in essence a Navy recruitment film. Its value to a modern audience is more for its historical footage of the pre-war Academy than for its storyline. Although the movie was generally dismissed as a "shoddy remake" of *Midshipman Jack* of three years earlier, Heflin stood out. "[T]he acting honors rest with Carey and Heflin," wrote one reviewer. "[Heflin] is a young actor of distinct promise, and I look forward to seeing more of him." Another said he looked "like a less dangerous James Cagney and has some impertinent charm."[18] Heflin would later corner the market in perky minor villains such as Parker and he showed more life and spark here than James Ellison, who never quite made the grade as a leading man. J.C. Jenkin of the *Motion Picture Herald* commented, "If they don't go headlining him pretty soon we are going to make a squawk about it."[19]

After only four films at RKO he was handed the lead role in *Saturday's Heroes*, a rousing, good-humored movie tackling the thorny issue of professionalism in college sports. Val Webster (Heflin), star player for Calton's football team, is dating the coach's attractive daughter Frances (Marian Marsh). He cannot make ends meet so he scalps tickets on the side. His sensitive best friend Ted is accused of being a ringer (a clearly overqualified player used to gain an unfair advantage) and is thrown off the team. Unable to live with the shame, he commits suicide. Incensed, Val speaks out against the hypocrisy of the faculty which accepts huge profits but turns a blind eye to what goes on. He teams with reporter Red Watson to expose the double standards with which the amateur game is riddled. He then moves to a small college with a hopeless football team and intends to coach them to victory, thus bringing attention to the central issue.

"For at least two-thirds of its running time," wrote one critic, "*Saturday's Heroes* is among the best sports films of the 1930s."[20] Heflin was enthusiastic and appealing as the young hero, with an easy smile one minute and socking Red Watson in the jaw the next. Sometimes showing flashes of temper and his trademark intensity, he received excellent notices. "Van Heflin and Marian Marsh carry the brunt of the story and act the leading roles with conviction. Heflin ... looks the part and brings the proper shade of restraint and vigor to the role."[21] Another critic remarked that Heflin was "well-cast, and with care can be worked up to more important roles."[22]

Director Edward Killy helmed over a score of movies. Few of them were particularly memorable; *Saturday's Heroes* was perhaps his best. Although amiable, the screenplay did not shy away from addressing an unappealing subject which is still under discussion today: the influence of money in sports and its effect on the status of the game. Sports lovers will no doubt enjoy the scenes on the field of play. The story was written by George Templeton, who was part of the winning freshman team at UCLA alongside a young John Wayne in the 1920s.

Heflin was later disparaging about his time at RKO. Frustrated by his lack of opportunity, he impatiently decided he would rather return to the New York stage than continue his Hollywood career. After six months of making "one B-picture after another" he beat his employers to the punch and marched into the front office, telling them he didn't want to stay. The executives tried to persuade him otherwise but he had made up his mind and promptly returned to New York.[23]

He went back to the theater and perfected his craft. It seems that he expected too much too soon from movies; after all, few actors make an instant impression. Most serve a long apprenticeship before finding a plum role. He was good in *Saturday's Heroes*; the reviews were remarkably positive for him personally; in some quarters he was already being billed as a "dynamic new screen personality,"[24] one "who has risen rapidly to screen prominence."[25] Perhaps if he had been less hasty to abandon films after so few attempts, he would have found his way in the medium and achieved success far sooner than he did.

It would be two years before he made another movie, his time taken up with *The Philadelphia Story* and its subsequent year-long tour. The Vernon Steele Production *Back Door to Heaven* (1939), filmed at the Kaufman Astoria Studios in Queens, New York, was written and directed by William K. Howard, who had scored a hit with *Fire Over England* two years earlier. Although perhaps appearing over-sentimental to modern viewers, this glum tale of the downward spiral in the life of Frankie Rogers nonetheless retains its power to move largely because of the honesty of the central performance by Wallace Ford. One feels certain that this overlooked actor put a great deal of his own feeling into this role, having suffered many hardships himself as a child.

Heflin gave a sensitive portrayal as small-town lawyer John Shelley, who seeks to help a childhood friend in the touching melodrama *Back Door to Heaven* (1939). He's seen here with Patricia Ellis.

The story is framed by scenes of Rogers' disadvantaged childhood which sets him on his difficult road; it culminates with a very strange school reunion where all the friends meet as adults many years later and Frankie is on the run from the police, having escaped from jail. Heflin played convincingly as the sympathetic but struggling small town lawyer John Shelley who tries in vain to save his friend from the gallows. Towards the end he has one short speech where he makes the case for mercy; he is nervous and often hesitant but emotional and heartfelt, in keeping with the character and situation. Here is a callow youth who is clearly more accustomed to drawing up deeds and conveyances than pleading for someone's life. Despite his relatively short screen time, Heflin's character was without doubt the most memorable characterization after the lead.

Despite his great Broadway success, Heflin was keen to re-enter movies for personal motives. Soon after *The Philadelphia Story* he learned that his father had cancer, which made him anxious to please him as much as possible. His dad had always longed to see Van make it big in the movies; he felt movie stardom made a bigger splash than a stage career. He was especially keen on the idea of Van living in a house with a pool, which to the father would be proof that his son had arrived. For his part, Heflin admitted that he hated swimming pools.[26]

He soon had an opportunity to get back into films and work on getting a swimming pool. Between the end of the Broadway run of *The Philadelphia Story* in March 1940 and the start of the ten-month tour that followed, he was offered the part of Cadet Rader in director Michael Curtiz's *Santa Fe Trail* for Warner Brothers. He showed to great effect as a villainous rival of Errol Flynn in a tale that eschewed historical fact in favor of entertainment. The usual Flynn cohorts were present (Alan Hale, Guinn "Big Boy" Williams) but the most memorable performances came from the veteran Raymond Massey as "God's Angry Man" John Brown and Heflin.

Despite its title, *Santa Fe Trail* took place solely in Kansas and purported to be based on the events which led to the Civil War. Screenwriter Robert Bruckner maintained that it should be "eight parts entertainment and two parts fact"; it could be argued that he ended up with a ratio more like nine to one. Herein is the main problem with this film; unlike others by the same team such as *Dodge City* and *They Died with Their Boots On*, it was less easy to suspend disbelief because the war, its causes and aftermath are still so contentious. As one critic observed, *Santa Fe Trail* was confident only in its rollicking action in true *Boy's Own* Saturday afternoon style, but far less assured in its treatment of the issues surrounding slavery.[27] It is also over-simplistic and is particularly damning of John Brown, who emerges as a madman intent on smashing the Union and starting the Civil War almost singlehandedly. His granddaughter took great exception to his portrayal and attempted to sue Warner Brothers for damages for defamation of character.[28]

It was rousing entertainment once it was taken on its own terms, most decidedly a crowd-puller, and proved to be Heflin's breakthrough role. Billed by the studio as "The Man You Hate to Hate!" he was incisive as the sly West Pointer with the seditious and dangerous anti-slavery opinions who gets into a fight with Jeb Stuart (Flynn) and is dismissed before graduation. He then throws in his lot with John Brown.

According to one report, Errol Flynn saved Heflin's life while on location: "only Flynn's expert horsemanship saved him from certain death." The two became good friends and Van often spent weekends on Errol's boat.[29]

Heflin was informed by Warners that he should "never play anything but heavies," but he was not about to be typecast. Versatility was his hallmark. There was one scene where he was required to shoot a child; Heflin objected strongly and Curtiz agreed to remove it. The next day he left Hollywood without seeing the rushes. Some time later he went to a mati-

Heflin scored a hit as renegade Cadet Rader in Warners' *Santa Fe Trail* (1940) with Raymond Massey (right) as John Brown. Heflin was such a convincing and oddly likable villain that he was soon billed as "The Man You Hate to Hate."

nee showing of *Santa Fe Trail* with Katharine Hepburn at a Texas movie theater. When it came to that scene, he saw himself shooting. "Next came a close-up insert shot where the young boy toppled dead from his saddle. I slunk down in my seat as the audience gasped."[30]

The two hastily left their seats and ran straight into a boy in the lobby who recognized him and starting shouting, "He'll kill me, he'll kill me!" His concerned parents and numerous "Texas giants" came running from their seats. According to Heflin, only the presence of Hepburn prevented a lynching that day.

Such was the power of the movies; he was ever after wary of playing too many heels. He also made sure he watched rushes whenever possible. So effective was he as Rader that other studios began to take an interest in him. Soon it was said that Warner Brothers must have been "kicking themselves all over Burbank for not hanging onto him." When he moved to MGM he was soon tipped as their "hottest bet for stardom." Warner Brothers reacted by giving him a three-picture deal to take effect once the year-long provincial tour of *The Philadelphia Story* was complete.[31]

High Hopes at Metro

Heflin was not, in his own words "swamped with offers" so "he telephoned MGM talent scout Billy Grady and requested a screen test." He did the test opposite Donna Mullinger, who later became Donna Reed. The young actress was signed instantly and two days later cast in her first picture; Heflin settled for a stock deal. "It worked out remarkable for her and good for me," he recalled.[32] Grady commented that it was "a piperoo for them both."[33] Heflin was offered $550 a week, $150 less than his stage salary. He accepted because, as he explained in his self-deprecatory way, he wanted to get a movie "name" and thought he was not handsome enough to rely on his looks or personality so would establish himself as an actor.

It was the beginning of an eight-year stint that initially brought him success but which ultimately did not make the best use of his talents. At first, the talk was of him being "scheduled for a big publicity build-up ... and [that he] may be Norma Shearer's leading man in her next film."[34] However Shearer was nearing the end of her career. In the event she only appeared twice more on the screen, her lovers were the more predictable Melvyn Douglas and Robert Taylor.

Heflin's first outing for the studio was going to be the crime drama *The Enemy Within*, directed by Richard Rosson. This was retitled *The Getaway* but Heflin is not in the finished movie. Instead he was cast in Joseph L. Mankiewicz's light-hearted production *The Feminine Touch* which boasted four appealing leads: Rosalind Russell, Don Ameche, Kay Francis and Heflin sporting an unfamiliar and unsuitable goatee that provided this smart comedy with much mileage for gags. He showed a natural timing and flair for the genre, very much underplaying. He was subtle where necessary and did not appear ill at ease. After his terrific success in the sophisticated highbrow comedy *The Philadelphia Story* it was unsurprising that he should be cast in a similar type of movie. The writer George Oppenheimer and director W.S. Van Dyke were past masters of the métier, and the often witty script benefitted from additional dialogue by Ogden Nash. College professor John Hathaway (Ameche) wants to publish his hefty scholarly tome *Jealousy in All Its Aspects and Universal Applications* to prove that it is possible to eliminate jealousy from all relationships. He approaches publisher Elliott Morgan (Heflin) and becomes sidetracked by his attractive secretary Nellie Woods (Francis). Then Morgan becomes infatuated with Hathaway's wife Julie (Russell). Thereafter the plot begins its predictable meanderings to reach its happy ending where suitably jealous husband is reunited with wife and suitably chastened publisher is matched up with his secretary.

Part of a cycle of screwball comedies, *The Feminine Touch* is a rarely seen movie which would be of great interest to students of the era and its genres. It was viewed at the time as an "ultra-modern" and "sparkling" comedy "with a background of literary bohemianism"; now much of the humor appears dated.[35] As ever in this form of comedy, the whole premise is flimsy; the "story had the weight of a damp feather," wrote one contemporary reviewer. However the actors work very well together in a fine ensemble showing. No one outshines anyone else, or tries. Much-loved director Major Van Dyke was known affectionately as One Take Woody; he was a larger-than-life character whose chief commercial and critical success was the *Thin Man* series. His early death at age 53 came a few years later; *The Feminine Touch* was one of his final films. Here the stylish "Gowns by Adrian," the song "Jealousy" and an appealing dream sequence in which Ameche and Heflin have a comical fight over Russell to the strains of a lush Franz Waxman score are all highlights. Once the story moves on to Morgan's country lodge retreat there are several delightful scenes involving Donald Meek, who watches as Ameche and Heflin chase each other around a tree and square up pathetically for a fight that adds an appealing element of pure farce to the ending. Heflin generally scores as a "fake sophisticate" with a roving eye. However the film as a whole is rather uneven. The combination of sometimes witty but often verbose dialogue interrupted by bursts of broad comedy is not entirely successful.

Fourth-billed Heflin was singled out by many reviewers for his "original and breezy performance."[36] One praised him as "an actor who is amusing in his suggestion of a lunacy most sanely aware of itself."[37] Another wrote that he "steals almost every scene he's in—even from Kay Francis, who has never done a better acting job.... Heflin is positively brilliant as the lecherous publisher..."[38] All agreed he had scored a hit and he was being noticed even among a cast of established stars. "The fourth member of the quartet is Van Heflin, a young man ... of whom we shall hear more. Mr. Heflin comes from the stage to play the neurotic wolf with style and dispatch, his is the rapier touch nicely contrasted with the sponge-like playing of Ameche."[39]

Heflin plays the unorthodox best friend of Robert Young (left) in *H. M. Pulham, Esq.* (1941). The subordinate "best friend" role became all too familiar for Heflin during his years at MGM. "I sometimes wish I never had a friend," he once commented wryly.

It seemed an auspicious start to his time at Metro—at least in the short term. But it also underlined just how limited his chances might be there. A glance at the Warner Brothers repertoire for 1941—*The Sea Wolf, High Sierra, Out of the Fog, The Maltese Falcon*—showed how much more scope he might have had elsewhere.

In his next movie he was again the ever-supportive best friend of the main character, a position that became rather too familiar during his MGM years.[40] King Vidor's *H.M. Pulham, Esq.*, adapted from the John P. Marquand bestseller, told the tale of stuffy, middle-aged Bostonian Harry Pulham. Born of a good family, he takes stock of his life while writing a résumé of his career for a school reunion. He begins to question his happiness and in particular recalls his greatest love Marvin Miles (Hedy Lamarr), an advertising copywriter he planned to marry; she felt stifled by the weight of his family tradition and he married his childhood sweetheart Cordelia (Ruth Hussey) instead. After many years he again meets Marvin but they are unable to re-connect.

This was essentially a lament for the road not taken in life and as such might have had profound things to say about the human condition. But the whole was presented in a generally light-hearted vein so that the dramatic impact was somewhat diluted. However its structure was interesting. There was intriguing use of internal monologues and the flashback sequences were cleverly interwoven, which at times made it engrossing. The final third of the movie appeared to drift, and plot-wise the outcome seemed to be signposted: In the end, Pulham goes back to his conservative and rich life. As one observer commented, "perhaps because it showed conventions and traditions triumphant over romantic freedom—it was not big box office."[41]

Heflin was not over-taxed as Pulham's best friend Bill Kent. They first meet at Harvard; he is introduced as a laid-back character, inclined to bookish pursuits with a healthy disregard for college sport, and in particular the mock heroics of the football "hero" "Bo-Jo" Brown (Leif Erickson). After World War I, Bill gets Harry a job at his New York advertising company where he first meets Marvin. The three are firm friends and Harry invites Bill and Marvin to the family home in Boston. Both feel out of place but Bill is very attracted to Kay. Later they all go sledging together with Harry's sister Mary (Bonita Granville) and Joe Bingham (Phil Brown). Joe becomes rather jealous of the time Kay and Bill are spending together. When Harry decides to marry Kay instead, Bill is best man, which is the last time he appears in the film.

Heflin's name is fifth on the cast list behind Charles Coburn. The thankless role of Bill Kent is underwritten; although there is hint of a romance between him and Kay, this does not become especially apparent, and his character is not developed satisfactorily nor is he central enough to the plot. However Bill is an important character quietly underscoring the satiric nature of Marquand's novel, and Heflin makes the most of his limited opportunities. He gives a living portrait of a personality who is seldom fazed by anything and has charm and a wry humor which carries him through life. In one early scene he enters the common room at Harvard where the football bores are gathered to pay homage to their "hero," who has hurt his leg in a tackle. Although he says little, Heflin's thoughts are manifest in his facial expressions and a roll of the eyes at the sycophancy of his fellow players. In other scenes he established a kind of cynical streak of humor and sideways manner of looking at the world. In total contrast to Harry Pulham, his life is not bound by convention. This contrast is not sufficiently brought out. Altogether he had only a few short scenes which he played with his usual ease; he also briefly got a chance to sing a song, "Where Do I Go from Here?" a question he might well be left asking after several years at MGM.

H. M. Pulham, Esq. was a prestigious film, and despite only being a supporting player Heflin was already being noticed. There was something different about him. Most critics were supportive and excited by the new star, and even the chary amongst them had to grudgingly admit his worth. "Heflin, like olives, is a cultivated taste…" commented Louella Parsons. "He has an unusual personality I must admit; [and he is] not conventionally handsome—but he has a way with the ladies."[42]

Metro announced that his next film *Joe Smith, American* would team him once more with Robert Young and Marsha Hunt. Heflin's part went to Harvey Stephens instead.[43]

At this stage of his career Heflin appeared comfortable but had not been challenged by any role. His next film *Johnny Eager* would change all that and point the way not just to his future direction but make the studios and the wider world sit up and take note that here was an actor of some considerable ability and promise. He was not the star of the picture but he would in many ways outshine star Robert Taylor (one of the biggest of his time), no mean feat for a young and relatively inexperienced movie player. It was a chance meeting on the lot with Taylor that led to his big chance. "He introduced himself and told me he had a story coming up with a good part for me, and that I'd better go after it. After that I rolled." In a few short years every actor would know to be on their toes if they ever had to share the screen with Van. Before long the word around Hollywood was "Watch out for Heflin."[44]

Four

"Watch Out for Heflin"

Eager *and After (1941–45)*

> "I liked the inebriated youth in Johnny Eager better than
> anything I have ever played. That young man interested
> me. He was so intelligent, with nothing evil in his make-
> up. He got involved with gangsters because of his one fail-
> ing—a love of drink. He was sensitive and an idealist."[1]

Johnny Eager gave Heflin a chance to shine in a part that could have
been made for him. He had the perfect sensitivity to understand the character thoroughly and make him entirely empathetic. He deservedly won
the Best Supporting Actor Oscar for his portrayal ahead of such stalwarts
as Walter Huston, William Bendix and Frank Morgan. He had a great facil-
ity for portraying drunkards and could run the gamut from slightly tipsy
to roaring drunk without ever striking a false note. No doubt his experience with his father, to say nothing of his seven years at sea, had given him
ample opportunity to observe the effects of drink both directly and indi-
rectly.

Mervyn LeRoy's *Johnny Eager* concerns the adventures of one-time
big shot Eager (Robert Taylor), recently released from the state peniten-
tiary. Under the conditions of his parole he must report regularly to the
D.A. To outward appearances he is a cab driver living in a small apartment
block with his young niece and a housekeeper (Connie Gilchrist); both
are paid stooges. Eager's real life takes place at the dog track where behind
the scenes he runs the whole operation as a big business exploiting every
angle possible and surrounded by a gang consisting of Marco, Julio and
Benjy. Heflin is newspaperman Jeff Hartnett, Eager's intelligent best friend
and confidante, invariably under the influence of drink no matter what
the time of day. He is almost like a mirror held up to Eager reflecting the

Heflin was outstanding as Jeff Hartnett, the conscience of hood Robert Taylor (left), in Mervyn LeRoy's *Johnny Eager* (1941). Frequently emotional, he made a real impact in a role that other actors disdained. It brought him a well-deserved Oscar as Best Supporting Actor.

troubles in his soul. "Why do I keep you around?" asks Eager at one stage. "I don't know—why do you?" asks Jeff. Eager is offhand with his girl Garnet (Patricia Dane) who doesn't like Jeff and feels strangely threatened by his intelligence and his very presence. His constant stream of quotations from classical literature infuriates her. When he likens her to Agrippina, it is the final straw. "Who is this Agry-pina dame anyway?" she demands.

In a very clever breakfast scene, Jeff nurses a hangover while gingerly smoking a cigarette. Garnet arrives and he tells her to go down to Miami until the heat is off; actually, this is the "brush-off" for her because he met Lisbeth (Lana Turner) the night before. Befuddled though he clearly is, and through a haze of smoke, Jeff looks at Garnet with concern. That says a great deal about his feelings with the subtlest of touches. After Garnet leaves, he speaks his mind, asking Johnny why he didn't tell the poor kid. Johnny is surprised, unable to understand how Jeff could feel sorry for someone he didn't like. Jeff tells him it is "possible to feel sorry for someone you don't like, if you've got any humanity." This raises the hackles of Eager and there follows a rundown of Johnny's egocentric philosophy of life. "Now I know why you keep me around," says Jeff when he has finished his diatribe. "Even Johnny Eager needs a friend."

Johnny always retains Jeff no matter what; there is an intensity to the relationship which seems mired in emotion, at least on Jeff's side, and a strong case can be made that this is in effect a homoerotic relationship as some have commented.[2] Johnny really seems to *need* Jeff around and he is practically always by his side. It is also noticeable how Eager is decidedly offhand with "dames," especially Garnet, to whose kisses he appears indifferent. Even the arrival of Lana Turner as the shapely Lisbeth is not enough to break the ties that bind Jeff and Johnny. At the end, when Lisbeth is packed off with her society boyfriend and Johnny lies dying in the street after a gunfight, it is Jeff who holds him in his arms and, with tears streaming down his face, hears his last words: He talks about the name of the highest mountain where they are going. The emphasis is on "we" and the implication is quite obvious: Whatever happens, they will always be together.

It might be argued that Jeff and Johnny need each other because each reflects what the other lacks. Johnny, ruthless and resolute, sees all his plans through, no matter who has to be trampled; he is cold, heartless even. Jeff is weak, irresolute, a hopeless drunk, but he is intelligent and above all kind-hearted. Each has a fascination for the other and they seek on some unconscious level to understand one another. It is a simple law that opposites attract.

Heflin gave a remarkably subtle, layered portrait of a deeply flawed personality. Always emotional, he is often close to tears and cries on more than one occasion. It was a risky strategy that only an assured actor would be bold enough to undertake. His very modern, naturalistic performance decidedly moves things on from the often stagey acting style of the pre-war era. "He interpreted the part with such vividness," wrote one critic, "that the scenes in which he did not appear were almost dull."[3]

Taylor and Turner were the big box office draws for the movie and the tagline "TAYLOR Is JOHNNY and TURNER Is EAGER!" neatly summed up the producer's (and the public) expectations alike. Heflin effectively stole the picture. He was distinctly modest about his achievement and credited Taylor and Mervyn LeRoy for giving him his chance.[4] Taylor was full of praise for the rising star: "I think it was one of the best performances to ever come out of Hollywood," he later commented.[5] The two became lifelong friends and after the war Taylor, who served in the Navy, gave Heflin flying lessons.[6]

Johnny Eager deserves to be considered one of the first film noirs and one of the most overlooked. Beside the two bona fide stars and Heflin, it had a memorable atmosphere, excellent, stirring music and great support from Edward Arnold as Lisbeth's politically ambitious stepfather. Also good were Paul Stewart, Charles Dingle, Connie Gilchrist and Lou Lubin. The weak link may have been the scenario of John Lee Mahin or James Edward Grant's story; the plot was rather contrived and often strained credulity. However, the whole thing was fast-paced and the combination of terrific actors and a literate and thought-provoking script ensured that there was plenty for the eyes to behold and the imagination to perceive so that cinemagoers would recall the film long after the credits rolled.

Many in Hollywood were suitably impressed with the new star. Legendary actress Gloria Swanson called his Jeff Hartnett "the best performance I can think of."[7] Moreover, he was a hit with the public and it most certainly brought him his "first avalanche of fan mail."[8]

Several other actors had turned down the role of Jeff in *Johnny Eager*; their reasoning was that the part "looked so shallow in the script." But Heflin showed them what could be done. He impressed the bosses at Metro so much that they "promised him a solo starring contract as soon as the war ended."[9] But their promise was not made binding and memories were short. On his return from the war he was left without a project for the best part of a year, and all his roles were subsidiary.

His next picture, *Kid Glove Killer* (1942), might have been a standard whodunit yarn but was lifted out of the commonplace by a perceptive portrait from Heflin and the lively direction of Fred Zinnemann making his feature debut. Heflin as Gordon McKay, head of the city crime lab, investigates a politically motivated assassination via tiny clues left by fibers on gloves. There is constant heavy pressure from the D.A.'s office to get a quick conviction and a suspect is soon in the frame; but McKay is not convinced and cleverly sets out to trap the real killer. Watching people in white coats peering into microscopes sounds like dull fare but this B-movie rattled along splendidly and maintained interest throughout. This was due in no small part to the genuinely intriguing nature of the investigation and the witty romantic byplay between Heflin and Marsha Hunt as his assistant, which is natural and engaging. The supporting cast could have been stronger and a few more character actors would have made this even more appealing. The quality of the two leads only emphasized the blandness of the second lead Lee Bowman.

Director Fred Zinnemann's feature debut *Kid Glove Killer* (1942) was an entertaining whodunit with attractive performances by Heflin as a police scientist and Marsha Hunt as his assistant. The movie proved so popular that Metro planned to make a series with the same characters but then the war intervened.

The critics were generous in their praise of the appealing star who one said "adds decidedly to his laurels with *Kid Glove Killer.*... [His] popularity as a screen luminary is progressively increasing."[10]

He impressed Metro bosses so much with his effective portrayal of the police scientist that it was intended to construct a series using the same characters, which would no doubt have been successful. But the war intervened.[11]

Marsha Hunt said she always loved working with Heflin and particularly enjoyed the experience of making *Kid Glove Killer*, which she remembered fondly. She thoroughly enjoyed the repartee with Heflin; their scenes had great vitality. She was also struck by the openness and adaptability of director Zinnemann, who summoned the cast and crew together beforehand to say that he welcomed any suggestions as to how the picture could be made better.[12]

An entertaining script by Allen Rivkin and John C. Higgins (adapted from an original idea by Higgins) found inventive ways to relieve the tedium of a bogged-down investigation. There are effective little touches like the target practice silhouette dartboard on the other side of the door and McKay's inability to hit any other than the right arm each time until the very end when the actual killer is standing in the doorway and he hits him for real. The rapid-fire repartee and equally swift fight sequences are all handled adroitly and despite his white coat and bookish air McKay proves to be a cool man of action when required. Already the Heflin hallmark of being totally at ease before the camera is very apparent. At no time does he appear to be acting. His natural humor and playfulness are manifest and his total believability is established before a word is spoken.

He was a detective of a different kind in *Grand Central Murder*, a bright and breezy whodunit in which he was almost the lead. Convict Turk (Stephen McNally) escapes at Grand Central Station while being transferred for retrial. He threatens his old girlfriend, stage actress Mida King (Patricia Dane), on the phone. Mida walks out on the show and heads straight for the private railcar belonging to her wealthy boyfriend David Henderson. A short time later she is murdered in the railcar. Suspicion immediately falls on Turk, but soon Chief Inspector Gunther (Sam Levene) has a room full of potential suspects. Enter private detective "Rocky" Custer (Heflin) who already has an interest in the case as he is working for the acquittal of Turk on the previous charge. Before long Custer has a bet with the inspector as to who can solve the case first.

A large but interesting cast made good use of a wordy but witty script by Peter Ruric and the scenes of Grand Central Station in New York (especially the underground area rarely seen) provided a great noir background. Most of the action takes place on three sets: police headquarters, where the suspects are first introduced; the theater where various strands of the story are developed, and finally the private railcar. It's told mostly in flashback at a fast pace. At times there is rather too much going on to make the proceedings coherent but Levene and Heflin furnish the humor and hold the interest. There is a wonderful character turn by the redoubtable Connie Gilchrist as a cigar-smoking, down-on-her-luck stage veteran.

Heflin breezes through the film with perfect assurance. All the little things such as the tilt of his black fedora and the way he handles his pipe whether lit or unlit made him seem totally at ease and in character. He is something of a ladies' man with a wry humor; the asides to his wife and assistant criminologist Sue (Virginia Grey) are subtly handled. The byplay with Baby Leroy (Betty Wells) work especially well; they flirt and gently undermine the inspector's attempts to conduct the investigation. Heflin worked superbly in conjunction with Levene who is constantly harassed and forever calling for another bottle of "pop." But as always Van proved what a generous and capable ensemble player he was. All in all this was a good vehicle for "the studio's most talented young player."[13] His reviews were glowing for his performance as the laid-back private eye.

"Van Heflin, deservedly so, is the fastest-climbing actor in Hollywood. Everything is slouchy, from his hat to his walk and his speech, but it is a pleasant slouchiness that catches the audience.... [Custer was] a role made to order for his talents."[14] He employed his "Oklahoma slouch" which, he said, was also known as a "cotton-patch walk." The verdict at the box office was very positive. *Grand Central Murder* proved an engaging diversion for wartime audiences. At this stage of his career Heflin really seemed to be on his way and was soon being billed as "one of the surest major stars of the very near future."[15]

After a run of roles that played to his strengths, he was back to more recognizable featherweight MGM territory as a replacement for Robert Sterling as one of the suitors in *Seven Sweethearts* (1942), starring 20-year-old Kathryn Grayson. This Frank Borzage musical, originally known as *Tulip Time*, was set in Holland (Michigan) during the Tulip Time Festival. The "plot" concerned the marrying off of the seven daughters of eccentric Dutch innkeeper Mr. Van Maaster (S.Z. "Cuddles" Sakall), who insists on maintaining the family tradition that they must all marry in age order. Enter reporter Henry Taggart (Heflin), sent to cover the festival. Naturally he falls for the youngest daughter Billie (Grayson) but is chased all through the picture and eventually trapped into an elopement with the eldest, the spoiled, stage-struck Reggie (Marsha Hunt). New songs included "Tulip Time," "Little Tingle-Tangle Toes" and "You and the Waltz and I," the latter two composed by Walter Jurmann with lyrics by Paul Francis Webster.

Although entirely predictable fare, this was made at the height of the studio's musical heyday and the team certainly brought off the spectacle with typical energy and panache. The result was a "gay, shapeless little picture," according to the *Miami News*, a "waltzy schmaltzy" confection which proved immensely popular during the dark days of the war.[16] Shooting took place entirely on the Metro back lot which added to the artificiality of the enterprise; surprisingly it was shot in black and white when this sickly sweet spectacle seemed far more suited to color. "Praise the lord and pass the saccharine," declared one critic, who also maintained that Heflin here was "a good actor wasted." Others noted that as the breezy newspaperman, "he brings another of his distinctive characterizations to the screen." He was certainly suitably gauche and likable and even maintained his savoir faire during the musical interludes.

However it is hard to disagree with the reviewer who wrote; "After it's all over, the tulips, Papa Van Maaster's double chin, Van Heflin's gamin face and Kathryn Grayson's singing seem to stand out instead of the usual cinema requirements of good story, direction, suspense and impressive characterization."[17]

While working on the movie, the young actor became firm friends with the producer, Joe Pasternak, who instigated a slight change in his appearance to make him look more like a leading man. Gone was the kink in Van's hair so noticeable in *Johnny Eager*; instead he looked more slick and polished. One might say he was given the MGM treatment. Pasternak also convinced him to buy a number of suits, which he reluctantly did. Heflin was uncertain of his ability to succeed as a leading man in such lightweight fare, believing he was not sufficiently handsome. Pasternak informed him that he did not want a pretty boy; "I want someone who can act," he said.[18] Pasternak gave a glowing tribute to Heflin, likening him to Spencer Tracy and commenting that every producer on the lot sought him out because he was a different type. He called him "the best actor in the movies in a long time."[19]

Next the rising actor got the plum lead role in *Tennessee Johnson*, originally known as *The Man on America's Conscience*. This was a biopic of Andrew Johnson, the man who followed Lincoln, and the first president to be impeached. Directed by William Dieterle, who was renowned for his many ambitious historical biographies, this was all set to be one of

1942's "most prestigious pictures."[20] The screenplay was written by Universal horror veteran John L. Balderston and Wells Root, adapted from a story by Milton Gunzberg and Alvin Meyers, and based on two years of intensive research including widespread use of the *Congressional Globe* in which Johnson's speeches were reported verbatim along with details of all the bills he introduced.

The story begins in rural Tennessee in 1830 as young Johnson, an illiterate runaway tailor's apprentice, arrives at the town of Greenville where the local blacksmith and others notice his shackles. Struck by his honesty and willingness to work, the smith agrees to take off his shackles

in return for repairing his clothes. Johnson is welcomed into the town and soon meets librarian Eliza McCardle (Ruth Hussey), who teaches him to read and write and later becomes his wife. Later he becomes involved in local politics, encouraged by Eliza. Johnson begins to rail against the vested interests and attempts to gain the vote for the landless. He is attacked at a meeting at the town hall and his loyal friend the blacksmith is killed. The townspeople are incensed and seek immediate retribution but Johnson convinces them to have faith in the law. The action moves on to 1860 by which time Johnson is a Tennessee senator. The movie then charts his difficult rise through the Civil War years, his appointment as Lincoln's deputy and ultimately successor, and his very public fall, instigated by his bitter rival Thaddeus Stevens (Lionel

Heflin gave a remarkable performance as Andrew Johnson, the president who followed Lincoln, in William Dieterle's *Tennessee Johnson* (1942). He convincingly aged fifty years, going from a callow youth to an old man returning to the Senate after years of turmoil. The political furor surrounding the film ensured that it was little-seen for many years. It is sometimes shown on TCM but has never been released on DVD.

Barrymore). The impeachment trial takes up much of the final third of the film.

This ambitious movie was judged a "well-knit and effective drama" at the time, and praised for its "patriotic values" and attention to period detail, especially in costume and set design. The direction by the veteran Dieterle was "typically interesting, painstaking and leisurely." However the producers were somewhat overwhelmed by the "welter of charges and counter-charges" which resulted, instigated by the latter-day supporters of Stevens who felt their cause was unfairly maligned.[21] Some took exception to the timing (World War II was being waged); Harold Cohen felt it was a "political mistake at a time like this" to reopen "such a dark chapter of history." Such worthy political sagas were unlikely ever to pull in the crowds seeking escapism during wartime. Still the same critic found it a "tense and honest drama ... sober and frequently affecting."[22]

Several outspoken actors including Zero Mostel and Vincent Price petitioned the Office of War Information, demanding that the movie be destroyed "in the interest of national unity." Although this did not occur, the brouhaha surrounding the film undoubtedly caused it to suffer both then and subsequently. Paradoxically, during the time of the McCarthy witch hunt, the German-born director Dieterle was suspected of being a communist sympathizer. He had a long and highly successful career with such hits as *Juarez, The Hunchback of Notre Dame, The Story of Louis Pasteur* and *The Devil and Daniel Webster. Tennessee Johnson* was one of his popular historical re-imaginings, based on actual events; the treatment was as dramatic as possible; for instance, in reality Johnson didn't attend his own impeachment trial but in the film the effect is more sensational because he does appear and gives an impassioned plea in his defense. The final defeat of the impeachment motion by a single vote cast by a member of the Senate who makes a miraculous recovery from a previous collapse seems like pure Hollywood. Dieterle had a sure hand when it came to drama; several key scenes are memorable including when Jefferson Davis gives his farewell speech, precipitating the walkout by the Southern Senators and the inevitable outbreak of the Civil War. As they all troop out they pass Johnson, his head bowed solemnly; he's the only Southern Senator to stay for the Union and he's labeled a traitor for doing so.

But whatever the dramatic qualities of *Tennessee Johnson*, the politics of the whole era seem to have conspired to sink the movie without trace. In the film Stevens is portrayed as vindictive in seeking vengeance on the former masters of the South, Johnson as their hero. Stevens was a lifelong abolitionist and champion of the cause of the freed slaves; his contention was that they should all have been given forty acres of land. Therein seems to lie the problem; the 1940s political view of the Civil War era seems entirely at odds with current thinking. Hence the movie has largely disappeared from public view because it is not deemed politically correct and suffered badly from a campaign of repression against it. But censorship is wrong; audiences ought to be allowed to make up their own minds and *Tennessee Johnson* ought to be seen and reevaluated, viewed in its time and context and appreciated as an historical artifact.

Whatever the merits or demerits of *Tennessee Johnson,* and despite its historical inaccuracies, on one thing all the critics were united: Heflin's performance as the title character was the best thing about it. He gives a very strong portrayal and he ages convincingly over fifty years, from his first appearance as an earnest, callow youth ashamed of his past, to the determined general of the Civil War, to the politician uncertain he can ever fill Lincoln's boots to the old man returning to the Senate reflecting on the once empty desks of the Southern Senators, it is a tour de force performance. He was "straightforward, illuminating and always perfectly keyed," said one critic; "[I]t is largely due to him that *Tennessee Johnson* is the good picture it is and has what fire it has," opined another. He "handles his role with outstanding sincerity and skill ... in a performance which is well-sustained."[23] The *New York Times* critic noted Metro's lack of appreciation of the talent in their midst: "Mr. Heflin, in a full-blown, carefully delineated portrait of a passionate man, gives decisive proof that his talents thus far have been haphazardly used."[24]

Heflin drew praise from all quarters. Particularly satisfying were kind words from his fellow actors. The great Lionel Barrymore gave a glowing and perceptive tribute to the rising star; he spoke of how Heflin had spent more time "living life than talking about it" and so could bring a much greater understanding to any characterization. Barrymore continued:

> [Andrew Johnson] is a meaty role, but a tough one for a young actor. But Van has borne out my opinion that a dramatic portrayal can always be made more effective if it is colored with ... knowledge of life. I think I have seen Van Heflin win his spurs.[25]

He handled all the tense dramatic moments with assurance, such as when he refuses to march out of the Senate chamber when the break with the senators came, in his stirring defense of his actions during his trial, and his heartfelt pleas to keep the Union together. The inauguration scene as vice-president when he appears to be drunk was another great piece of observation. All in all he gave an insightful portrait of a complex human being. His Johnson emerges as an essentially honest but wronged man,

Van worked well with Judy Garland in *Presenting Lily Mars* (1943), his final movie before war service. He never forgot an impromptu concert Judy gave at Dick Powell's house with just a few couples present in 1954. "Only once in a lifetime do you ever get to hear anything like that," he remarked.

mistrusted by Congress but ever loyal to Lincoln's legacy and the Union, "whose quick temper is his worst enemy."[26]

Presenting Lily Mars was a large-scale Joe Pasternak production which had all the elements of another great MGM musical success. Loosely based on the novel by Booth Tarkington, this was essentially a starring vehicle for arguably the studio's greatest asset, Judy Garland. Under Norman Taurog's direction, "through seven, eight or nine reels she sings, dances, recites, cries, laughs, moons, rejoices, clowns and otherwise covers a repertoire that looks like a marathon screen test."[27] As the same critic remarked, she was required to do everything "but stand on her head and juggle eight rubber balls." It was a lot to ask of a super-talented but emotionally scarred 21-year-old who had been driven hard on the MGM treadmill for eight years. (In view of the burden of expectation on such young shoulders, her nervous breakdown five years later came as no real surprise.) Taurog was a former child star himself; once he quit acting, he enjoyed a long career as a director which included such high spots as *Young Tom Edison* and *The Adventures of Tom Sawyer* and Elvis movies such as *Girls! Girls! Girls!*

Judy as the star-struck small-town girl who dreams of making it big was "glamored up" for this movie in an attempt to transition her to more adult roles and away from the "girl next door" image. Heflin is the successful New York impresario John Thornway who wearies of her constantly bombarding him with auditions but in time gives her chances and then predictably falls in love with her. With music by the Tommy Dorsey and Bob Crosby Orchestras and appealing songs such as "Mirage," "Tom, Tom the Piper's Son" and "Kubaika" sung by the exotic Marta Eggerth, this was a moneymaker that played to capacity audiences in both America and Canada; it also performed well overseas. It may have been mere "lush monotony and ornamental dreaminess" but the magical power of its young star was undeniable. "GARLAND and HEFLIN EXCITINGLY TEAMED FOR ROMANCE!" exclaimed the posters, and audiences seemed to agree. The combination of "America's famous singing star and America's most acclaimed young actor" was judged a great success and showed that at this stage at least Heflin's star was on the rise and Metro were beginning to realize what an asset he was.[28] Although some felt he was not at his best, others had a different view; one said he "gives one of his best performances to date." Another was generous with the praise but mistook him for Van Johnson: "[O]ne of Hollywood's most personable young actors is given a role deserving of his talents, and again makes a swell job of it. If he was good in former pictures he is terrific now."[29]

There were times in *Lily Mars* that Heflin seemed under-used if not superfluous to requirements. Often he had little to do but practice his double-takes, react to Garland and smile uncertainly while she sang such romantic numbers as "When I Look at You" directly at him in a nightclub scene. One reviewer called him the "cream in the coffee of this delightful movie," but went on to comment that he was an actor who was "much too important to play a musical lead."[30]

Even recent commentators have noted that Garland "completely steals the show, outshining not only her fellow performers but also the material itself." Judy was happy and healthy during filming, and consequently she was at her prettiest. Several female admirers have noted that she looked especially good teamed with Van and his "rugged all-natural looks," and remarked that the two had chemistry.[31]

Ironically, when Heflin first signed at MGM he was told by Louis B. Mayer in no uncertain terms that he was not leading man material and that he would "never get the girl at the end of the picture." It must have given the rising star some satisfaction to see his image growing as something of a heartthrob. Already he was quietly proving the doubters wrong. In one film he courted Kathryn Grayson and was chased by Marsha Hunt; and in *Presenting Lily Mars* he was the love of Judy Garland, the biggest name at Metro.

His own romance was somewhat different from those on screen. For some time he was going out with actress Diana Barrymore, daughter of John. According to her autobiography *So Little Time* he proposed to her and she turned him down; "the very next day" he married Frances Neal. "Diana's memory is just a year out of context," he remarked. "I married Frances a year later."[32] He first met RKO starlet Neal around 1940 but it was not until they were both guests at the Pasternak ranch that their relationship progressed. After spending much of the day together, he called her the next evening and asked if he might drop by. When he arrived, he suggested that they go for a drive along the beach. Frances agreed. As she flung a coat around her shoulders and started for the door, Van asked her to marry him. But later, while driving to Malibu, she kept reasoning aloud that she shouldn't marry her yet because he didn't even know her and they couldn't be sure how compatible they were. Van smiled, assuring her that he knew her far better than she thought. "For fifteen years I've known the kind of girl I wanted to marry someday," he said. "What she'd look like. How she'd act. She's you, Red."[33]

They married on May 16, 1942, at the Westwood Congregational Chapel in Los Angeles. The simple, low-key ceremony was performed by the Rev. Mark S. Hogue. A few relatives and friends were present including Frances' parents and Van's mother; his father had died the previous year. Joe Pasternak was best man and his wife Dorothy was matron of honor. "The bride wore a light draped wool aqua suit with accessories in brown. Her aqua hat was trimmed with black and her only flower was a white orchid."[34] They honeymooned in Del Monte. Frances, the 20-year-old daughter of an army surgeon, had been mostly raised in Texas. She took to modeling in her teens and was chosen for *George White's Scandals of 1940* on Broadway; she made a few films at RKO beginning with a bit part in *Citizen Kane* (1941). As a result of her appearance in *Thirty Seconds Over Tokyo* (1944) as a girl in an Officer's Club, she "landed a fat MGM contract," but with increasing family commitments was unable to accept.[35]

After Heflin's great success in *Johnny Eager* and critical acclaim for *Tennessee Johnson,* he desperately wished to play Father Chisholm in A.J. Cronin's *The Keys of the Kingdom* for David Selznick. "I am holding my breath," he said, "I am almost afraid to mention it." Spencer Tracy also coveted the role "more than any other since Father Flanagan in *Boys Town*," but he acknowledged he was "not the perfect type as described" in the novel and also told friends he thought Heflin would be ideal. Neither got

the part which went to Gregory Peck (it was his second film), who was nominated for an Oscar.[36]

War was declared on December 7, 1941, and Heflin, a reservist since college days, joined the Field Artillery. He trained at San Luis Obispo, Camp Roberts in California and later in the Caribbean. At Camp Roberts he was hurt, went to the hospital, then was put on limited service and sent to Culver City for a spell. Keen to be where the action was, he transferred to the 9th United States Army Air Force and saw service as a combat photographer in France and Germany.[37] As a second lieutenant he was attached to the First Motion Picture Unit where he joined many fellow actors. He became an expert with firearms, gaining "a

Lieutenant Van Heflin was an operational flyer over France and Germany during the Second World War. He was "one of the most popular officers to come out of Hollywood ... rated A-1 swell guy by the Air Corps boys under his command."

marksman's rating with the carbine and an expert's bars with the service rifle."[38] Based in Chester, England, for a year, he became "one of the most popular officers to come out of Hollywood ... rated A-1 swell guy by the Air Corps boys under his command."[39]

He also made some Army training films during the war including *Land and Live in the Jungle* (1944). Filmed in Panama, it outlined the correct methods of survival after crash-landing a military aircraft on one of the many densely vegetated Pacific islands then under enemy control. It showed the procedure for making shelter, signaling, conserving water and surviving for some weeks.

Heflin had a very narrow escape in wartime London: He ordered an army blouse and a pair of trousers at a tailor's; "on his way for a fitting he learned that the shop had been hit by a robot bomb and destroyed."[40]

Serving in the armed forces, Heflin missed out on a number of roles including Jimmy Blake in the Universal comedy *Between Us Girls* (1942) which was handed to Robert Cummings, and as Lao San Tan in Metro's *Dragon Seed* which went to Hurd Hatfield instead.[41] The latter film seems unthinkable to a modern audience in that all the main roles in this historical Chinese drama are played by Caucasian actors including Katharine Hepburn and Walter Huston. Heflin was also set to star in *Men at Sea* and opposite Ann Sothern in *Big Hearted Maisie*, a Maisie series entry in which the popular Brooklyn wisecracker character adopts a baby.[42]

In August 1942 Heflin was voted "Most Promising Star of Tomorrow" in the Exhibitor's Poll for *Motion Picture Herald*.[43] But his future was looking uncertain: Actors *not* called on to serve their country could stay at home and play the hero in film after film. Heflin had to pick up the threads of his career three years later. It was not until 1946 that his next movie was released. He wondered with good reason whether it would be business as usual or if the public had forgotten him.

Five

Radio Days (1934–60)

"The pictures are better on radio."

From the early 1920s until the mid–1950s, radio was the most popular form of mass entertainment in the United States as it was globally. The early twentieth century saw the development of the crystal valve set and the wireless was born. Radio works in a far more subtle way than cinema and especially television. Sound has the ability to create visions and feed the imagination. Radio engages the imagination like no other medium because all the work is done in the brain; the ears are the conduit for ideas. The ultimate power of radio was proved in 1938 when Orson Welles made a broadcast about an invasion from Mars which left the nation panic-stricken. During the war the propaganda value of the medium became all too apparent to those in occupied Europe and beyond.

From his earliest acting days Heflin had worked on radio; he had a great voice for it. He tried hard to hide his strong Oklahoman accent but it "poured out like rich syrup."[1] As a struggling young actor playing inter-mittently on and off Broadway in the 1930s he started to receive steady work in a variety of radio shows. He made his debut on CBS in 1934 in *The Court of Human Relations,* a series of human interest dramas. In an episode entitled "My Heart Stood Still" he played "an ex-convict afraid to marry the girl he loves because he thinks society will stigmatize her."[2] For most of 1935 he was acting far more regularly on radio than on stage.[3] As a result of *A Woman Rebels,* his first movie, he signed a long-term radio contract in 1936 with Sam Briskin.[4] He appeared in *Way Down East* with Agnes Moorehead and joined the cast of many popular serials; he had a regular role as Sammy in *The Goldbergs* starring Gertrude Berg as the matriarch of a Jewish family in New York.[5] In 1939 he joined the cast of *Meet the Dixons,* a long-running saga of small-town life set in Minnesota; for the next five years he played Bob Dixon opposite Arlene Francis as

Betty.[6] This show had started on NBC in October 1932; when it transferred to New York it was revamped and became *Bob and Betty*.[7] During Heflin's long run in *The Philadelphia Story* he played in several other radio programs daily; often three times a day plus rehearsals for each, and he sometimes managed to slip in an extra broadcast or two for good measure. At the time he said he was lucky when he got four hours sleep.[8] He played crime reporter Bob Shellenberger in *Central City*; Adam Waring in *The Man I Married*; and Slim Delaney in *Our Gal Sunday*, which followed the travails of an orphan girl from Silver Creek, Colorado, who marries an English lord.[9]

After the war, one of the first radio assignments of the returning Lt. Heflin USAAF was close to his heart: the charming *Parade* by Arch Oboler, a special tribute to his own Army Air Force on its 38th anniversary. He was convincing as Captain Henry G. Stelling of Merrill's Marauders in "Burma Incident," part of the CBS series *The Doctor Fights*, broadcast in July 1945 while the conflict in the Far East was still being waged.

He became a mainstay of postwar radio and from 1947 made several first-rate contributions to an overlooked genre which might be termed "radio noir." He was a recurring presence in the long-running and fondly recalled mystery series *Suspense* and was the first to portray Raymond Chandler's famous private eye on the medium in *The Adventures of Philip Marlowe*.

Suspense, billed as the "Theater of Thrills," was an effective series of hour-long mystery-crime dramas. One of his earliest was "Three Blind Mice" in which he played Arthur Lockwood of the publishing firm of Lockwood, Bentley and Walsh. One of the partners is found dead and the other is on Death Row charged with his murder. This series had the sort of smart dialogue, tricky dames, ever-present threat of murder and air of mystery and menace familiar to all fans of film noir. The voiceover alone could have come from some forgotten gem of the era: "Even at the restaurant they seemed to know I was on my way down; the waiter sat me at one of those dime tables usually given to out-of-town ribbon clerks..."

Suspense's "Wild Oranges," adapted from a novella by Joseph Hergesheimer, was an enthralling yarn in which he starred as John Woolfolk, a rich yachtsman who heads into a cove on a deserted shore where he encounters "an eerie trio.... Lichfield Stope, owner of a run-down plantation, who is imprisoned by fears ... and his daughter Millie," who are both in thrall to their demented servant Nicholas.[10] One of the most memorable episodes was "Three O' Clock," from a 1938 Cornell Woolrich short story. The story involved Paul, whose calculated revenge on his wife (who he thinks is cheating on him) backfires. It was a clever and tense story, effectively an inner monologue, but beautifully realized by Heflin, who brought it to life so vividly that it lived in the imagination.

He relished his role in Lou Huston's "The Murder of Aunt Delia" in which he played Dort Sharples, "a completely vicious and evil character" with "a soft spot in his heart for one thing—money." Aired in November 1949, this intriguing tale begins in the Arizona desert where he thumbs a ride from a man who admits he jammed on his brakes on an impulse because of the resemblance of the hitchhiker to himself. The driver is on his way to visit his invalid aunt in Santa Barbara, whom he hasn't seen since childhood, and from whom he stands to inherit a great deal of money. A plot soon takes form in Dort's mind and he pumps the unsuspecting driver for the minutest detail of his past life. Before they have driven a hundred miles, Dort is sure his fortune is made.[11]

Heflin was excellent in "The Murder of John Dillinger" and as a newspaperman whose articles about murder make him a candidate for it in "The Thirteenth Apostle." He also impressed in "Song of the Heart" and the adaptation of Alexander Pushkin's unusual short story "The Shot." There was unusual depth to his role as escaped murderer Sam Newcombe, a stowaway, in "The Mystery of the Marie Celeste": He was by turns weak, violent and charming in a genuinely imaginative and atmospheric interpretation of what might have happened aboard that enigmatic vessel. His final entry was "Too Hot to Live" by which time the series was nearing its end. *Suspense* was one of the most popular shows on the air and over the years attracted a remarkable array of acting talent and garnered numerous awards. In 1946 it won a special citation of honor from the George Foster Peabody Awards for Outstanding Contribution to Radio, and another citation in 1949 for its "casting and music" which placed it "head above the competition."[12]

In April 1947 Heflin was offered the title role in NBC's *The Adventures of Philip Marlowe* based on the novels of Raymond Chandler; the first episode aired in June as a summer replacement for *The Bob Hope Show*. Early on in the proceedings, the decision was taken to dispense with a live audience to help give the show more authenticity. However the pilot episode performance was witnessed by nineteen of Los Angeles' top detectives who declared themselves very satisfied with the results. They were further impressed by Heflin's diligence; he had taken a keen interest in all police procedures.

He appeared in fourteen episodes of *The Adventures of Philip Marlowe*, of which only four survive: "Who Shot Waldo?" "Red Wind," "King n' Yellow" and "Trouble Is My Business."[13] These are currently available on CD and as mp3 downloads. They demonstrate for the iTunes generation how Chandler's distinctive style comes alive in Heflin's throaty and lived-in tones:

> There was a rough desert wind blowing into Los Angeles that evening. It was one of those hot, dry Santa Anas that come down through the mountain passes and curl your hair, make your nerves jump and your skin itch. On nights like that, every booze party ends up in a fight, and meek little housewives feel the edge of a carving knife and study their husband's necks. Anything can happen when the Santa Ana blows in from the desert" (excerpt from "Red Wind").

Heflin took pains with the role; he began by visiting Chandler at his La Jolla, California, ranch and talking with him all afternoon, which gave him a good idea of the author's view of his greatest creation.[14] He then took a midnight ride through Los Angeles' famous Skid Row with two of the city's best detectives, which gave him an insight into how the department operated. They drove to the river bed to look for vagrants and he followed the officers when they arrested drunks, broke up rows in beer joints and went through a second-floor flophouse where the beds cost 25 cents, the air reeked and a drunk lay on the corridor floor.[15] He also kept copies of Chandler's books by his bed and read and re-read them for weeks prior to the first broadcast. Once the series of weekly shows was underway, he really felt he knew his character; "He's tough," he observed, "yet sensitive and intelligent. He's tough-minded and lives by his mind and his muscle. But ... in Marlowe, the man, there is a guy with a heart.... Of all the detective characters of fiction, to me, Marlowe is the least fictitious, the most credible ... human and humanly admirable."[16]

Initial reviews for the series were mixed; some found it flat and Chandler was predictably "not enthralled." Some commented that Heflin "struggled with an awkward script" by the perfectionist Milton Geiger. But others said that he and co-star Lurene Tuttle "did a great job" and most agreed that Heflin "gets increasingly better as an actor."[17] Hearing the recordings now, one is struck by how well-suited he was to the role; his husky, masculine voice conveyed the toughness coupled with the intelligent, sensitive heart he identified in his Marlowe. It is one of the eternal regrets that he never got to portray the character on screen. By September his film commitments meant that he had to leave the series. Over a year later the show returned with a new actor, Gerald Mohr, and a different team of writers was brought in. *The New Adventures of Philip Marlowe* was fairly successful and was revived during the summer of 1951.

Van, Marlene Dietrich and Claude Rains record the CBS Radio version of *Madame Bovary* in 1948. Heflin had a long radio career beginning in his early days as a struggling actor in New York. It was estimated that he made over 2,000 recordings.

Heflin was often called on to reprise his film roles on radio, which he did in *Johnny Eager, Presenting Lily Mars* and *Shane* among many others. Sometimes he played a different role and showed his range as Boulanger the lover of Marlene Dietrich in a CBS version of *Madame Bovary* with Claude Rains as Charles. On other occasions he appeared in radio versions of popular films in which he had not starred such as *Night Song* with Merle Oberon, *The Seventh Veil* with Anne Baxter and *Vacation from Marriage* with Deborah Kerr.

He was a natural for airwave adaptations of the many plays and best-selling novels of the day; he was good as the struggling bacteriologist in Sinclair Lewis' *Arrowsmith* and as George Boswell in James Hilton's *So Well Remembered* (he appeared at the invitation of the author). In *So Well Remembered* he is married to a "cold, selfish woman who deserts him and moves in with another"; she is also "responsible for the death of their only child." Despite all this, he forgives her and lives again through her son by her second husband, in whom he instills his own thwarted ambition to be a member of Congress.[18]

He was effective in many short dramas such as "Why Keep Your Heart in Cold Storage," a sentimental but nonetheless heartfelt story of Thanksgiving about Jordan, an ex-army bum (Heflin) who is down on his luck searching for work. He meets Mr. Green, "half busybody and half saint," who takes him in and gives him a job. Truculent and bitter initially, he resents Green's prying into his affairs, but eventually realizes he has a lot to be thankful for. Sponsored by Hallmark Cards for their *Playhouse* series, this breezy tale avoided mawkishness because of the combination of Heflin's gruff tones and subtle acting style which made the other players (apart from Will Geer as Mr. Green) seem flat by comparison.

He appeared as Morris Townshend in *The Heiress*, adapted from *Washington Square* by Henry James. It starred Olivia de Havilland, reprising her famous film role as Catherine Sloper with Louis Calhern as her father. This was only shortly after the movie version in September 1950. *The Heiress* was a masterful film and a successful adaptation of James, whose detached, emotionally bound world has not transferred well to cinema by and large. Radio was an appropriate medium to capture some of his psychological complexity and Heflin appeared more naturally suited to this difficult role than Montgomery Clift had in the film. His Townshend is nuanced and he is able to convey more layers of meaning and implication in a single word or phrase than many actors manage in a lifetime of trying.

Heflin would have done more radio work if possible and in 1947 had to pass up the chance for a regular show of his own because Metro disapproved, claiming it interfered with production.[19]

He made a number of recordings for the *Lux Radio Theater* including Noël Coward's *Brief Encounter* with Greer Garson; and won praise for his part in *The High Wall* with a young Janet Leigh. He twice played opposite Ida Lupino: in a version of *The Strange Love of Martha Ivers* and in the famous courtroom drama *Ladies and Gentlemen.* He was equally at home as a guest stooge on *The Charlie McCarthy Show*, as the narrator of documentaries or the star of historical dramas. He narrated *Document A/777* by Norman Corwin, which took the form of a Bill of Rights. It was effectively a blueprint for democracy among emerging nations in the post-war period and was broadcast worldwide and heard on Radio Malaya, among others.[20]

Having portrayed one president on screen, Andrew Johnson, he went two better on radio and played the first and second presidents. He was outstanding as George Washington in Maxwell Anderson's acclaimed play *Valley Forge* and as John Adams in *John Adams and the American Revolution.* Heflin was always convincing as historical figures and was heard as Tom Edison and Damon Runyon as well as many explorers and early adventurers into whose questing spirits he was able to provide real insight.

By the mid–1950s, television had begun its inexorable rise in popularity which would eventually see the decline of radio in both quality of production and more importantly in the public perception. In time it degenerated into merely a vessel for pop music; soon plays, novels, mysteries and ideas largely disappeared as everything moved wholesale to the visual medium. But radio had left an indelible mark on the imagination of millions and can still work its magic today, given the chance. Heflin was reluctant to work on television; besides, he had what a recent critic has called "one of the best voices of any actor of his generation."[21] In a way his voice was already familiar to Americans long before he became a movie star. He was a prolific radio actor: Taking into account his early soap operas, he was estimated to have made around 2,000 appearances over the years. He honed his craft there and could use his distinctive voice to great effect.

Increasingly, old radio shows are becoming available on CD and for download so that present and future generations might gain a valuable insight into social history and begin to appreciate a once great medium that gave so many Hollywood stars of his era a steady and lucrative income for so long.

Six

Dissatisfaction at MGM
(1945–49)

"The role of Athos in The Three Musketeers is bound to be secondary one. D'Artagnan has to be the star. In Madame Bovary I was one of Jennifer Jones' three lovers." [1]

Heflin found a changed environment on his return to Hollywood after his honorable discharge from three years of war service in 1945. He'd been voted the Most Promising Star of Tomorrow; now tomorrow had arrived and it was more a case of "Van who?" The scene had altered considerably in his absence and all the momentum of his career had drained away. New, young and handsome stars had been discovered in the meantime—including the other Van, Johnson—and it was very difficult for Heflin to recover any of the ground he had lost. But as a trained actor he was not about to be defeated. He acknowledged that he was not handsome, nor so young, but that he had great stage experience on his side. He was never concerned with being a star; for him the part was the important thing. Not himself, the marquee or the fan mail—"just the job of making the character real." He undoubtedly succeeded every time. [2]

There were a number of scripts awaiting him—but they were all for studios other than the one to which he was tied. He was offered the role of Sam Wainwright in Frank Capra's *It's a Wonderful Life* and a part in *Love Lies Bleeding* for Paramount. [3] His part in *It's a Wonderful Life* devolved to Frank Albertson; but *Love Lies Bleeding* eventually became *The Strange Love of Martha Ivers* and boded well for his immediate future because this time he was the lead. [4]

By August 1945 he had been home from his army service for three months without an offer from MGM. [5] It was already clear that the more interesting ideas emanated from other studios. *The Strange Love of Martha Ivers* and *Possessed* were loan-outs to Paramount and Warner Brothers respectively. Several ideas were considered by his own studio including a role in *The Hoodlum Saint* (ultimately played by James Gleason) and the starring role in *The Postman Always Rings Twice* opposite Lana Turner.[6] This might have led his later career into other, very different and fascinating directions, but the role was assigned to John Garfield instead.

While waiting for his employers to employ him, he purchased a home on a two-acre site in Brentwood (a neighborhood familiar to many of Hollywood's glitterati): 116 Tigertail Avenue, the name of which fascinated him.[7] The house had extensive gardens where he grew fruit. His eldest daughter Vana Gay was born in June 1943 and his second daughter Cathleen Carol (always known as Kate) two years later.

His dissatisfaction at MGM effectively began as soon as he returned from the war when he was informed that his salary would still be at the same level as when he left. In typical penny-pinching style his bosses hid behind the wording of his contract stating that he had "not fulfilled the two years elapsed by serving in the armed forces."[8] He threatened to test the validity of his contract legally but several other returning servicemen actors also brought attention to the issue and the studio reluctantly rectified the situation, increasing his salary threefold.

Metro offered him *Bridgit,* the story of an embittered composer who is helped by a child-angel played by everybody's favorite poppet Margaret O'Brien.[9] Then that deal fell through and it was not until January 1946, after eight months of idleness, that they finally presented him with *Till the Clouds Roll By.*[10] This was the lavish color musical biopic of songwriter Jerome Kern which might have turned out very differently. Initially Kern was all set to give the studio carte blanche to tell his tale; tragically, while he was walking on Park Avenue one day he suffered a cerebral hemorrhage and died a few days later without regaining consciousness. His estate was less forthcoming and MGM balked, fearing lawsuits; hence the producers changed tack and constructed a light-hearted storyline which bore little resemblance to reality.[11]

The film begins and ends with scenes from *Showboat* and is told in flashback by Kern (Robert Walker) from the back of a taxi cab. Heflin is introduced early as James Hessler the fictional arranger and best friend along with his young daughter Sally (Joan Wells). There follows a desultory version of the great composer's life which is interspersed with his many songs. The narrative takes a back seat and the movie becomes merely a showcase for the most popular singers of the day to deliver his most famous songs: Angela Lansbury sings "How D' You Like to Spoon With Me"; Judy

Garland delivers "Look for the Silver Lining" while washing up; Lena Horne sings "Can't Help Loving That Man" and "Why Was I Born?" Other stars appear including Dinah Shore, Kathryn Grayson and Van Johnson; the whole thing finishes with a big production number in typical MGM style with Frank Sinatra singing "Ol' Man River."

Whenever the plot is required to re-emerge between the songs, the movie appears to flag considerably; Robert Walker was a fine actor but his part is so blandly written that he could do little to bring Kern to life. Despite the fact that Hessler is an entirely fictitious character, he appears more real thanks in no small part to Heflin, who does well to imply more than the material gives him to work with and creates a believable personality. One reviewer called his portrayal "superlative" and the movie was a huge success, earning $4,000,000 in the U.S. and Canada alone. But because of its huge budget it made an overall profit of only $700,000.[12]

Over ninety hours of material—some 500,000 feet of film—was shot of the wastes of Antarctica by the U.S. Navy and released as *The Secret Land*, which received the Academy Award for Best Documentary of 1948. This survey of half a million miles of the icebound territory charted Rear Admiral Richard E. Byrd's twelve-year expedition, beginning in 1935. Photographed by Navy, Marine and Coast Guard cameramen, this covered Operation High Jump and showed the harsh environs in which 4,000 men battled 100 MPH gales and all the aspects of life in the frozen wilderness. Among the images of ships, planes and helicopters there were dramatic scenes of rescues at sea which were some of the first to be seen on screen. The enterprise was narrated by Captain Robert Montgomery, Lieutenant Robert Taylor and Lieutenant Van Heflin who, it was said, "give additional punch to the stirring incidents."[13]

Green Dolphin Street, based on the novel by Elizabeth Goudge, charted the involved tale of the lives of four main characters. Marianne Patourel (Lana Turner) and her sister Marguerita (Donna Reed) live with their father Octavius (Edmond Gwenn) and mother Sophie (Gladys Cooper) on the Channel Island of St. Pierre. The man whom Sophie once loved, Dr. Ozanne (Frank Morgan), returns to the island after many years with his son William (Richard Hart). William immediately falls for Margarita but is never certain which sister is which. Timothy "Ty" Haslam (Heflin) has eyes for Marianne but she is unaware of this. Haslam gets into a fight and suffers a knife wound; he kills the other man. His arm is tended by Dr. Ozanne, who does not inform the police as he should by law; Haslam then sneaks aboard the ship *Green Dolphin* bound for New Zealand to escape the law. Captain O'Hara (Reginald Owen) allows him

MGM *présente*

LE PAYS DU DAUPHIN VERT

d'après le roman d'ÉLIZ. GOUDGE
GREEN DOLPHIN STREET

LANA TURNER
VAN HEFLIN : DONNA REED
Mise en scène VICTOR SAVILLE

HET LAND *van de* GROENE DOLFIJN

Metro labeled Heflin "ungrateful" for asking for his release from his contract and he was relegated to second lead in *Green Dolphin Street* (1947). In Europe his stock was much higher as reflected in this Belgian poster which emphasizes him at the expense of the bland Richard Hart.

to stay on the ship and he sails to begin a new life. Meanwhile Marianne persuades her father to finance a Navy career for William.

Two years pass and William comes home on leave; his father dies but William is urged by the ambitious Marianne to sail the same day, which he does. He travels to China where he is robbed; instead of reporting to the consulate, he gets on board another ship, the *Green Dolphin* sailing to New Zealand, and Captain O'Hara allows him passage. In New Zealand he meets and becomes friends with Ty, who remembered his father's kindness and invites him to join him in his successful lumber business. Some years pass and William writes to Mr. Patourel asking for his daughter's hand in marriage. In his drunkenness he writes Marianne when he means Marguerita.

Marianne sails to New Zealand. As the ship docks, William is expecting Marguerita and is heartily disappointed when he sees Marianne. Ty urges him not to show his disappointment and to love Marianne as though it was her he wanted all along. William agrees. But their life in the colony is hard; they suffer earthquakes, a tidal wave and a Maori uprising.

A sweeping historical saga, the novel of *Green Dolphin Street* had been read by twenty million people. The film itself was two years in the making and when released was billed as "the most heralded picture of the last ten years" (trailer) and compared to *Gone with the Wind*. Katharine Hepburn was initially to star; the director insisted on Lana Turner instead. With dark hair she did well as the self-centered Marianne; "she's become a good actress," remarked Heflin.[14] There were attempts to "deglamorize" her, and she crawled through the mud several times for director Victor Saville while filming the earthquake scenes. However, in the 140-minute film she still managed to go through "thirty-two lavish gowns."[15] Saville was British and moved to Hollywood after the war; mostly a producer, he also directed a number of films including *The Good Companions* (1932) and *The Green Years* (1946). The little-known actor Richard Hart was lacking in star quality in the central role of William Ozanne; although handsome and dashing enough, he had little real feeling. Indeed, it was said all over the studio that the love scenes between Van and Lana "will start more hand-holding in theater balconies than spring fever."[16] The supporting actors did well; the veterans Dame May Whitty, Reginald Owen et al. were their reliable selves; and Donna Reed impressed despite drawing the short straw. However the effects were truly breathtaking and it was difficult to disagree that "the best performances are turned in by the studio's technical staff."[17] The reconstruction of Wellington and St. Pierre on four huge stages of the MGM lot was something to behold and made this the largest-ever construction at the studio up to that time. Filming began at the Klamath River in Northern California but a planned location shoot at Catalina Island was abandoned due to the weather. Despite the massive cost of the production, set designers were quite ingenious, utilizing only used lumber and other salvage materials.[18] The effect was stunning. Especially impressive was the link between St. Pierre and the convent by a beach path impassable at high tide.[19]

Heflin played an interesting character. Throughout, he is in love with Marianne, and does everything to ensure her happiness, even encouraging William to marry her despite the fact he had made a mistake in his drunkenness. Outlandishly dressed, his quiet assurance and ability to make allies among the Maories makes him a thoroughly convincing frontiersman of New Zealand. There is one scene when Marianne is newly arrived from England and William is trying to be attentive to her; both are standing doing various tasks. Haslam (Heflin) is sitting at the table between them smoking a pipe; he glances casually from one to the other as they talk. Between puffs his feelings and observations about the two are quite palpable. Although Hart and Turner are doing all the talking, Heflin, not speaking, is doing all the acting, mostly with his eyes which were always expressive.

Green Dolphin Street, an ambitious epic, may have just missed its mark, although contemporary audiences did not think so. For the most part it is engrossing and sometimes moving; the acting is good, the costumes and settings exactly in keeping. The stirring romantic music of Bronislau Kaper adds to the whole effect; his song "On Green Dolphin Street" lives on as a jazz standard recorded by Miles Davis among others. As mentioned, there were some spectacular special effects for the era, particularly apparent in the earthquake scene which won an Oscar for the inventive effects department.

Despite being relegated to second lead, Heflin attracted attention as the strong, resourceful Ty Haslam, reserved but able in his unassuming way to surmount many obstacles in the nascent colony. It would have been interesting to know what he might have made of the character of William; but when asked by a reporter on set if he would like to swap places with Hart he gave a rather too emphatic "No."

In truth, he had already asked for his release from his contract. Metro declared him "ungrateful, stating that now he wanted to sell his talents to competitor studios after they had groomed his image."[20] But what had they groomed his image as? In their view he was not a leading man nor was he a character actor; he seemed to be a nearly man, the ubiquitous best friend once too often. He had every right to feel aggrieved that he was not treated with the same respect on his return from war as those who had stayed at home.

Interviewed at the time, he revealed how intensely self-critical he was, finding fault with many of his past performances. "If I ever see a picture in which I think I'm good, I'll be the deadest actor ever," he commented. The interviewer observed the perfectionist actor:

"We chatted in Van's dressing room while he nervously manipulated hooks with which he had drawn on his boots for a scene in *Green Dolphin Street.* Van is a trim, athletic-looking (but sedentary) man with a square-jawed baby face, a small mouth, thinning hair, and friendly, direct blue eyes."[21]

Green Dolphin Street was Metro's most popular film of the year and also did very well at the British box office. It definitely bolstered his reputation; furthermore he was soon in such vaunted company as Spencer Tracy and Clark Gable on Hollywood's Top Star list for 1949.[22]

After the success of *H. M. Pulham, Esq.,* Metro was keen to film other bestsellers by John P. Marquand. Heflin was announced as a replacement for Robert Taylor in the intended production of *So Little Time.* His co-star would be Angela Lansbury with support from Audrey Totter and Tom Drake; the producer Carey Wilson.[23] The movie never materialized and attention turned instead to another novel, *Polly Fulton.* Released under the title *B.F.'s Daughter,* this charted the lives of several characters from 1932 to the war years. Polly Fulton (Barbara Stanwyck) is the spoiled but spirited daughter of industrial tycoon B.F. Fulton (Charles Coburn); she is unhappy unless she can do something for somebody. She's engaged to prominent but socially conservative lawyer Bob Tasman (Richard Hart) but he cautiously puts off the wedding until he can win a partnership in the firm. Polly then meets a "brilliant but impoverished" economics professor, Tom Brett (Heflin), and impetuously marries him much to the chagrin of Tasman and the great disappointment of her father. She sees Tom as someone who she can really help and secretly advances his career using her money and influence. This brings him to prominence when the war begins. (The role of Polly was originally intended for Katharine Hepburn.)

This was a fine starring vehicle for Stanwyck in a "portrayal marked by poise, assurance, and dramatic vitality" according to one critic, who also commented: "Heflin is ideally cast as the sardonic young economist."[24] Not as brittle as usual, Stanwyck appeared more at ease and her character was one of her most sympathetic and perhaps least well known. This was the second Stanwyck-Heflin venture. They worked well together on screen;

they seemed to have a natural chemistry and a mutual respect for each other as actors. However Stanwyck was very much on her guard with him; she did not need to be told to "Watch out for Heflin." Between takes on the set as she fanned away his cigarette smoke, she cracked, "You're not going to louse up my close-up."[25] Apparently she considered him "a pal who was a worthy target of practical jokes and before filming a scene ... where he has to carry her over the threshold she hid weights in her mink coat," causing him to stagger as he lifted her.[26]

Veteran director Robert Z. Leonard did his familiar unobtrusive job and the screenplay by Luther Davis was witty at times. Only the stylish costumes by the ubiquitous Irene were nominated for an Oscar. The movie did decent business and deserves to be more widely seen today. It's an appealing drama, romantic, often witty and sometimes profound. The romance is handled expertly by the two leads who are the chief reasons for its success.

Heflin makes Tom Brett a living, breathing character: appealing, intelligent but penniless. He could go places, she reasons, with her help; but this is the source of all their later trouble because of course he wants to get there on his own. She is well-meaning and only motivated by a desire to help and put her money to good use. Their early scenes together in the speakeasy, at the Metropolitan Museum and at her father's house are handled with skill and humor. Tom is introduced with some unusual chat-up lines which nonetheless intrigue her. He invites Polly and her friend Apples to lunch and afterwards, as he shakes hands with Polly, he keeps hold of her hand. "Please stay," he says plaintively. "If you stay, I'll explain technocracy to you." So begins this offbeat romance. She is quite beguiled by him even though he is preaching sedition in her father's eyes. He is the antithesis of the staid Bob Tasman, which is why he appeals to her so much. The previous night she had talked with Bob about the house he wanted her to see at Pyefield, New Jersey, complete with iron animals on the lawn.

The scene in the museum establishes their curious romance. With his hands in his pockets he leans nonchalantly near the exhibit of a knight in armor; she is looking ahead reflectively. He explains about his nervous stomach before lectures, how he loves to talk until the early hours and that he has no money but he does have a future. He then offhandedly suggests they should get married. "It ruins all my plans ... but I love you," he says.

In the scene where she takes him to meet her father and break the news to him about their marriage, he enters carrying a cigarette absent-mindedly and is half-thinking about where to put it. As expected, the meeting does not go well: His playful wit is at odds with the practical business sense of B.F. "I haven't any money, practically none," he says. "I guess that covers most of the questions..." The scenes during their honeymoon in a snowbound cabin in Minnesota have the same humor and charm. When it comes to carrying her over the threshold, he is hardly romantic.

The second of three movies Van made with Barbara Stanwyck, *B.F.'s Daughter* (1948), directed by Metro stalwart Robert Z. Leonard, was an appealing romantic drama nicely underplayed by them both.

Again he makes subtle use of little things to establish character: the cigarette which prevents him from shaking hands with love rival Bob Tasman at the theater; playing with the silver spoon distractedly in the speakeasy while falling for Polly; and turning the lecture tour rejection letter around in his hands while looking at it thoughtfully.

Some critics dismissed it as too glossy and a far cry from the original controversial novel. Others believed it was "brought to the screen with fidelity, intelligence and taste," and another said it was "one of the most satisfying, thoroughly entertaining films to come from the MGM lot in some time."[27] Whatever the verdict, it ought to be viewed again now to be appreciated on its own terms. The two leads ensure that *B.F's Daughter* is an unusual and engaging romantic drama. They complement each other well; the lack of romanticism gives the movie its appeal, subtlety being the key word of both actors.

Away from MGM he relished the chance to play a dashing romantic lead for a change in Universal-International's big-budget production *Tap Roots*. Based on the bestseller by James H. Street, this told the story of the Dabney clan in rural Mississippi; it was founded by Big Sam and after his death headed by Hoab (Ward Bond). The fiercely independent-minded Dabneys aim to maintain their neutrality at all costs during the impending Civil War; they are even prepared to fight for it. When the war arrives, Hoab declares the 20 square miles of Lebanon County unilaterally independent which brings down the might of the South upon him and raises the ire of the North. His spirited red-haired daughter Morna (Susan Hayward) is engaged to Clay MacIvor (Whitfield Connor), "whose nature is somewhere between a snake's and a rat's."[28] Local newspaperman and ne'er-do-well Keith Alexander (Heflin) is also in love with her, so much so that he is willing to run contrary to his supposedly shallow nature and fight for her father's lost cause. Hitherto he had more reputation as a ladies man and notorious duelist who settles arguments with his two formidable weapons, pistols called Alpha and Omega. When the fight comes, MacIvor shows his true colors: He organizes the forces against Hoab and his followers.

Often dismissed as a "poor man's *Gone with the Wind*," this Walter Wanger production was filmed in lush Technicolor among the Smokey Mountains of North Carolina and Tennessee which passed for Mississippi. Among the fine supporting cast, Boris Karloff stood out as Tishomingo, a Choctaw Indian friend of the family. Julie London appeared as Morna's sister Aven, and there was sterling support from the redoubtable Arthur Shields, Richard Long and Russell Simpson.

A criticism often leveled at Heflin was that he couldn't wear clothes but in Universal's *Tap Roots* (1948) he looked every inch the southern gentleman and roué. Here he courts the feisty Morna Dabney (Susan Hayward). This engaging but curiously overlooked adventure was directed with spirit by veteran George Marshall.

Described at the time as an "intensely moving and turbulently exciting" epic and "one of the best of Hollywood this year,"[29] *Tap Roots* benefitted from great cinematography by Winton C. Hoch and Lionel Lindon. Director George Marshall's varied career included such diverse fare as *Destry Rides Again, The Blue Dahlia, The Mating Game* and the *How the West was Won* segment "The Railroad." Here he handled the action and romantic scenes with equal assurance; the effect was enhanced by the sense of place: the well-realized locations; the setting of the big house and the tree with its inscription which starts and ends the movie. Scenes of battle in and around the swamp as McIvor's forces close in, allied to the stirring music of Frank Skinner, provided an exciting climax.

"Heflin makes a gallant lover as the straight-shooting Keith," said one critic. With his stylish clothes and easygoing manner (to say nothing of his pencil moustache) he is every inch the Southern gentleman and roué. He is an ultra-cool character at the beginning and maintains his savoir faire throughout. He is also a capable leader of the rebels. A criticism often leveled at Heflin was that he couldn't wear clothes but he looks smart in *Tap Roots*, although even here he goes through swamps, fire and battle and is disheveled by the end. A Canadian reporter interviewed him at the time of the film's release, noting how handsome he looked in his blue serge suit: "You look a lot better in real life than in any film of you I have seen," he remarked. "I generally do," grinned Heflin. "I usually seem to make the worst of it in any film."[30]

Susan Hayward has been dismissed as being not quite Scarlett O'Hara although she had nevertheless been one of the many who had tried for the role back in 1939. Here she is suitably tempestuous, feisty and credible as the type of Southern belle men would fight over.

Heflin again plays a complex character who, when weighed in the balance, is not found wanting. He reveals that he is more of an altruist who is willing to risk his life for a cause; that cause was his love for Morna. At the end, when all is lost and her father disowns her because he thinks she has brought shame on the family, Keith rushes to her defense and movingly asserts that he has never loved her more.

Every other studio appeared to have a much higher opinion of Heflin than his own and *Tap Roots* provided him with a far more satisfying role in keeping with his status. At such times he must have relished the life of a star. One disgruntled reporter watched the shooting of a love scene on a sound stage at Universal; all afternoon the two leads kissed and hugged passionately. "Both seemed to be enjoying it," he remarked sullenly, "and I suppose it's as pleasant a way as any of making large bundles of money.... This must be getting mighty tiresome, I observed crossly [to Heflin between takes]. 'My no ... not with Miss Hayward. I could do this for weeks and weeks.'"[31]

After proving a natural romantic hero in *Tap Roots* for Universal, Heflin was back to the day job playing the second lead in *The Three Musketeers* for Metro. Alexandre Dumas' adventure has been filmed so often over the years to be almost too familiar to require description. Ever since silent days this seventeenth-century tale that combines adventure, romance and buffoonery in equal measure has had a timeless appeal to filmmakers. Each generation has their own version; the franchise was recently revived and reinterpreted for the twenty-first century with a big-budget movie and television series.

The 1948 MGM version has cast perhaps the longest shadow as it seems to capture the spirit of the novel and has an appealing cast headed by Gene Kelly as D'Artagnan; the others were Athos (Heflin), Porthos (Gig Young) and Aramis (British character actor Robert Coote). Angela Lansbury was Queen Anne with Frank Morgan as Louis XIII. Originally Sydney Greenstreet was penciled in as the scheming Cardinal Richelieu but ill health forced him to retire and the part went to Vincent Price. Lana Turner refused at first to play Lady de Winter but was told that if she did not, "she would be blackballed from Hollywood for life." which forcibly illustrates the power of the studios.[32]

The plot revolved around D'Artagnan, youngest of the swordsmen of the Paris musketeers loyal to the crown of Louis XIII. There are numerous intrigues involving two of Queen Anne's diamonds, which Richelieu persuades the duplicitous Lady de Winter to steal from the Duke of Buckingham, prime minister of Britain (even though the post did not exist in 1625). It emerges that the mysterious Lady de Winter was once the wife of Athos (Heflin); she deserted him and was branded with a fleur de lys on her shoulder, the mark of a common criminal. In England she kills the Duke of Buckingham and is caught and given over to the custody of D'Artagnan's love Constance (June Allyson). Constance feels pity for her charge, who pleads for a means to end her life. She smuggles a knife to Milady between the pages of a book. By the time the Musketeers arrive, Constance has been fatally knifed and Lady de Winter has fled. The Musketeers follow her to France and track her down to the old estate that once belonged to Athos. There they capture Lady de Winter, who is beheaded. At the end the Musketeers are rewarded with monies and restoration of lands despite having acted on their own in executing de Winter.

The Three Musketeers is a colorful, rousing adventure with plenty of action; there are some battles and numerous swordfights. The costumes by Walter Plunkett are particularly fine: the velvet tabards and doubloons, to say nothing of the cloaks and hats with plumes of feathers of the Musketeers, each in their own color with livery for the horses to match. Heflin with his red-brown hair looked dashing in his cobalt blue ensemble. The bright cinematography of Robert H. Planck was Oscar nominated. The Robert Ardrey screenplay tends too much towards the saccharine. The use of Tchaikovsky's music for the clinches was rather typical of the whole ethos at Metro. The budget was vast and there is no denying the star power and sheer exuberance of *The Three Musketeers*, which made it MGM's second highest grossing movie of the 1940s.

As regards the acting, there is really only one actor in it, namely Heflin; unfortunately, the spotlight is on Kelly. Even during several key scenes when Heflin is talking, the camera is on Kelly. In all there is rather too much of Kelly, who spends most of the first forty minutes mugging and the rest merely overacting. He has natural agility and athleticism but his appeal soon wears thin, and the desire to sit through the movie to the end depends to a large extent how much of Kelly one can stand.

It was said at the time that Kelly and Heflin "heckled each other during filming," and judging by some of Heflin's comments afterwards, it was around the time of making this film that he felt his disillusionment at Metro complete. MGM promised him leading roles before he went off to war, and now he was reduced to playing feed man to a hoofer.

Kelly and Heflin were taught how to handle their swords by the Belgian fencing champion Jean Heremans, who also appeared in the film.[33] There was much hilarity among the press fraternity when the two stars were rehearsing their swordfights wearing their ordinary clothes and without their toupees.[34] There were a great number of extras and lots of horses and Heflin also rescued a runaway horse on set.[35]

As the drink-addicted Athos, Heflin shone. His performance was rather too good for the film, which was for the most part played on the same predictable level. Again he excelled in getting to the emotional heart of a drunkard and making him seem far more than pathetic. His ability to project emotion, vulnerability and pain in a few seconds of screen time makes him seem "the most Byronic of the musketeers," as a recent critic observed.[36]

Much fun was had on set at times especially between Lana and Heflin, who were good friends. She "adored Van" and during filming she kept kidding him, calling him "a great thespian" and almost ruined the scene where she is about to be beheaded, saying, "Oh, please Vannie honey, don't take my head. You wouldn't do that to your sweet little old Lanita! Oh, my sweetie Heffie—not my head!" Heflin couldn't stop laughing and quipped to the crew, "Let's just strangle her instead and get this over with!"[37]

Reporter Vivian Meik was on set during the filming of two sequences which, despite their brevity in screen time, were grueling work and took most of the day to shoot. Actors were required on set six days a week from seven in the morning until six in the evening and had an hour for lunch. She was introduced to Heflin between scenes in his dressing room and was distinctly impressed by his "sound American good manners and good breeding—and solid, decent hard work."[38]

Between the rumbustious *Three Musketeers* and director Vincente Minnelli's colorful adaptation of *Madame Bovary,* Heflin worked on Fred Zinnemann's intense noir *Act of Violence.* That all three films were made under the aegis of Metro around the same time says a great deal for the strength of the studio system. The fact that Heflin could be equally effective in all three says everything for his great ability as an actor.

Heflin won acclaim as Charles Bovary opposite Jennifer Jones' Emma in Vincente Minnelli's luminous and popular adaptation of Gustave Flaubert's *Madame Bovary* **(1949).**

Gustav Flaubert's *livre sur rien* (book about nothing) *Madame Bovary* was fashioned into something by Minnelli. Jennifer Jones was cast in the central role of the vain, selfish Emma Bovary with Heflin as her ever-loving husband Charles. Flaubert (James Mason) appeared in an opening scene re-enacting part of a court case that occurred because of the controversial nature of the subject matter at the time it was written; he narrates the drama. Mason expressed the view that such a novel was not possible to bring to the screen but Minnelli opened out the book and retained much of the French provincial background and characters. Minnelli's Hollywood-inspired treatment may have been some way removed from the "unpalatably caustic" original, peopled as it was by a host of unsympathetic characters, but he nonetheless fashioned a sumptuous and handsome movie from unpromising material. The film was a flop but it has gained in reputation in the ensuing years and many have been encouraged to discover for themselves the interminable ennui of the French nineteenth century writers.

Emma (Jennifer Jones) is a dreamer who lives on a peasant farm in rural France. A mere drudge, she longs to be whisked away by a romantic hero on a white horse. One day a young doctor, Charles Bovary (Heflin), visits the farm and immediately falls in love with her. They marry and go to live in a small town. They have a daughter but Emma becomes bored with provincial life and begins to long for the bright lights. At a grand ball she meets dashing Rodolphe Boulanger (Louis Jourdan); furthermore she is deeply embarrassed by her drunken husband. She has an affair with Rodolphe and starts to incur debts from moneylender Lhereux (Frank Allenby). One night she arranges through Lhereux to settle her debts and elope with Rodolphe. She waits outside his shop; Rodolphe's coach appears but drives straight past; Emma is distraught. Later, when her debts become very large, she goes to Rodolphe asking for money; he refuses. She starts an affair with Leon Dupuis. All the while, Lhereux is demanding payment. Things come to a head when their house and contents are set to be auctioned; by now, Charles knows everything—he is a ruined man. In a final desperate act Emma takes arsenic poison at the chemist's shop. She reaches home and collapses. Charles tries to revive her but she dies.

Minnelli's film is exquisitely realized. Jennifer Jones came in as a replacement for the pregnant Lana Turner. She works hard as Emma, suitably distracted and self-seeking, seemingly oblivious to anyone's pain except her own.

Heflin is an utterly convincing Charles Bovary. From his early spellbound infatuation to his final humiliation he remains true to character. At first he is the smitten young medic who encounters Emma in the kitchen of her peasant farm; he is entranced and unable to see anything but her. Once married, he is completely unaware how dissatisfied his wife becomes in a short space of time. He is blind to anything but her beauty and does not question her happiness because he never questions his own.

Film adaptations of historical novels are notoriously variable and always subjective; each reflects the interpretation of their director. Minnelli had his own vision in mind. Hence his Emma is seen by some as a "bitch-heroine of [her] time" and his Bovary "softened out of all recognition from the original, so much so as to make him Emma's victim rather than the cause of her suffering."[39]

Heflin handles the scene during the ball masterfully. The proud Charles enters with his wife, who immediately attracts attention. She dances with all the men during the evening as Charles at first looks on and overhears the conversation. "Who is she?" asks one haughty young buck. "Some country doctor's wife," sneers another. He makes his way to the bar as Emma continues dancing; she is in a whirl of ecstasy as she dances with Rodolphe. Eventually the drunken Charles staggers down the steps onto the ballroom floor. "Emma!" he calls repeatedly. "I want to dance with my wife…" He stumbles into the dancing couples and lurches towards someone else he thinks is her. By the time he reaches her and holds out his arms to dance with her, the music has stopped, everyone is staring and Emma runs out in tears.

At first studio executive David O. Selznick did not want Heflin for the part. Selznick felt he was not romantic enough. But director Minnelli insisted. Selznick was infatuated with Jones and did not want anyone or anything to take attention away from her. Minnelli, in common with other directors, resented Selznick's interference.[40] In the event, many agreed that Van stole the picture despite the apparent dullness of the role.

The cinematography and set design department rightly won Oscars for *Madame Bovary*; Minnelli's eye for detail was especially apparent; every object seemed to be suffused with symbolism. The lustrous score by Miklos Rosza added to the high drama. Several set piece scenes were handled wonderfully: The raucous peasant wedding at the muddy farm encapsulates all that Emma was trying to escape; her failed elopement, waiting for Boulanger's coach and trudging back to the house alone is effective. The highlight is the waltz scene where the dancers are in such a whirl of frenzy that all the picture windows are smashed ecstatically.

Elsewhere there were some changes from the novel which seem in retrospect unnecessary; for instance, there is one scene in which Charles, egged on by his wife, attempts to perform an operation on the club foot of Hyppolite (Harry Morgan). Finally he refuses, knowing he is not qualified; he shames her by walking away through the crowd of eager onlookers. In the book he performs the operation, which turns out to be a disaster for the unfortunate cripple and professionally for himself. Working within the restrictions imposed, the makers fashioned a very good version of a difficult novel. Everyone emerged with credit, especially Heflin. Always able to make dull interesting, he surpassed himself here. His Charles Bovary is easily mocked but always true to himself. Blinded by love, he is ultimately a tragic and touching figure.

East Side, West Side, based on a bestseller by New Yorker critic Marcia Davenport, told of a love triangle spiced with murder among New York's smart set. Brandon Bourne (James Mason) is the wayward husband of Jessie (Barbara Stanwyck). When he meets his ex amour. Isabel Lorrison (Ava Gardner), they resume their affair. Meanwhile Jessie falls under the spell of an attractive ex-cop and war hero, Mark Dwyer (Heflin). Brandon promises that he will never see Isabel Lorrison again, but she contacts Jessie to say that he is now with her. Jessie confronts Isabel in her apart-

A rather drawn-out melodrama, *East Side, West Side* (1949) only came to life when Van shared scenes with the Amazon Beverly Michaels; especially memorable was the fistfight they had in a car. It was his final movie after eight years at MGM.

ment. Later that day Isabel is found dead. Suspicion falls on Brandon, who found the body, but Mark helps the police find the real murderer.

The critics were not generally enamored of this "unadulterated and very slick domestic drama" which "consumes [nearly] two hours and seems almost twice as long," wrote one reviewer, who nevertheless singled out Heflin for praise.[41] Stanwyck, Mason and Gardner were center stage; Heflin and Cyd Charisse as girlfriend Rosa were on the second rung. But Dwyer is a pivotal character, especially once the murder investigation begins. The scenes between Van and Barbara have an appealing naturalness; their ease of playing together seems very apparent, especially in the kitchen scene where he dons the apron and cooks her dinner.

The cast gave *East Side, West Side* its allure and lifted it out of high-class soap opera as one critic noted: "No company is quite as adept as MGM at presenting basically uninteresting material with such style, and such a strong cast, that it cannot fail to entertain."[42]

Oddly enough, one of the unknowns—the "Amazon" Beverly Michaels—made more of an impression than others in the starry cast. Her unusual bearing and tight-lipped deadpan delivery of her lines brought a whiff of noir, as some commentators noted: "Her scenes with Van are the only lively interludes in a crawling-paced, verbose and spurious photoplay. Then, when a murder mystery temporarily snaps *East Side, West Side* out of its lethargy; the ex-cop and the big blonde stage a wing-dinger of a fist fight" [in a car].[43]

Heflin was happy to be reunited with director Mervyn LeRoy, who had been so instrumental in his earlier successful years at Metro. His character is resourceful and appealing, and he plays the role in a relaxed mode. However by now he was heartily sick of playing "the friend of Robert Walker or someone else." As he commented dryly, "Sometimes I wish I never had a friend."[44] He had now seen out his contract and sought new pastures. Although Metro did not give him his full release, the divorce was final and he never made another film for the company.

Towards the end of his time at Metro, there were signs the studio was trying to find him some decent vehicles, but their choices often displayed confused thinking about which direction best suited him. For instance, one idea they bought with him in mind was *The Skipper Surprised His Wife*, a national magazine story by Commander W. J. Lederer. The featherweight yarn concerned a "navy commander who, when his wife breaks her ankle, takes over and proves that he can run the household as well if not better than his wife." The skipper role was later assigned to Robert Walker, who had just been released from a sanatorium. MGM then cast Heflin opposite Betty Garrett in a documentary; tentatively announced a period costume drama, *Alexandra*, in which he would join Angela Lansbury and June Allyson; and contemplating putting him, Lana Turner, Gregory Peck and Donna Reed in a Civil War drama, *The History of Rome Hanks*.[45] All three projects were abandoned. Dore Schary's personal project for the studio was to bring *Lost Boundaries* to the screen starring Heflin. Set in Georgia, this told the partially true story of a black man who passes for white and the problems he has when his employers discover the truth. However the studio was not ready for it and Schary dropped out. The Mel Ferrer film was later released by the little known Louis de Rochemont Productions.[46] Heflin was slated to play one of the three "fathers" of Margaret O'Brien in the sentimental melodrama *Big City* but the part went to Robert Preston instead.[47]

His final projects at Metro were to have been Westerns; one was an epic set after the Civil War, *The Outriders*, with John Hodiak; the other was *Ambush* with his friend Robert Taylor. However, Heflin had already terminated his contract and Hodiak dropped out of *The Outriders*; Joel McCrea and Barry Sullivan took over the leading roles. Hodiak then replaced Heflin in the "strictly routine" *Ambush*.[48]

Away from Metro, several ideas came Heflin's way. Independent producer Benedict Bogeaus intended to adapt *The Wall Between* for the screen. The novel by Elsie Oakes Barber concerned "a glamorous social butterfly who becomes a minister's wife and does great work in getting better housing conditions for the poor." Heflin was offered the role of the minister, with Dolores Moran as his wife. The film was never made. (Only one of Barber's novels was ever filmed, *Angel Baby* in 1961.[49]) Frank Rosenberg wanted Heflin or Lew Ayres for the starring role in *Man-Eater of Kumaon*, based on adventurer Jim Corbett's famous book about a vicious tiger. Eventually this Shaff Productions venture settled for the lackluster Wendell Corey as the man of action and also featured Sabu. In 1950 Heflin was in the running to play Romeo opposite Olivia de Havilland in *Romeo and Juliet*. Both were somewhat long in the tooth to play Shakespeare's teenage lovers: Olivia was 33 and Heflin 42. The film was never made.

Heflin had a special interest in the much-anticipated filming of Tom Wolfe's novel *Look Homeward, Angel* which was postponed many times. Michael Curtiz lined up a producer, Arthur Ripley, who had a script that adhered to the original with Heflin as Ben, Robert Mitchum as Luke and Walter Huston or Frank Morgan as the old man. Many others wished to be involved including Kirk Douglas and Richard Widmark. Ridley had "discussed it thoroughly with Wolfe's mother," but the main stumbling block was expense.[50] Heflin's suggestion was that the studios should get together on the project and use all these actors, and find an unknown for the boy with Ethel Barrymore as the mother and Raymond Massey as the father. His vision was "to make it as an all-industry picture to show the world what could be done here with cooperation." He further suggested that the profits should go to the Motion Picture Home. His ideas fell on deaf ears. Ripley sold the story to David O. Selznick, who in turn sold it for a profit to Paramount, where it languished. The film was never made.[51]

One of the other interesting ideas would have seen him on screen alongside Spencer Tracy, with whom he was often compared. Veteran producer Carey Wilson intended to make a movie based on the three 1924 murder trials of Harold Hoffman. Sydney Boehm, who had covered the case at the time as a Hearst reporter, was assigned as the screenwriter. Heflin was set to play Hoffman with Tracy as the Brooklyn lawyer Samuel Leibowitz who tries to free him. Unfortunately, this tantalizing film was never made.[52]

In 1949 Heflin shocked the Hollywood establishment by asking to be released from his contract two and a half years before it was due to expire. Although he had actually been seeking his release since 1946, the studio agreed to reduce his commitment to twelve weeks a year. Heflin declared he was grateful to MGM for giving him a movie "name." However, looking back on his time there, he later seemed bitter about his perceived lack of success, especially as a romantic figure. "I was rejected by more women in five years than any man in history," he joked. Undoubtedly Metro was not the studio suited to an actor of his caliber; he was a square peg in a round hole. The feeling was that anyone could have played most of the parts he was assigned and his frustration was understandable. But he was a thoroughgoing professional who always gave his best no matter what he was called on to do. Although the studio frittered away his talent, he could point to some successes along the way including *Johnny Eager, Tennessee Johnson* and *Act of Violence*. He also proved to be far more of a romantic leading man than he actually remembered; and the big-budget success of *Presenting Lily Mars, Green Dolphin Street* and *The Three Musketeers* certainly put him into the public consciousness and boosted his reputation, nationally and internationally.

But such an outstanding actor needed an environment that worked to his strengths. The general lightweight tenor of the films made at MGM and the lack of starring roles left him dissatisfied and unfulfilled. He was by no means alone in his dissatisfaction; many other stars including Ava Gardner, Lucille Ball, Jimmy Durante, Irene Dunne and Myrna Loy also sought their release in this post-war period. The studio once boasted of having "More stars than there are in heaven," but the figures tell their own story: In 1945, 175 stars were under contract; by 1951 this was down to 72.[53] The power and prestige of the big studios was fragmenting and actors were no longer satisfied with being made to dance to their employers' tune.

By the time he left Metro Heflin was making $3,000 a week. He reckoned that as a freelancer he could make nearer $10,000 and more pertinently he would have the chance to choose only the film roles which appealed to him and be free of any straitjacket a studio might deign for him to wear.

Seven

Possessed by Noir
(1946–51)

"Some fellas do it for millions of dollars. I did it for $62,000.... But I loved you; you gotta give me credit for that."

—Webb Garwood, *The Prowler* (1951)

Heflin had an unerring capacity to explore the dark side and was naturally suited to the world of noir. He could be a glib villain or a wronged man backed into a corner; desperate or cool; a man of action or thought and often conflicted. Whatever part he was required to play, he always convinced and in this genre in particular he gave great insights into the heart of darkness as much as the heart of light.

Johnny Eager was in essence his first venture into noir territory; his portrayal of the booze-addicted, Shakespeare-spouting Jeff Hartnett was a *tour de force* which earned him an Oscar. Strangely this did not lead to more offers in a similar vein. Both *Kid Glove Killer* and *Grand Central Murder* pointed the way to better things but these did not materialize at MGM. Only one of his great performances in noir, *Act of Violence*, was made under the auspices of his home studio; of the others, *Possessed* was made at Warner Brothers; *The Prowler* by United Artists and *The Strange Love of Martha Ivers* on loan to Paramount.

Adapted from the novel *Love Lies Bleeding* by Jack Patrick, *The Strange Love of Martha Ivers* was Heflin's first completed postwar venture. Initially he was penciled in for the part of the weak character, Walter O'Neil. But then this role went to Kirk Douglas and Heflin was awarded the strong male lead, Sam Masterson. This effective piece of casting proved just how able an actor he was: He could play strong or weak with equal conviction, and it spoke well for his chances to be considered a more natural leading man in the future.

Toni Marachek (Lizabeth Scott) models for the approving Sam Masterson (Van) while Martha Ivers (Barbara Stanwyck) looks on in *The Strange Love of Martha Ivers* (1946). The enchanting Lizabeth was nervous in only her second film, but Van put her at ease and as a result their scenes had an easy naturalness. "He was very kind and helpful to me," she said.

The movie is set in Iverstown where 12-year-old Martha Ivers, heiress to the Ivers fortune, is attempting to run away from her domineering aunt (Judith Anderson). She meets another youngster, Sam Masterson, and they sneak on board a freight car. The police catch them, having been tipped off by their other friend Walter O'Neil acting under the instruction of his ambitious father (Roman Bohnen). When Martha returns home, there is a confrontation. Later that same night Mrs. Ivers begins to beat a cat on the stairs. Martha picks up a poker and hits Mrs. Ivers, who takes a fatal downstairs fall. When Mr. O'Neil arrives, Walter backs up Martha's story about a stranger entering the house and killing Mrs. Ivers.

Eighteen years later, Sam Masterson crashes his car while entering the city limits of Iverstown. He pulls in for repairs and, asking around town, finds that Walter and Martha are married. Walter is the local district attorney and has political aspirations. But they hide a dark secret: They sent an innocent man to his death for the murder of Mrs. Ivers. Sam meets Toni Marachek (Lizabeth Scott) who is on parole for stealing a fur coat. Walter finds out that Sam is back in town and wants to know why; he has him beaten up and even spoils the budding romance with Toni. Martha and Walter believe that Sam has returned to blackmail them for what happened all those years ago when they were children and subsequently. They are prepared to go to any lengths to stop him from telling.

Heflin was excited at the prospect of making *Martha Ivers*. This was his first movie after the war, almost a year after his discharge and four years since he had seen the inside of a studio. "I feel like a kid the night before Christmas," he said. "I can't sleep. I'm so glad to get back."[1] Having been away so long, he was quite nervous. As he later explained, co-star Barbara Stanwyck helped in her no-nonsense way: "She was great to me. I was scared to death, couldn't remember my lines, and had no feeling of security. Barbara didn't pull any punches. She let me have it. It was what I needed."[2]

Whatever she said to him certainly did the trick; he found his confi-

Director Lewis Milestone, Kirk Douglas, Heflin and Barbara Stanwyck enjoying a coffee break between scenes of *The Strange Love of Martha Ivers*, Van's first project after the war.

dence and employed his usual approach of thinking himself into a role by deciding which animal a given character most resembled. This idea was suggested to him by an old director when he was first learning to act and he was having difficulty getting to the essence of certain roles. Seeing each one in animal terms appealed to him. "It was so simple," he commented, "it surprised me. Now here in Hollywood, the first thing I do when I'm cast in a role is to decide which animal I'm going to be, and after that I have no trouble." In *Johnny Eager* he had been a "kind-hearted sheep dog" but in *The Strange Love of Martha Ivers* he was undoubtedly a panther.[3]

At the time the critics were not kind to *The Strange Love of Martha Ivers*. One labeled it "a disagreeable story about essentially disagreeable people with criminal tendencies."[4] *Time* magazine's reviewer wrote:

> *Martha Ivers* has been described ... as a stealthy plot of murder, false witness, assault, lust, perfidy and tender love. The summary is too modest. The picture also includes some tidy touches of sadism, juvenile delinquency, blackmail, civic corruption, adultery and dipsomania.[5]

Heflin emerged as the strongest character; he was, said one reviewer, "impressive as the dogged Sam who isn't afraid of anything." In such a highly melodramatic film his "moving manner of quietness and restraint" was noticed.[6] One reviewer said that he came over as "a cross between Dana Andrews and Alan Ladd," with whom he was touted as one of the "best box office bets in the business."[7]

Helfin had rejected many scripts before selecting *The Strange Love of Martha Ivers*. He was drawn by the story that he described as terse, dramatic and forthright. "When I read Sam," he explained, "I knew he was for me. Sam is a guy you meet every day. He knows the score. He's painted in a number of colors. Not just as black or white. It's the Sams that promise a long life as an actor."[8]

Director Lewis Milestone suggested Heflin do a complicated coin trick of rolling a fifty cent piece across the back of his hand to establish the character as a gambler and to give him an edge. But Stanwyck was not about to be upstaged by anyone: "Any time you start twirling that coin," she remarked, "I'll be fixing my garter—so be sure you don't do that when I have important lines to speak."[9] He afterwards felt in his self-critical way that he had used it too often; "six times when twice would have done."[10] But the coin trick was very popular with audiences and "theater managers have written him that customers have dropped half dollars on the floor, trying to copy it, and have gone searching for their money during the performance."

Heflin said that, after his long absence from movie sets, "I was rusty on my technique, not as smooth as I should have been." As usual he was over-analytical about his performance. "Some of the technique I used, to make the guy seem easy-going, went too far. In underplaying or, as I prefer to call it, not over-dramatizing, you can be so cockeyed easy that you don't project anything." The critics, however, disagreed. One wrote: "Heflin, who probably knows more about acting than any two other people in the picture, is excellent.... At any rate every emotion that [he] has comes across to the audience by close coordination between body, mind and voice."[11]

He got on well with his co-stars. Lizabeth Scott was nervous appearing in her second movie but he was, she said, "Very kind and helpful to me,"[12] This was Kirk Douglas' debut; he had been warned to watch out for Heflin, but the two men got along well. Heflin later introduced him into the Hollywood Golf Club where the young actor was overawed to be in the company of such heroes as Clark Gable.[13]

Hedda Hopper noted that at the preview of the film, Heflin was the one principal player who did not receive applause when first appearing on screen; however, "after the show the whole theater lobby was buzzing about the terrific performance Van gave."[14] The writer was nominated for an Oscar and the director for a Cannes Film Festival award, but both lost out. None of the actors were nominated; Heflin did win accolades from the Australian *Walling's Weekly* for his "outstanding performance."[15]

His next project while awaiting employment at his home studio was a Hal B. Wallis production for Warner Brothers. *Possessed* begins with Louise Howell (Joan Crawford) wandering the streets of Los Angeles in a daze in the early hours of the morning. "David?" she asks forlornly of total strangers; she waits for the streetcar absent-mindedly. She drifts into a café where concerned patrons arrange for her to be rushed to a hospital. So begins this intriguing noir which tells her story in a series of flashbacks from a hospital bed.

It emerges that Louise has been employed as nurse to Pauline (Nana Bryant), the invalid wife of wealthy industrialist Dean Graham (Raymond Massey). Pauline is demanding and begins to be paranoid, accusing Louise of having an affair with her husband, with whom she constantly argues. Louise is hopelessly in love with David Sutton (Heflin), an ambitious structural engineer, but he ends the affair once she harps on the subject of marriage. Louise cannot accept this. Mrs. Graham dies under mysterious circumstances; the verdict is accidental death, although Dean believes it was suicide. Louise becomes convinced that she has murdered her. She continues to look after Graham's two children Carol (Geraldine Brooks) and Win. When Graham proposes to her, she accepts but tells him she is not in love with him. They are married, and David reappears after the ceremony. He is by now a valued friend and employee of her husband. Louise is still obsessed with him and is unable to accept that he doesn't love her. She feels increasingly persecuted, then begins to hear voices and suffer hallucinations. She sees David and Carol together and imagines they are lovers laughing at her behind her back. Still possessed with thoughts of him, she goes to great lengths to dissuade Carol from marrying him. Then she goes to his apartment and sees him packing his suitcase; he and Carol are to be married that very night. When she produces a gun he does not think she is being serious. She thinks he is laughing at her and shoots him dead. All this is recounted from her hospital bed in flashback chiefly in the form of a conversation between the two doctors studying her case.

Possessed, originally entitled *The Secret*, was an inventive study of psychosis. It's a wonderfully crafted film, beautifully directed in a near semi-documentary style by Curtis Bernhardt with expert cinematography by Joseph Valentine. The script by Silvia Richards and Ranald MacDougall

Louise Howell (Joan Crawford) suffered at the hands of egotist David Sutton (Heflin) in director Curtis Bernhardt's beautifully realized *Possessed* (1947). Both actress and director were unlucky to miss out on the Academy Award.

The blasé David (Heflin) sent Louise (Joan Crawford, right) over the edge in *Possessed.* **Here a trip to the theater with her step-daughter Carol Graham (Geraldine Brooks) is not such an enjoyable occasion for Louise.**

is incisive and witty; the subject is sensitively handled and characters well-drawn. The dramatic score by Franz Waxman is especially fitting with clever use of the music of Schumann at key points. Schumann was a deeply romantic but psychologically disturbed composer whose work had about it a beautiful dramatic melancholy. He spent some time in an asylum and suffered hallucinations mirroring the mental problems of the central character in this film. "For the other girls, Gershwin, or something light and fluffy," says David as he plays the piano for Louise, "For you, Schumann."

Crawford gives a bravura performance; she really seemed to be suffering the mental anguish of Louise Howell and later admitted how difficult she had found the role (which she considered her best). She spent time visiting mental hospitals in an attempt to understand case histories. It was apparent just how much she cared about what she did: "By observing the film queen between takes it was easy to see why she has bounced back on top again. She conferred with her wardrobe girl about minor dress matters ... while doing this she discussed the next scene with Heflin in the minutest detail. She also mulled over previous scenes with keen analysis."[16]

Her co-star Heflin was generous in his praise:

> Damn, I knew Joan had perfected the art of projecting her personality but I never took her that seriously as an actress until I found myself up against her in [*Possessed*]. She outplayed me, Raymond [Massey], everybody in the cast—and she was up against some experienced competition. Yet she carried the day.[17]

Some have accused her of over-acting. This is possibly true on other occasions, and perhaps her wide-eyed, slightly manic style might seem excessive at times. But here she finds the central truth of Louise and makes her an entirely sympathetic character. Her downward descent is terrible to see.

Some critics felt the picture was too geared towards Crawford. Bosley Crowther observed that the supporting characters were too quickly sketched in; he particularly lamented the lack of scope given to Heflin "who is eminently worth it" and felt that both he and Massey "are given much too short and casual shrift."[18] However, it made perfect sense to concentrate on Louise and her intense suffering. The chief complaint might be the lack of delineation of Pauline; and even she, it could be argued, probably worked better kept as a shadowy figure and the uncertainty about her demise in the mind of Louise and the audience.

Heflin as David Sutton gives a remarkably laid-back performance which lends his scenes with Crawford an extra tension. She is all keyed up, he appears blasé. He is casually cruel and thoughtless; while she is fearful and obsessive. No matter what she does, she is unable to get him to love her or even to see her. "Why don't you love me like that?" she asks sadly as he eulogizes over a parabola. "I'm much nicer than a girder and a lot more interesting."

Despite his rejection of her, David keeps turning up at intervals and each time she feels worse. Whatever advances she is making are immediately reversed. After she is married, he is a visitor at their house discussing engineering plans with Dean, who is unaware of their previous relationship. When she is alone with David she starts to question him relentlessly about his activities and what he was doing while away in Canada. She asks him to kiss her like he means it a little bit. He gives her a peck. "I didn't mean for you to mean it that little," she says, deeply hurt. Both handled this scene expertly; the characters' motivations and feelings were obvious. David is cruel and mocking, but it is unclear whether or not he is aware of her parlous mental state. Generally he appears not to be until near the end when she confronts him in his room wielding a gun.

The wedding scene is a good example of his approach to the role. He arrives late and asks where the refreshments are. He plays the scene in a blithe manner; he becomes friendly with Carol, they exchange banter; he is completely relaxed and seemingly oblivious to Louise. But all the time he is really well aware of her. *His* presence there can only be explained (in her mind) one way: He is there to torture her. She begins to believe that everyone is against her.

Some believed Heflin was too cool in many of his scenes, too much like a *femme fatale*. However, that was how he was directed to play them and it was entirely appropriate as the character is in effect *un homme fatale*. Despite appearing bland and unconcerned on the surface, Heflin is able to convey much meaning in a glance or in some of his interpretations of the barbs in the dialogue, so that we are aware of much beyond what is written. It is obvious that a vulnerable character like Louise would by her very nature become obsessed with someone of inflated ego like David Sutton; and Heflin makes a memorable character study of a shallow and heartless man. He was quoted as saying that this was the best part he'd ever had.[19]

Heflin had other opportunities in the noir genre but for various reasons they did not come to fruition. Apart from the lead role in *The Postman Always Rings Twice* which went to John Garfield, he was also asked to test for *The Asphalt Jungle* in 1949. Heflin knew he was wrong for it; "so did the director John Huston." As he observed wistfully at the time, "I just wanted a chance to work with Huston once, I may never get it again."[20] (He never did as director but Huston was co-producer of *The Prowler*.) Heflin might have joined his good friend Robert Taylor in the F.B.I. thriller *The Bribe* but he had already ended his MGM contract by then.[21] There was another mooted project with Taylor, *Bedeviled* by Libby Block, which told the story of "an unknown composer (Heflin) who is married to Lana Turner. She goes after Bob Taylor, who is in love with Angela Lansbury.... Things become so complicated that Van ... just ups and shoots Lana to take her off Bob's hands...." So went the publicity for this enticing-sounding movie which unfortunately was never made.[22] He was touted as the possible star of the British-produced noir *Britannia Mews* which became *The Affairs of Adelaide* but his role went to Dana Andrews.[23] He vied with Kirk Douglas for the leading role in *The Raging Tide*, "an exciting story about a new kind of gangster" based on the novel by Ernest K. Gann; both lost out to Richard Conte.[24] In 1950 Heflin saw Sidney Kingsley's *Detective Story* on Broadway and announced that the starring role in the film version was "the thing he wants most" but he lost out to Kirk Douglas that time.[25] The following year he was sought for *Darling Jenny* with Dick Powell and Anne Baxter, which never materialized.[26]

Fred Zinnemann's *Act of Violence* was a powerful noir which reached into the heart of darkness more than most. Thoroughly compelling, this was a taut and contained story which distilled guilt, hatred, the anger of betrayal, and all the bitterness of revenge but ultimately left viewers with a strong sense of hope and redemption. The screenplay, actors, cinematography and direction were pitch-perfect and there were no weak links. All in all this was a gem of a movie which has begun to be appreciated more fully in recent years. Its resonance emanates from its timeless themes which seem almost Shakespearean and give insights into the complexities of human nature and motivations.

A limping, trenchcoated Joe Parkson (Robert Ryan), a determined look on his face, walks upstairs to his hotel room. He heads straight for the top drawer of the bureau from which he takes out a .45 pistol, then heads back out into the night. So begins *Act of Violence*, and the very starkness of the image speaks volumes. His intentions are clear but where is he heading, and why? Miles away in sunny small-town California, Frank Enley (Heflin) is being given a civic award by the town council. It soon becomes apparent that Parkson is on his way to the town and that Enley is his target. First he visits Enley's house; he is not there but his young wife Edith (Janet Leigh) answers. Parkson discovers that Enley is on a fishing trip; he drives up to San Bernadino, hires a boat and waits for a chance to shoot him. Enley is made aware that someone is asking after him and realizes instinctively he is in danger. He cuts short his trip and returns home. Eventually Frank confesses to his frightened wife all that happened. During the war they were in a POW camp in Germany; a group of prisoners, including Parkson, were all set to escape, but were betrayed by Enley, who told the Germans where the tunnel was. He did so because of their promise of food (the inmates were all starving). The Germans also said that they would not seek reprisals. Although the Germans kept the promise of food, they shot the escapees; Parkson was wounded in the leg. Enley flees to Los Angeles where he hopes to hide at a crowded convention. But Parkson follows him there. The drunken Enley meets faded prostitute Pat (Mary Astor), who introduces him to a shady lawyer (Taylor Holmes) who listens to his story and suggests a drastic solution. On waking from his drunken stupor, Enley is appalled by his own actions and runs out into the night, desperate to make amends.

The ending worked particularly well because there was no big wordy confrontation scene between the two main characters. In a sense, it had all been said, so action was the essence of the final scene. Hunter and hunted do not meet until near the very end so tension is built up further.

Things do not finish in the expected manner: The climax is both compelling and uplifting. All along, the audience is made to feel for the characters. Sympathies switch from Enley to Parkson and end with a true appreciation and understanding of both.

The making of *Act of Violence* was a great experience for all concerned, not least Fred Zinnemann, who said that although he had been making films for fifteen years by then, this was the first time he really felt "in command" as a director. As he acknowledged, one of the reasons for his supreme confidence in the project was because "the actors were so good."[27] It would be hard to imagine a better cast. Originally but rather improbably, Clark Gable was approached for the role of Frank Enley; he backed out.[28] Robert Ryan was loaned out by RKO. Heflin and Mary Astor were still available at MGM, but not for much longer; both left within the year. Despite the relatively small size of her role in *Act of Violence*, Astor relished the chance to be challenged again as an actress in a creative environment:

Act of Violence (1948) with Heflin and Robert Ryan (right) was a terrific noir about betrayal in which Heflin gave a devastating character study of a man disintegrating under his own guilt.

Playing some of the scenes with Van Heflin, working with an artist like Zinnemann—after years of literally *nothing*—was a tonic. The way we worked,
talking about it, thinking about it, using, discarding, trying something else.
It was great, it was the way it ought to be—always.... After this drab, black
and white wonderful little picture, I went back to the picture postcard sump-
tuousness of *Little Women*.[29]

Shooting took place in many Los Angeles locations, often at night
which heightened the dramatic noir effect: the streets deserted save for
the solitary figure of the desperate Enley, who is finally coming to terms
with what he did in the prison camp. These scenes are Expressionist; there
is no dialogue, just the music, the stark streets and the actor, walking as
if in a daze. His despair is writ large in his face, his demeanor and the long
cry of anguish that he gives in the tunnel.

This was one of Zinnemann's most powerful films. It was widely
praised at the time. "[A] realistic, tight study in fear, hatred and revenge"
said *Time*. "Zinnemann gets as much power out of his lens as if it were a
fire hose nozzle."[30] Heflin took a risk playing a very unsympathetic role
but it was said that it "could win [him] an Academy Award—or it could
make you despise him in the part." Enley was a difficult character to pitch
correctly and called for an actor of subtlety, one who could make full use
of "voice inflections, facial expressions and action of the eyes, instead of
depending largely on the script."[31] Heflin's gamble paid off; the critics were
uniform in their praise for his "effective portrayal of a man slowly going to
pieces." One remarked that he "scores in a role many actors would shun."[32]
Enley is a desperately weak man who cannot live with himself or what he
has done. Faced with the consequences of his actions, he is ultimately
destroyed from within. Heflin charts this destruction so clearly that he
makes him real and understandable. It is a devastating portrait of human
weakness.

Joseph Losey's *The Prowler* has been described very accurately as
"an inventive study of a shallow, athletic materialist," and by novelist James
Ellroy as "a masterpiece of sexual creepiness, institutional corruption, and
suffocating, ugly passion."[33] This extraordinary film taps into an undercur-
rent of desperate longing for the American dream among those who never
quite make the grade via the honest route; who feel aggrieved at the perceived injustice of the hand they have been dealt in life. Some go through
every day of their existence and merely grumble at their lot, kicking at the
dirt; others, like Webb Garwood, take action.

The story begins with Susan Gilvray (Evelyn Keyes) reporting a prowler
to the police. Webb Garwood (Heflin) and Bud Croker (John Maxwell) arrive

to investigate. Garwood is instantly attracted to Susan and assesses her marital situation, intending to come back later anyway. Before long the two begin an affair, interrupted every night by her staid middle-aged husband, a late-night radio DJ, signing off his show with the words "I'll be seeing you, Susan," and a song "Baby," which is Garwood's cue to leave. Not content to put up with this, he concocts a scheme to murder her husband and make it look like self-defense, blaming it on the mythical "prowler." He does so; and in the court case which follows, the verdict is accidental death. Susan has her suspicions and confronts Webb, who immediately placates her; he convinces her they should leave for Las Vegas to start up a motel which he has always longed for. They marry and go to the motel for their honeymoon. Once there she drops the bombshell that she is four months pregnant. This sets Webb's mind racing; others will begin to ask questions once the child is born, and realize that her husband was still alive; also that he was impotent. The only course of action is to hide out somewhere until the baby is a few months old and then announce the birth.

They make their way to Calico, a Mojave Desert ghost town which Bud once mentioned. There are complications with the birth and they need to find a doctor in a hurry. Webb drives to the nearest town and shows the doctor his police badge to convince him to attend. Susan now realizes what has happened and tells the doctor to leave with the child and tell the police about her husband. Webb makes a desperate drive to get out and runs straight into Bud and his wife, who are on their way to visit them. He tries to back up and drive the other way, but the police are by now in hot pursuit. He is cornered and runs up the side of a hill. He almost reaches the top when he is shot and falls back down to earth.

The script by Dalton Trumbo (under the guise of Hugo Butler) has been described as "over-subtle" which is hardly a criticism because the very subtlety of the script helps to give this film its timeless appeal.[34] Based on an original story by Hans Wihelm and Robert Thoren, the combination of the sordid and the matter-of-fact way in which the events are described help to give this tale its power. "Out of some sleazy excitements," one reviewer observed, "*The Prowler* has snapped a steel-grained documentary of degradation to life size."[35] The ordinariness of the middle-class surroundings and seemingly comfortable houses and ordered lives hides a well of discontent and thwarted dreams. Such men as Webb Garwood will always think their goals are within easy reach. In Susan Gilvray he finds a woman who is a willing but unwitting accomplice; one who is just as desperate for the life she dreamt of as he is, and almost prepared to risk everything to reach it.

Director Joseph Losey's *The Prowler* (1951) "snapped a steel-grained documentary of degradation to life size," wrote one reviewer. Heflin gave an amazing portrayal of human weakness and was ably assisted by Evelyn Keyes as the equally desperate Susan Gilvray. It's a remarkable movie, still not fully appreciated.

The reviews were uniformly excellent, and Heflin's personal notices especially glowing;

"In his customary skillful fashion…. Heflin has created another memorable role, this time as a psychotic cop with an idea that life has been systematically arranged with the breaks against him. Step by step, he develops his alternately brutal and sympathetic characterization while the Machiavellian wheels whirl almost audibly in his head."[36]

Overall this was one of Heflin's most satisfactory and perhaps most timeless films. The obvious comparisons in storyline and execution are *The Postman Always Rings Twice* and *Double Indemnity.* However there was something very different about *The Prowler* which set it apart, as Harold Cohen stated:

An unheralded melodrama of indecent people impaled on a grisly tale of greed and lust, it turns out to be a thing of expressive craft and cunning that whips up waves of sting and bite. The commonplaces have been carefully

Some were opposed to Heflin playing the role of the unscrupulous cop Webb Garwood in *The Prowler*. Van admitted that the character appealed to him because "he's someone I could possibly have become."

avoided in this highly articulate symposium of human weaknesses, and the picture is drilled with a curving suspense and a wily everyday realism.[37]

And as David Thomson perceptively observed, "[T]he density of Losey's film and its view of American opportunism owes a lot to Heflin's grasp of character."[38]

Van was very enthusiastic about *The Prowler* from the beginning. There was something about the central character that held a fascination for him despite what it might mean for his homely image. Although he said some people objected to him playing the part, he admitted that he liked the character "because he's someone I could possibly have become."[39]

With his usual thoroughness he had studied police procedure with the Los Angeles Police Department in order that he might more authentically appear as an officer of the law. For the police he was rather too convincing and some in the department regretted that they had been quite so cooperative with the filmmakers.[40] Keyes, who had a financial stake in the film, made personal appearances to promote it. She considered this her best performance, and the critics agreed. So did Van, who thoroughly relished the whole experience and had nothing but praise for his co-star (who he said did a honey of a job) and for the director Joseph Losey.[41] The film was shot in only seventeen days; the cast rehearsed for five days. *The Prowler* was a work of love.[42]

The taut screenplay, excellent cinematography, compelling story and all the actors ensured this was a memorable noir, although it's been strangely overlooked. The music was very apt: the dramatic main theme by Lyn Murray and the cloying romantic ballad "Baby" that recurs throughout at telling points. The use of the disembodied radio voice of her husband (in reality the writer Dalton Trumbo) was also very cleverly done. His drawling voice spouts his ironic homilies about the cost of living going down, then his parting words "I'll be seeing you, Susan" is both Webb's cue to leave and an incentive to commit murder. When the newlyweds go to the ghost town of Calico for the birth of their child, there is a moment where they are almost happy; the sun is shining and they believe they can get away with all they are planning. They play some records that once belonged to Susan's husband; when one song ends, the voice of the dead man floats across the desert saying his usual goodbye "I'll be seeing you, Susan." They race to switch the record player off but too late; they realize that they will be found out sooner or later. This was a very well-handled scene in which they turn from bliss to sheer terror in a few seconds, and the nightmare underlying their romance is laid bare.

Heflin was perfect as Garwood. Early on, he establishes the character's confidence: Although he is a cop, he saunters nonchalantly into Susan Gilvray's house as though he owns it. It is the small touches like tossing his flashlight in his hand that makes it seem as though he is in control. When he comes back to the house, he sits down without being asked and puts his feet up. Before long he is complaining bitterly about his lot, how he had been a good basketball player but missed out on selection and was done out of four years of college. The next time, he appears in civilian clothes. His hat is on top of the radio; he grabs a beer and pops peanuts in to his mouth; he even breaks into her husband's desk with her hairpin, ostensibly for cigarettes but it is then that he sees his will. Later, when he is playing hard to get, there are a series of scenes in his apartment, where Heflin shows great skill in doing very little but saying everything. He is lying on the bed in his dressing gown; the phone rings, it is Susan; he looks at it and lets it ring, then answers after a pause. He is offhand and lets her do most of the talking. Then he hangs up abruptly and starts to shave with an electric razor. When the phone rings again, he looks up lazily from his fitness magazine and lets it ring a few times. It is Susan again, and she is quite frantic by now. Again he puts her off. Finally she comes to see him and he explains exactly how things are: They cannot see each other, it is not possible. She leaves crestfallen; he bounces onto the bed and laughs, throwing a discarded letter into the light fitting. Now he knows he has her exactly where he wants her and she will go along with anything he proposes. With small touches and subtlety of observation, he establishes everything about the devious nature of his character. His supreme nonchalance says it all.

Black Widow (1954), a lesser noir, is discussed in the following chapter. Several chances to make more in this field came Heflin's way during the 1950s including the starring role in *If I Should Die* for Universal-International.[43] The picture went through several title changes, first *Appointment with Death* and finally *The Big Story*; eventually Heflin's part went to Jeffrey Hunter, who fell ill. It was then handed over to George Nader. The end result was strictly routine by all accounts. He would have co-starred with Karl Malden as head of a big crime syndicate in Phil Karlson's *Experiment with Crime* from the novel by Philip Wylie. The movie was never made.[44]

Heflin appeared in only a handful of bona fide noirs but all were top-notch and much enhanced by his presence in a leading role. It is one of the eternal regrets that he did not make more but the ones he did are testimony alone to a true interpreter of modern angst and the zeitgeist of noir.

Eight

Freelancer (1950–55)

"I would prefer my mistakes to be my own, and not those made by my studio." [1]

In 1950 Van "startled the Hollywood Establishment by asking MGM to relieve him from his contract."[2] But ever since his discharge from the army, he had cherished the aim of freelancing. After finally leaving the employ of his studio, he practically succeeded.[3]

Eventually he took up the offer of several short-term contracts, initially with Universal. However, he also wished to be the best actor he could possibly be and to that end decided to go back to college. He enrolled at UCLA for a Master's degree in the Technique of Acting in Screen, Stage, Radio and Television, with the eventual hope of gaining a Ph.D. He even wrote a thesis which he later intended to publish as a textbook for drama students.[4] This was all part of his avowed aim to "spend his twilight years in a small college campus as a professor of drama." As he observed, "I can't think of a finer way of life after a career in this hectic, mad rat race we call the theater." He acknowledged that acting could not be taught, it was one of the talents that you are born with; you either have it or you don't. But he knew he could teach youngsters a few tricks of the trade. As a tutor he would have been in demand and in 1954 received an offer of $15,000 yearly to lend his name to a chain of eight dramatic schools along with six weeks of lectures to students.[5] He had lectured on acting on occasion; for instance, at his old alma mater in April 1947 for a career conference convention.[6] However it was not easy for him to find time for studying, and he had to interrupt his classes while making *My Son, John* and then later when appearing in *The Shrike* on stage.[7]

His first freelance venture was *Tomahawk* (1951), originally entitled *The Battle of Powder River,* a better than average Western based on true-life character Jim Bridger, a pioneer, trapper and scout. In common with a number of forward-thinking movies of the time, this reflected a fairer depiction of the Indians. The tide of feeling had turned and some of the great wrongs done to them were beginning to be addressed.

Set in Wyoming Territory in the mid–1860s, the story begins with the Laramie conference trying to make peace between the cavalry and Indians. As ever, the latter understand only too well what the white men don't say. Predictably, the government violates its own treaty and builds a cavalry fort on traditional Indian hunting grounds. Additional trouble is aroused by garrison officer Lt. Rob Dancey (Alex Nicol), who seeks to cause chaos. Dancey previously killed the father of Bridger's Cheyenne wife and baby plus Monahseeta's (Susan Cabot) father, who was a chief. Julie Madden (Yvonne de Carlo), who arrives with a traveling show wagon, is escorted by the hateful Dancey. Out of spite, he kills an Indian boy which leads to reprisals by the Indians and culminates in a Sioux charge on the white men.

Bridger is presented as a somewhat airbrushed figure but nonetheless Heflin manages to bring the tough frontier scout to life and make him an entirely sympathetic character. His antithesis is the "sneering racist" Dancey. The presence of Yvonne de Carlo, although appealing, is not vital; she is more of a hindrance than anything. After going riding in Indian land, she inadvertently causes the death of a brave, and this precipitates an attack.

For some reason *Tomahawk* was billed as a Rock Hudson movie when it was released on DVD and it is presented the same way on YouTube. This is a distortion of the facts: Hudson has a blink-and-you-miss-it bit part. It's also a great disservice to Heflin. It perhaps says more about revisionism than anything else.

While filming *Tomahawk*, Heflin "narrowly missed death when a fishing boat overturned in the rapids of Snake River" but he managed to reach the bank after a hard battle. He was lucky to get away with only "facial cuts and numerous bruises."[8] The crew spent two months filming in the Black Hills of South Dakota, mostly in and near Rapid City. During Van's time there, he proved a hit with the residents: "He made fourteen speeches, found people 'wonderful' and ... went fishing with the local citizens. He dined with the mayor, editor, and chamber of commerce president and became an honorary Sioux citizen."[9]

About 160 townspeople were hired as soldier extras and fifteen or twenty were invited to a local theater each day to view the previous days' filming. Five hundred Sioux Indians were brought from their reservation and their chief Ben American Horse "ceremoniously adopted Van as an honorary grandson, Looking Horse. The chief's own grandson, a paratrooper of that name was killed in the … war." Heflin was moved by the ceremony and deeply honored; he also learned to speak the Sioux language.[10] De Carlo was also made a member of the tribe at the elaborate ceremony in a meadow of the Black Hills, with High Eagle, Ben Chief and Bad Bear looking on. The Indians wished to show their gratitude for the months' employment of their people.[11]

Heflin received other honors, including a $75 Stetson from the rodeo committee of Belle Fourche, a gold nugget in Deadwood, and a tomahawk from a seven-year-old Sioux boy. He was also invited to speak in Rapid City "before the Kiwanis and Rotary Clubs, Veterans of Foreign Wars, American Legion, a bankers' state convention and other groups." He even found time in his public relations whirlwind to help dedicate a new lighting system at the Gutzon Borglum carvings at the Mount Rushmore Memorial, acting as emcee for the occasion.[12]

Even in this film which gave him limited chance, he made Bridger a sympathetic figure and invested him with emotion. Although *Tomahawk* may not be true to the historical facts, Heflin gives a real and believable portrait; his "thoughtful, introspective quality" combined with his naturally strong ability to handle the action sequences meant that he was as usual convincing and held the whole thing together. As one critic commented, he "steals the show from the Indians and the cavalry."[13]

Week-end with Father was Heflin's most appealing comedy, almost a decade after his previous venture into the genre. He had lost none of his timing and made a great showing with Patricia Neal and a cast of children and animals. Jean Bowen (Neal), a widow with two boys, and Frank Stubbs (Heflin), a widower, with two girls, take their summer vacation together at a children's camp. The situation is complicated by the presence of Frank's fiancée Phyllis Reynolds (Virginia Field) and the camp's ubiquitous physical training instructor Don Adams (Richard Denning), who has eyes for Jean. Introduced to their prospective father, the boys are unimpressed with the out-of-shape "Daddy" Stubbs' attempts to compete in any physical adventures: He knocks down all the markers during a cross country hike and has to replace them in the dark; he makes a hash of the egg and spoon race, and comes last in the sack race. Meanwhile the girls Annie and Patty (Gigi and Janine Perreau) are introduced to their new brothers Gary and Shorty (Jimmy Hunt and Tommy Rettig) and by the end of the night all are howling in despair at how much they hate each other.

Breezily directed by Douglas Sirk, *Week-end with Father* was one of a run of post-war romantic comedies using the well-worn device of a

Heflin (suit and tie) showed his range in Douglas Sirk's charming comedy *Weekend with Father* (1951), proving effective with a cast of children and animals. With from left to right: Virginia Field, Patricia Neal and Richard Denning.

widow and widower and/or suitor and the effect on the children. Sirk was dismissed in his day as a glossy soap opera director but has since undergone a renaissance in reputation; he is now considered one of cinema's supreme ironists, feted for his "paradigmatic dissections of conformist 1950s American society."[14] His oeuvre included such sumptuous fare as *Magnificent Obsession, Imitation of Life* and *All That Heaven Allows. Weekend with Father* is considered among his lesser efforts but below the surface it provided its own ironic commentary on its era. There are some clever scenes when the couple first arrives at the camp and engage in witty interplay with the desk clerk as their marital situations lead to confusion.

The screenplay was handled in a spirited fashion which pitched the laughs just right. It did not veer too much towards over sentiment or slapstick, but was witty and astute and must have raised a lot of knowing laughs among divorcees. It also proved popular with children. "It pays to get the kids on your side," Heflin observed. "They're your movie audience of the future."[15] The film also makes some sly asides at the curiously insecure self-image of the average male, the kind who tries to impress women with his hyperactive but thoroughly annoying physical prowess or those who try desperately to prove how fit they are but only prove the opposite. Either way he fails and is a figure of fun to all concerned.

Heflin chose to do a comedy as a change of pace and showed he could handle any assignment as an actor. In the same year as he was appearing in this light drollery, he played a tough western scout in a vivid Western and a murderous policeman in a classic noir.

Week-end with Father is little-known today but fondly remembered by those who first watched it as children. It was one of the biggest box office successes of the year and especially popular with families. Students of recent social history would find much to discuss here and a DVD release of this minor gem is long overdue.

Unfortunately Heflin never attempted another comedy, although *Count Three and Pray* was effectively a comedy Western. He had a natural ability in this area, never playing for laughs, but always staying true to the essence of a character. He would surely have succeeded in all kinds of comedies, which would have shown his diversity and allowed him to be more than grimly intense as he sometimes appeared to be in a series of downbeat roles later in his career.

Leo McCarey was the producer, director and co-writer of *My Son John* so he might be said to be almost entirely responsible for the result. The film begins with the Jefferson family going to church with two sons who are both about to leave to begin Navy service. A third son, John (Robert Walker), works for the government in Washington. A week later John arrives for a visit. He immediately gets across with his father on the subject of politics, makes cutting remarks to the local priest Father O'Dowd (Frank McHugh), a good friend of the family, and then goes to meet his old university professor with whom he spends all afternoon. His mother is concerned about him and fears he might be in trouble. Things come to a head when he makes fun of his father's patriotic song about bashing the communists. FBI Agent Stedman (Heflin) arrives, ostensibly asking about a bill for a previous car accident, but in reality to find out about John. In time, after much emotional argument, it becomes obvious that John is a spy. His mother goes through torment trying to straighten him out; her suspicions take her to Washington to discover the significance of a certain key. Stedman approaches her among the Washington monuments and proves beyond doubt John's involvement with a spy ring when the key opens the door of the apartment of a girl who was arrested for her part in the affair. Thereafter Stedman catches up with John, who has gone back to his parents' house. He escapes, then later returns and appears to have a change of heart on his course of action when he overhears his parents talking in an upstairs room. He goes to his office and starts to record a speech for the students of his old alma mater. Leaving the office he hails a cab; there is a car following which rides alongside and fires several shots. The cab overturns. Stedman reaches it in time to see John and hear his last words. The students hear the tape-recorded speech in which he exhorts them all not to follow his path.

Renowned stage actress Helen Hayes ended seventeen years of retirement to appear in *My Son John*, enticed, so she said at the time, by the prospect of working with McCarey. This was Walker's final film and he died while it was being made; his remaining scenes were shot in semi-darkness with a body double and interspersed with excerpts from *Strangers on a Train*. Consequently the ending had to be altered, which gave the quasi-religious finale a decidedly eerie effect (the shaft of light by the lectern with the disembodied voice of Walker floating over the audience of students). The mixture of diatribe and confessional made for an awkward climax to an overlong and often hysterical movie. At the time the only complaint the makers received was from the American Legion who took exception to the father coming home drunk from one of their reunions. Remarkably the screenplay received an Academy Award nomination, and the movie was voted one of the Top Ten of the year by the National Board of Review. But *My Son John* divided opinion then as now. It was described by one advanced critic as "a timely film of unusual merit and high dramatic intent."[16] Another labeled it a "laborious indictment of communism," and further commented, "Propaganda, to be effective, must be crisp, vigorous and informative—this is slow, sloppy and downright embarrassing."[17]

The death of its star also robbed *My Son John* of a satisfactory ending. There are a number of scenes showing John on the phone; his lips are moving but no sound is heard. The inserted clips from *Strangers on a Train* appears obvious, especially those showing John in a car lighting his cigarette with the infamous lighter. Two endings were considered; in one alternate ending, Heflin would have narrated John's speech to the assembled students. The ending as it stands is merely a masked shot of Bruno Antony's death scene from the Hitchcock classic; Heflin has to react to someone who is not there.[18]

Weighing in at just over two hours, *My Son John* is a wearisome exercise in heavy-handed dogma, unrelenting in hammering home its message. Helen Hayes emotes well, but there is rather too much hand-wringing and her character is altogether too pious and self-righteous at times. The husband is a bullying patriarch who seems to wear ignorance as a badge of honor; Dean Jagger makes him singularly unattractive. The other two sons are merely cyphers. John is immediately suspect because he is rather sneering about religion. Great emphasis is placed on his difference from the other two sons who were expert football players; "You never played football, did you..." says his mother in an insinuating tone, as if the very fact of not liking sports and spending too much time reading is bound to make one a subversive, and by implication gay. Indeed there is a strong case to be made that John's problem is that he is gay, as many other commentators have noted. But any kind of deviance from the norm is what is being attacked.

John is not allowed to develop enough beyond the limits of the script; but Walker has some fun, especially in his delivery of lines. There is a scene where his father harangues him for not being religious; John asks if he believes every word of the Bible. "Every word!" his father says with a shaking voice like a fire and brimstone preacher. Riled further he bashes his son on the head with the Bible. "What page was that on?" asks John nonchalantly. Heflin's Stedman is a quiet and strangely reassuring presence in this hysterical picture; his "easy naturalness" is never more noticeable or required. Unfortunately he can do nothing to save the movie from drowning in its own absurdity. No film is more deserving of its obscurity as *My Son John,* but the views of Washington and its monuments are appealing.

South of Algiers (originally known as *Mask of Pharaoh*) teamed Heflin, one of the finest American actors of his time, with a British counterpart, Eric Portman. Retitled *The Golden Mask* on its U.S. release, this Anglo-French production was originally to be filmed in Egypt; however, unrest following the revolution there made this impossible. The picture was about to be shelved but then it was discovered that Tunisia and Algeria would provide suitable backgrounds necessitating only a few changes in the story. The rest of the film was shot at the Associated British studios at Elstree in England over a five-week period.

Archaeologist Dr. Burnet (Portman) has a burning desire to find the lost tomb of Marcus Manilius and the priceless Golden Mask of Moloch, but his employers will not fund his research further. American novelist–amateur archaeologist Nicholas Chapman (Heflin) offers to accompany Burnet, hoping to use the material they find for a series of magazine articles. At first Burnet is reluctant to work with a hack writer of "cheap trashy books," but his curiosity gets the better of him and he agrees. Burnet and

Chapman travel to North Africa where they are greeted by Burnet's daughter (Wanda Hendrix) with whom Chapman falls in love. Petris (Charles Goldner) and his accomplice Kress (Jacques Brunius) are also intent on getting their hands on the mask and they follow Burnet's caravan across the Sahara.

Director Jack Lee, brother of the novelist Laurie Lee, began his career making documentaries during World War II. A sense of realism is present in all his movies, of which *The Wooden Horse* and *A Town Like Alice* were the most successful. Lee considered *South of Algiers* "old hokum but quite fun" and brought to the project his familiar understated style, love of narrative and abiding interest in essentially ordinary people showing heroism in adversity.[19] As ever, the environment became part of the film; it was like a travelogue at times. This gave it a rare authenticity. The intelligent screenplay by Robert Westerby meant the plot steered clear of clichés and sensationalism.

There are many shots of travels by camel in the Sahara and the contrasting bustle of the marketplace in Tunis, many tribal dancers including a male belly dancer in the street and a cavalry charge by desert soldiers. Other scenes were filmed at Djemila and at the ancient ruins of Carthage, and the site of a Roman amphitheater. The use of authentic local music and the cinematography of Oswald Morris added to the effect. There was an appealing encounter between Heflin and two nomadic children with a donkey. He buys the donkey to help them out and then gives it back to them; they latch on to him for all time. Most of the cast did well and the verdict was that "Heflin is the best in the lot."[20]

Portman and Heflin worked well together; there were no egos on display and their mutual respect was very apparent. In an introductory scene Portman is inspecting an enormous statue of Marcus Manilius; Heflin enters and circles. Both men circle the statue and each other; in turn they make observations about it; slowly they do a circuit of the statue. There is a huge crack in the side of the statue; Heflin rescues Portman just in time as the whole thing collapses. These introductory scenes are quite brief and simple but are subtly played. Their collaboration hints at what these two might have achieved in a more ambitious venture, say a Rattigan play. *The Golden Mask* is a good film—far better than its reputation and obscurity suggests—although in the final analysis some judged the exotic background to have been "better than the story."[21] However, it is interesting both for this background and to see two great actors together. Heflin with his "persuasive ambiguity" creates yet another utterly credible and likable character for his gallery of intrepid adventurers.

Heflin (left) as Nicholas Chapman with Eric Portman as Dr. Burnet in *The Golden Mask* (1953), a decent adventure set and filmed in North Africa. Portman was one of the foremost British actors of his time but never quite got his due. Heflin was in many ways his American counterpart and the two became friends.

Portman and Heflin had much in common. Both were thoroughgoing professionals from the stage who cared deeply about their craft; both were essentially character actors who were never quite leading men. They had a similar ability to connect with their characters' emotional being, to really live their part, and both had great voices. They were also heavy drinkers who loved sailing. Temperamentally they were intense, moody, and quick-tempered but singularly talented. Portman reflected on his time working with the American star: "[W]e got to know each other really well. Some people found Mr. Heflin an aggressive man and they thought he and I would clash, but we got on splendidly and formed a friendship which I think will last."[22]

The Syrian government banned *The Golden Mask*, fearing it would "offend the Arabs." (This was a time of tension in the region, especially in French colonial Algeria.) But no one seemed to be particularly put out. The four months of location shooting was not exactly idyllic; "The bugs are boundless and bouncy," Heflin commented. Nevertheless he was joined by his wife Frances from February 10, 1954.[23] "We got out of Tunis just in time," he observed. "It's cold, cloudy and windy on the Sahara. We had snow yesterday."[24] He returned from his time in Africa with a tropical disease from which he took a while to recover. He was ordered to adopt a strict diet and decided to rest and recuperate all summer.[25]

His next project, *Tanganyika*, was an adventure set in British East Africa in 1903. The presence of so many wild animals belied the fact that the whole enterprise was filmed on the back lot at Universal Studios. Directed by Andre de Toth from an original story by William R. Cox, this was a reasonable adventure, although somewhat let down by use of back-projection and the insertion of stock jungle footage of lions, tigers, crocodiles and hippos "under a heavy shower of Technicolor."[26] Undeserving of its reputation as "a stinker through and through," the movie had plenty of action and even here Heflin managed to create a believable character. His John Gale is a prototype Indiana Jones albeit more down-to-earth.

As the film begins, the actor's familiar throaty voice hovers over the opening shots of a safari. But this is a different kind of safari because Gale is hunting a white man: Abel McCracken (Jeff Morrow), who is stirring up trouble among the Nukumbe tribe. On the way he discovers Dan Harder (Howard Duff), shot with an arrow by the Nukumbe, and removes the arrow. A house is under attack by the same tribe; inside is teacher Peggy Marion (Ruth Roman) and her niece and nephew; their father has been killed. With help from Gale and his men, the attackers are driven off. Gale decides to take Ruth and Harder back to Nairobi where he has a lumber business with his partner Duffy. Harder is actually the brother of McCracken and later meets up with him but realizes he is now a dangerous man intent on murder. There are numerous adventures on the way involving encounters with tigers, lions and hippos. Eventually McCracken is outsmarted and defeated by clever use of dynamite dropped at intervals to sound like a creeping barrage of the British Army.

Considered a thrilling adventure on its release, *Tanganyika* now appears dated both technically and ethically. Little more than a B-movie jungle yarn intended to keep the children entertained on a Saturday afternoon, this is the kind of picture which must have seemed old-fashioned in 1954. De Toth had been making such films since the late 1930s in his native Hungary before decamping to Hollywood during the war. Over a thirty-year career his high spot was the 3D *House of Wax*; many of his movies were standard actioners of which *Tanganyika* is a fair example. Reviews at the time were mixed. The *New York Times* critic was suitably scathing and accurate in his assessment of film and star: "It's a good thing for *Tanganyika* ... that African scenery speaks and Van Heflin can act.... Mr. Heflin's persuasively blunt emoting threads this synthetic travelogue from start to finish."[27]

That Heflin managed even here to rise above the proceedings is no surprise. His no-nonsense acting technique made the often absurd story appear credible. As he once commented wryly, "I learned a long time ago that an actor is judged by his material—not by his performance.... I've been given a lot of bad material and worked to make it good without receiving any credit."[28]

Heflin often played the action hero at Universal. From *Tap Roots* to *Tomahawk* to *Tanganyika*, he was always handed the good leading role and given more respect than he had ever had at Metro.

Woman's World dealt with the hitherto overlooked and often unseen influence of women in business, in this case the automobile industry. Sid Burns (Fred MacMurray), Jerry Talbot (Heflin) and Bill Baxter (Cornel Wilde) all vying for the job of general manager are invited to interview along with their wives over a long weekend in New York by Gifford Motors CEO Ernest Gifford (Clifton Webb). The character of their wives is brought under scrutiny, each one exerting a different kind of influence on her husband. Bill and Katie (June Allyson) are thoroughly content with their life in small-town Kansas and have no real desire to move. Elizabeth Burns (Lauren Bacall) is convinced that advancement, would be the death of her husband Sid. Talbot's wife Carol (Arlene Dahl), the most ruthlessly ambitious of the three, will go to any lengths to advance her husband's career. During the course of the weekend, they are invited to the house of Gifford's wise sister and eventually a general manager is chosen.

Beneath the glossy exterior with its starry cast, lush color and stereoscopic sound, this was an intriguing insight into the unheralded importance of the distaff side in corporate life. Previously, movies about big business tended to be male-dominated affairs which featured women in peripheral roles as mere supports to their spouses, organizing dinner parties and wearing evening gowns. *Woman's World* attempted in part to show the subtle but considerable influence which a man's wife has, not just over her own husband's career but over the lives of his business colleagues.

Effectively directed by Jean Negulesco, this employed a witty and perceptive script by Claude Binyon (and several others) from a story by Mona Williams, and made excellent use of its New York background. The tone is set by the title song "It's a Woman's World" by the Four Aces, whose smooth romantic sound conjures up the whole ethos of their era. Viewers

Director Jean Negulesco (left) chats with Lauren Bacall and Van during the making of *Woman's World* (1954), an artful satire of contemporary mores with an excellent cast. This underrated gem deserves to be far more widely known.

see the city from above as Clifton Webb intones in his wonderfully clipped voice, reflecting on the beauty and excitement of New York. His commentary continues in a satiric vein as one of the latest cars is shown in all its '50s glory and he cleverly sends up the era's obsession with objects and prestige. Less a paean to consumerism, *Woman's World* is at heart a satire full of shrewd observation and dry humor. "Look, you can see daylight," says Burns to his wife as they are driving through a tunnel, having just been arguing about the state of their marriage; "I saw daylight years ago," says his wife acerbically.

Talbot has the most showy and glamorous wife of the three. When all three couples are about to take the elevator together to the formal introductory function to meet the CEO, she notices what the other two women are wearing and makes an excuse to go back to her room to change her outfit. When she emerges downstairs later in her eye-catching dress with plunging neckline and flouncy sleeves, she stops at the entrance; all the men turn her way and conversation stops. She goes straight up to Gifford and flirts outrageously. Soon Talbot arrives, turns to his wife and says, "I never saw you come in, darling." Gifford rejoins, "You're the only one who didn't."

Over the course of the weekend they all go to a number of social functions in between tours of the factories and sightseeing excursions for the wives. Meanwhile their husbands are being sounded out by Gifford; they are shown testing plants and such nifty inventions as a car that maneuvers itself sideways into a tight parking spot. Baxter speaks his mind when asked questions; he is not a yes man. Burns often says what he thinks Gifford wants to hear. Talbot speaks less but makes what he says count.

Carol Talbot spends most of her time dancing and flirting with Gifford. The relationship between Talbot and his wife is established in subtle ways. In one scene he is shaving with an electric razor in the bathroom while Carol is floating around their hotel room. "I've fallen in love," she announces. The sound of the razor stops. "How's that?" calls Talbot in a quiet, concerned tone. "I'm in love with New York," she says. Talbot's annoyance with his wife later boils over and he asserts himself. He begins to realize that, far from being an asset, his wife is a handicap to his career. In a scene at the house of Gifford's sister, all three candidates are asked about their wives. At the mention of this, Talbot sits down; Baxter tells Gifford that his wife comes first; Burns, despite his promise to his wife to the contrary, says he would do anything for the job. Talbot tells Gifford he would rather not have the job if it meant his wife had to have a say in things.

The ironic denouement of *Woman's World* is entirely in keeping with its satiric nature. All in all, this is a seldom mentioned but significant film which captures the whole zeitgeist of the 1950s. Several scenes such as that showing the mayhem at a fashion house clothes sale at great reductions cleverly sent up the madness of consumerism. The performances were universally perfect and the script a delight. It made a sharp, contemporary comment on its own mid-century time which would provide social historians with enough material for several theses.

Hedda Hopper mentioned that there had been talk of tensions and arguments on the set but found no evidence of this when she visited. Negulesco had a distinguished career but is often overlooked when plaudits are handed out. Although popular at the Venice Film Festival, he never won an Academy Award. After a colorful early life he began his directing career with *The Mask of Dimitrios* (1944) and tackled a taboo subject well in *Johnny Belinda* (1948). His most successful years came in the 1950s with the appealing, polished movies *How to Marry a Millionaire* (1953) and *Three Coins in the Fountain* (1954) which he completed immediately before *Woman's World.*

At the opening of *Woman's World* Heflin received the honor of being invited to leave his footprints for posterity in the forecourt of Grauman's Chinese Restaurant to add to all the other stars. It was one more bit of proof that he had arrived. He was riding high in the 1950s, an actor of great reputation, much admired by his peers. Always sought-after, he appeared in five films over a six-month period in 1954. "There's a saying in Hollywood," said Hedda Hopper, "that when Van Heflin's name appears on more than two shows a year, everything is all right in the industry."[29]

The jury is out as to whether *Black Widow* is a film noir. Many of the elements that constitute the genre are present including a wronged central character who appears doomed and a *femme fatale.* But the full force of CinemaScope and Technicolor worked against its own appealing air of mystery and the treatment of the story strayed too close to melodrama at times to qualify.

An ambitious girl, Nancy Ordway (Peggy Ann Garner), befriends writer Pete Denver (Heflin) at a party, and he takes her to dinner. His wife Iris (Gene Tierney) is out of town at the time. Nancy visits Pete's apartment several times to read her work to him. Some weeks later she is found hanged in the bathroom. Police Lieutenant Bruce (George Raft) eventually concludes that her death was not suicide but murder. Suspicion immediately falls on Pete, who tries desperately to prove his innocence. He uncovers a web of deceit that Nancy has woven involving their actress friend Lottie Marin (Ginger Rogers) and her playwright husband Brian Mullen (Reginald Gardiner) in the upstairs apartment. Time appears to be running out and he is the only suspect in the frame so he is determined to clear his name and find the answers.

The story begins promisingly. Pete is a quiet personality but he quickly becomes determined once he is backed up into a corner. Tension builds as he sets out to find the truth. Unfortunately the action begins to flag and the film loses its way as regards direction, making the climax veer too close to soap opera. Several puzzling aspects are left unexplained and some of the characters are not sufficiently developed, like Nancy's suspicious uncle Gordon Ling (Otto Kruger). Ginger Rogers was a fine actress and well suited to the genre as she had already proved decisively in *Storm Warning.* Her performance here is curiously overblown and she alters her voice unnecessarily. Another weak link is Reginald Gardiner, who is too old to be convincing as husband to Ginger and lover of Peggy Ann Garner.

Gene Tierney has little to do as Pete's doubtful but understanding wife. George Raft is George Raft.

This was Heflin's picture and he made the most of his role; however the plot, direction and character development were sadly lacking and effectively wasted an excellent cast. The much darker and deeper film which briefly emerges soon vanishes again in the glare of 1950s gloss and its preoccupation with color and widescreen.

Three key scenes could have given this film the sense of direction it needed. In one, the clearly harried and increasingly desperate Pete (Heflin) questions Claire Amberly (Virginia Leith), artist friend of the dead girl, and her brother John (Skip Homeier). The first time he visits, he is confused and only partially assuaged by her story. On his later visit he becomes forceful and quite violent towards her, grasping her around the neck. He is now under pressure and the audience begins to think that he was more than capable of killing Nancy. In a later scene he questions a hatcheck girl Anne (Hilda Simms); she is both observant and helpful, describing a man she saw with Nancy and giving Pete his next lead. But then the momentum flags and the ending is pure Agatha Christie, with all the protagonists in one room. This makes the final scenes appear very stagey.

Black Widow was based on the novel *Fatal Woman* by Hugh Wheeler and adapted for the screen by Nunnally Johnson, who also directed. Johnson usually scored with his screenplays such as *The Grapes of Wrath* and *How to Marry a Millionaire,* but misses the mark here. He directed only a handful of movies, of which this was only his second attempt. Perhaps his most interesting was *The Three Faces of Eve* (1957). *Black Widow* came over at its best like a noir version of *All About Eve,* with an ambitious but seemingly naïve girl a catalyst for murder. It occasionally sparked into life in Heflin's capable hands, but the excellent cast was largely wasted and the enterprise never caught fire, displaying much of the formulaic nature of later noirs.

Adapted by Leon Uris from his own best-seller, *Battle Cry* was a starry war drama which told the tangled tales of the lives of a group of American Marines during World War II. It begins with their recruitment through basic training at San Diego to various scenes of action on Pacific islands, especially Guadalcanal, narrated by the sergeant (James Whitmore). As much emphasis was put on their romances and off-duty lives as on the war itself so that although it was based on actual events it possessed a 1950s gloss which made it seem far less immediate than *Wake Island* or *Guadalcanal Diary* to which it owed its template. It was a good movie which had some convincing action scenes and a decent part for Heflin as Major, later Colonel Sam Huxley, nicknamed "High Pockets." Aldo Ray had the central role as a corporal who loses a leg; Heflin's chief cause for complaint was that he did not get top billing.[30] Such a slight wounded his pride but things were soon rectified when his star status was restored. Despite good performances, especially from Heflin and Nancy Olson, the verdict of the critics was mixed. It was variously described as an "interminable cheapie epic with both eyes on the box office" and "probably the most boring marine movie ever made."[31]

Filming was not a particularly enjoyable or well-organized affair. The cast and crew assembled at Vieques Island, Puerto Rico, in February 1954. According to young cast member Tab Hunter, the battalion was housed in a makeshift tent city, nicknamed Camp Hollywood, "where we shared cold showers and outdoor latrines. It teemed with scorpions, field mice, and billions of mosquitoes." Although shooting was scheduled for a mere eighteen days, a week passed without sight of a script. Said Hunter, "All we'd been given on leaving Los Angeles were ten pages, mostly action stuff. After several scriptless days on location, Van Heflin blew his stack. I expected him to grab a radio, crank it up and holler, '*We need words, dammit! Words!*'"[32]

Raoul Walsh was a veteran director of action films and his forte was shooting such scenes; the script was someone else's department. Days passed and the cast members were encouraged to make up their own dialogue. Eventually Walsh cabled Warners and a screenplay finally arrived. The rest of the filming went smoothly and the action sequences in particular were well choreographed.

As for the acting, Heflin, Olson, Ray and Whitmore stood out. Heflin had several key scenes which he played with his usual skill. In contrast to the other characters, Huxley's home life is not actually seen, so it is necessary to establish the kind of life he has with words only. He does this in a subtle scene with his second in command. He enters the office in his shirt sleeves and begins by putting on his coat, symbolic of his heavy burden of responsibility. Everything is done at a slow pace and his natural approach makes all he says seem real and heartfelt. He talks movingly of the last hours he spends with his wife before sailing; despite all the times he has sailed before, there is the same well of emotion beforehand, each time never knowing if it will be the last. He talks about how she goes into the other room so he cannot hear her crying. All the time he is putting on his coat, fastening the buttons, fiddling absentmindedly with his cigarettes, tying his belt and finally putting on his cap. "What makes a woman go on loving a man she can't even claim belongs to her?" he asks rhetorically as he opens the door and leaves.

The stirring music of Warner Brothers stalwart Max Steiner was augmented with "The Halls of Montezuma" for the most patriotic moments and strains from "I'll String Along with You" during some of the more tender interludes.

Several intriguing movie ideas came Heflin's way during the 1950s but for a variety of reasons they never materialized. In 1950 his was one of a number of names in the running to play Captain John in Jean Renoir's meditative version of Rumer Godden's novel *The River*, set in India; others included Glenn Ford, James Mason and Robert Walker.[33] Eventually the role devolved to an unknown Thomas E. Breen, who was too bland by far to capture the psychological complexity required. Heflin would have given this philosophical venture an extra dimension.

The previous year he was all set to star as Captain Mike Dillon in Universal's *Sword of the Desert*, an adventure tale about the foundation of the state of Israel; the part went to Dana Andrews instead.[34] In *White Sheep* for Universal he would have starred opposite Ann Blyth and for the little-known Panoramic Productions he was set to film *A Matter of Life and Death* in Spain along with Susan Hayward and Faith Domergue; neither of these movies were made.[35] In 1953 he turned down the key role of William Keefer in *The Caine Mutiny* because he felt that once the censors had been through the script, they had taken away all the humor and lessened the role, which later went to Fred MacMurray.[36] Another abandoned project was George Sherman's first independent production *File 246* co-starring Shelley Winters, to be shot in Rome.[37]

George Stevens wanted Alan Ladd to play Jett Rink in *Giant*. Ladd refused because it was not the starring role; he wanted to play "Bick" Benedict. Heflin was then offered the part of Jett and William Holden desperately wanted to play Benedict; neither were chosen and the roles famously went to James Dean and Rock Hudson, who were both nominated for Oscars.[38] As far back as 1950 Jerry Wald wanted Heflin to appear in *Rebel Without a Cause*.[39] He had another chance to appear with Spencer Tracy in *Henry Menafee* but the movie was never made.[40] He might also have appeared as Professor Jerusalem Webster Stiles in *Raintree County* for which Nigel Patrick was nominated for a Golden Globe Award. Director Jean Renoir suggested Heflin to play Vincent Van Gogh; this was a role he particularly coveted.[41] However, after much discussion, Renoir eventually dropped the idea and a different script, *Lust for Life*, was handed to director Vincente Minnelli, who cast Kirk Douglas.

There was the tantalizing prospect of co-starring with Humphrey Bogart in *River of the Sun*, an adventure to be shot in Brazil, based on the novel by James Ramsey Ullman and also featuring Aldo Ray. However the project was dropped.[42]

So many opportunities came his way which for various reasons he rejected. He was choosy and sometimes his reasoning was not easy to understand. He refused most scripts he received; in October 1956 it was said that he had "read thirty-one scripts since February and turned them all down."[43] He might have had the role of Ivan in *The Brothers Karamazov* which went to Richard Basehart.[44] In 1958 he was invited by Bill Mauldin to do an army comedy, *Up Front*; around the same time, Burt Lancaster wanted him to co-star in *The Naked and the Dead*, adapted from Norman Mailer's best-selling anti-war novel. Lancaster sent Heflin the script, which he perused while on vacation in the High Sierras; it was to be produced by Lancaster's independent company Norma Productions and the suggested director was the great Fred Zinnemann. Heflin turned both projects down. (*The Naked and the Dead* employed a number of the same cast members as *Battle Cry* to which the finished result bore an uncanny resemblance.[45]) Other abandoned projects included Phil Karlson and Irving Levin's *The Smouldering Sea* co-starring George Peppard and based on U.S. Anderson's novel.[46] He even considered producing his own films and planned to be co-producer with David Heilwell of *Precipice*, from a screenplay by Philip MacDonald. He scouted locations in Acapulco and Mexico City but the project did not come to fruition.[47]

All things considered, the films he made as a freelancer were something of a mixed bag. Most were good, some bad and others indifferent; however, some were outstanding. *Shane* has proved to be one of the most timeless Westerns ever made.

Nine

Shane and After (1953–59)

"Shane *was made with a lot of integrity.*"
—Ben Johnson[1]

If George Stevens' original casting intentions had been followed through, then Montgomery Clift would have been the mysterious stranger seen riding into view at the beginning of *Shane* and William Holden and Katharine Hepburn the homesteaders who welcome him. But Holden was unavailable and suddenly the whole project was almost abandoned. Then the erstwhile director went to Paramount head Y. Frank Freeman and asked him which actors he had available and under contract. In three minutes he came up with three names: Alan Ladd, Van Heflin and Jean Arthur. And the process of making one of *the* most timeless Westerns began.

Heflin was more than happy to accept the role which re-united him with Jean Arthur as his wife almost twenty years after the two appeared together in the Broadway "flop" *The Bride of Torozco.*[2] He had great respect for directors, and especially so for George Stevens. "I'm your man!" he said when he was asked, before he had even read the script.[3]

Filming began at Jackson Hole, Wyoming, in July 1951 amidst the splendor of the Grand Teton Mountains and ended in October. However the movie was not released until 1953, spending sixteen months in post-production. During that time there was extensive editing and it was made to fit the new Cinerama format.[4]

The plot of the movie is simple and familiar. A stranger, Shane, arrives on horseback at the ranch of Joe Starrett. Like the other homesteaders, Starrett is being ordered by Ryker and his cohorts to get off "his" land. Unwittingly Shane is drawn into this conflict and helps Starrett and the homesteaders. Along the way he builds up a rapport with little Joey and the Starretts, but he cannot stay.

Based on the novel by Jack Schaefer, *Shane* was taken from actual events during the Johnson County War in Wyoming in 1862 after the Homestead Act came into being, and was shot in a similar locale in the same state. The memorable fight sequence at Grafton's store-saloon was one of the action centerpieces of the movie. The filming of this was a little too authentic as Heflin recalled shortly afterwards: "Part of the routine called for me to take a 'punch' in the stomach, double up and then receive a blow on the chin. Unfortunately, Alan bumped into me as I was doubled up, and pushed me forward—right on to the stunt guy's uppercut. My teeth bit right through my lower lip."[5]

He had to have stitches in his lip when it was all over, but for Alan and Van it was the start of a lifelong friendship.[6] On the surface they appeared so dissimilar: Ladd the blond-haired Greek god who played the unsmiling lead of many a film noir, war movie and melodrama, was a major star; Heflin the "homely, ruggedly handsome" character actor from the stage who had spent time studying his art. But they found a definite connection in their shared Oklahoma background; there was a mutual respect and ease in one another's company. Heflin had, as Ladd's biographer observed, "most of the other qualities Alan had always been drawn to" and he also had the sensitivity to understand and appreciate all Ladd's qualities and insecurities. The two men became "as close as brothers." Heflin later spoke about their friendship:

> One of the sadnesses in my life is that Alan and I never had the opportunity to work together again after *Shane.*... But we talked about it a lot. And although actors usually go their separate ways after a movie is completed, Alan and I remained very close. God, how I loved that man.[7]

Ben Johnson played the sneering Chris Calloway, whose earliest retort about "sodypop" sets up a memorable fight. Johnson was also a native of Oklahoma and enjoyed immensely working with Alan and Van. The three spent many happy hours together fishing on the Snake River and surrounding lakes, and caught a lot of rainbow trout.[8] With Jack Palance they all had some fun drinking; but their families were on location too, including Frances and the children and Alan Ladd's son, so a jovial atmosphere prevailed on set. Despite the bonhomie amongst the cast, Jean Arthur often kept herself aloof and on the final day of shooting left the set without saying goodbye to anyone.[9]

It is not necessary to know that it took 116 takes for Alan Ladd to shoot straight in front of Joey; or that Jack Palance had trouble riding his horse; the finished movie is a perfect distillation of the essence of the struggle for the west. There is a real sense of the isolation of the homesteads and

The funeral of Stonewall is a moving turning point in *Shane* when Joe rallies the other homesteaders to stay and fight. Left to right: Heflin, Jean Arthur, Brandon de Wilde and Alan Ladd. Timeless and critically acclaimed, George Stevens' masterpiece has never stopped making money since its release.

the importance of the instilled notion of community which keeps them together in the face of their many hardships.

The casting too was faultless. Ladd gave his best performance as the enigmatic Shane; Stevens' "infinite patience" undoubtedly brought out the best in his star. Ladd gave the character his own "large measure of reserve and dignity" which made his acts of violence echo all the more profoundly. He also possessed what Leo Genn termed "an indefinable aura of sadness" which is an apt description for actor and character. Shane is a gunman who comes from nowhere and goes to nowhere; he has no roots, no family.[10] He recognizes the innate goodness of the life of Joe Starrett and his family; he longs to be part of such a world and set of values. But he knows he never can and his silence comes from sadness—sadness that is too deep for words.

Heflin was perfectly cast as Starrett. Strong but slightly dim-witted, he is a farmer to his core. "Someone's coming, Pa," says Joey as Shane first rides into view. "Let 'em come," is Starrett's laconic response as he goes on hacking at a tree stump. He is not sure what to make of Shane at first but when the stranger stands with him and his family as Ryker and his men threaten them, he is full of good will towards him and accepts him as one of the family instantly. Starrett's honesty and integrity shine through, and although he is not always able to articulate the whys and wherefores he keeps the other homesteaders together in the face of Ryker's bullying tactics, mostly through his own sheer determination not to be beaten. In the scene at the dance when he sees Marian and Shane dancing together, the look that comes over his face reflects that he is aware of the growing feelings of his wife for the stranger. In some way he seems to accept it because he likes him so much himself; the whole family has fallen under Shane's spell.

Jean Arthur was a fine actress and also one of the most reclusive; prior to *Shane* she had made her last film three years earlier and at the age of 51 considered her movie career to be at an end. However she was coaxed out of semi-retirement as a favor to Stevens. Her casting as Marian Starrett was another coup and one of the reasons the dynamic of the four leads worked so well. Her style was emotional but often subtle; she proved effective time after time over the years in so many roles despite the personal agonies she went through for every single one. In *Shane* her fraught emotional state at the turmoil of their harsh life and the turbulence of her own feelings about the stranger are apparent. She had a similar emotional center to her acting as Heflin; both were veteran stage players. Here again was a reason Ladd was so effective as the title character: His coolness, aloofness and above all his silence worked as a perfect counterpoint to their natural emotionalism.

Brandon de Wilde was a naturally ebullient child actor who had the ability to convey so much emotion and to instill great empathy in the audience. The movie is seen from his perspective which gives it the timelessness that is so marked. It is hard to avoid the tears from falling at the end as he shouts after Shane, "Shane, come back!"

Over the years there have been many and fulsome tributes to *Shane*. One of the movies' greatest fans is Woody Allen, who praised its poetry and elegant flow. He admitted to having seen it at least twenty times and in a wide-ranging 2001 interview for the *New York Times* discussed it at length. His favorite films were mostly European, he said, and he was not a fan of Westerns, but he considered *Shane* a fine movie regardless of genre and rated it above *High Noon* and all others.[11] Biographer Andre Soares, writing on the 60th anniversary of the film's release, spoke eloquently about its subversive quality: "how unheroic its heroes are, how complex the lives and minds of the common people; how civilization can be just another manifestation of barbarism; and no matter their righteousness, how hollow human victories can be."[12]

Shane is much more than the sum of its parts (the epic grandeur of the mountain setting, the compelling fight for life against the odds and above all the great performances of all the actors involved). It all came together over two years to create something that ought to live while men ever struggle. The heart is stirred by the landscape, the people, their story, and above all the sweeping, majestic score by Victor Young. Epic, expansive and full of feeling, it speaks forever to our humanity.

Ladd, Heflin and Jean Arthur were all passed over for Academy Awards for *Shane*, which is difficult to comprehend. The simple reason stated was studio politics. By the time the movie was released in 1953 all three had left Paramount so the studio would never back their nominations.[13] (Heflin was nominated for a BAFTA as best foreign actor.) Young's sumptuous score didn't receive any award but "The Call of the Faraway Hills" will be heard long after everyone has forgotten who won the award that year.

After the success of *Shane*, Stevens was keen on working with Heflin again and assigned him the lead role of Captain Jake Cutter in *The Comancheros*.[14] The director had bought the rights to the novel by Paul I. Wellman about maverick white men stirring up trouble with the Apaches and he wanted Cary Grant to co-star as Paul Regret. But filming was postponed. Twentieth Century–Fox later bought the rights from Stevens for $300,000. Marlon Brando expressed an interest in the project but the movie was eventually made by Michael Curtiz in 1961 with John Wayne.[15]

Heflin was a late replacement for Glenn Ford in *Wings of the Hawk* after the latter had fallen off his horse.[16] Based on a novel by Gerald Drayson Adams, this was the swift, bold tale of Irish Gallager (Heflin), a gold prospector whose mine is commandeered by corrupt Mexican administrator Colonel Ruiz and his Federales during the revolution of 1910–11. Gallager saves the life of guerrilla leader Raquel (Julie Adams), the fiancée of the Insurrectos' weak leader Arturo (Rodolfo Acosta). Raquel falls in love with Gallager. When Arturo is deposed as leader, he is spurred by jealousy and turns traitor, offering to guide Ruiz's men to the Insurrecto camp. Numerous adventures culminate in Orozco's counterattack on Juarez.

Heflin made a convincingly rugged, no-nonsense action hero and carried the whole yarn with admirable help from Julie Adams. The other actors did not register so well, and interest waned when the two leads were off-screen. The action consisted mostly of ambushes, kidnappings and counter-attacks and ended in a large explosion. Filmed in 3-D and directed with verve by Budd Boetticher, this was shot partially on the Universal back lot and also in the Simi Valley and at Burro Flats in the Simi Hills. *Wings of the Hawk* is an entertaining Western very much of its time but had little resonance beyond the events it described, although the idea of a woman as leader of the rebels gave it a twist, and there seemed to be a natural chemistry between the two stars.

The Raid (1954) is an overlooked film based on the novel *The Affair at St. Albans* by Herbert Ravenal Sass, which was taken from actual events about a party of Southern renegades who planned to cause havoc in a small town in the United States near the Canadian border. It would be the first in a series of such raids in order to decoy Union forces from the front during the Civil War.

Seven Southern officers escape from a prisoner of war camp in Vermont in October 1864. One is wounded and left behind by the others as they head across country. The remaining six head for a rendezvous with sympathizers at an isolated farm in neutral Canada. They have a plan of

Hugo Fregonese's *The Raid* (1954) was a tense, thoughtful Western based on true events. Heflin starred as a Confederate officer torn between what he sees as his duty in a time of war and his feelings for Union army widow Katy Bishop (Anne Bancroft) and her son Larry (Tommy Rettig, seen here).

action that Major Neal Benton (Heflin) will enter the nearby town of St. Albans alone to reconnoiter and prepare the way for the others to drift in over the next few days. He poses as a Canadian businessman interested in money-making opportunities and property in the area. He lodges at the hotel run by widow Katy Bishop (Anne Bancroft) and soon builds a rapport with her and her son Larry (Tommy Rettig). The other guests include Captain Lionel Foster (Richard Boone), who is immediately antagonistic towards the newcomer.

One of Neal's men, Lieutenant Keating (Lee Marvin), starts drinking and becomes trigger-happy during a church service. Before the shocked congregation, he is about to shoot the preacher; Neal thinks fast and shoots Keating, not wishing to jeopardize the mission. For this act he is feted as a hero and worthy citizen of St Albans. Larry, like the other townspeople, is in awe of him. Plans for the raid continue and groups of rebels are brought into the town; there are moments of great tension when they coincide with a Union Army Day celebration. Meanwhile Neal is taken to the heart of the community and especially Katy and her son; he has conflicted loyalties but is resolute in the course he has to take.

Directed with gusto by Hugo Fregonese, *The Raid* was a tense and engrossing tale which had an air of authenticity lacking in sundry other Westerns at the time. This was an even-handed treatment of the novel by Sass and reflected more accurately on the inhumanity of war itself. Neal is seething with hatred at what the Union troops did to his land and family, but his actions in causing more mayhem only compound the misery of everyone else. For a while he begins to think with love and tenderness towards Katy and her son, but his mind is made up and he is a soldier first and last. Heflin reflects the conflicting emotions of his character with his look and demeanor. His eyes as always register all the variety of emotions he is going through. His instincts to love the widow of a Union soldier run contrary to all his military tenets in a time of war which he sees as a fight for the survival of his country.

He is a man of swift thought and action as befits a major. Ruthless both with himself and his men, he leaves one to die and shoots another who puts the mission in jeopardy. The background characters are well drawn by an excellent supporting cast, especially Anne Bancroft as Katy; the appealing Tommy Rettig as her son; and Richard Boone as the awkward Captain Foster who longs to be a hero.

What set the film apart from many other Westerns of the era was its thoughtful and thought-provoking treatment of the effect of war on the country at large. Vermont was far from the scene of war but there is the same direct sense of involvement reflected in the interest which each daily bulletin posted at the town hall engenders in the population; the sons of the town are fighting too. Wonderful cinematography by Lucien Ballard and the stirring music of Roy Webb added to the drama at key moments. There was plenty of action throughout and the chaotic burning of the town was vivid. However there were few actual deaths on screen which added to its believability; practically all the main characters were still alive at the end.

Although Heflin had agreed to appear in *The Calico Pony* for Columbia, he received an offer from Paramount to star in *The Maverick*. However, the Paramount deal was postponed and finally abandoned so he was free to make *The Calico Pony* after all. Retitled *Count Three and Pray*, this was an entertaining Western produced by Ted Richmond and Tyrone Power's independent company Copa Productions. Power appeared in the trailer promoting it.[17]

Former rebel-rouser Luke Fargo (Heflin) and two friends arrive at his home town in the South after the Civil War, in which he fought for the Union. He makes for the parsonage with the intention of taking up residence as the preacher. He soon encounters Lissy (Joanne Woodward), a spirited orphan "of about fourteen or fifteen" who is squatting there. He seeks to rebuild the church in the face of bitter opposition from the townspeople who consider him a traitor. His most formidable opponent is Yancey Huggins (Raymond Burr), the storekeeper who lost two brothers in the war and holds sway in the town; he is the repository of all the residual post-war surly resentment and bitterness. Huggins courts Georgina (Allison Hayes), the haughty daughter of Mrs. Decrais. Huggins is a counter-jumper in the eyes of the Decrais family, but Georgina nonetheless is "nice" to him in order to maintain the genteel façade of their life. Georgina was once keen on Fargo, and Huggins begins to get jealous of the attention she pays to him on his return. Old flame Selma (Jean Willes), a prostitute with a good heart, also hopes to rekindle her love for Luke. But the real "romance" of *Count Three and Pray* is between Luke and Lissy, who he never considers in a romantic way. If anything, he feels responsible for her. It is the very unconscious nature of their non-romance that provides the story with its light heart.

There are several key scenes which Heflin handles adeptly. He holds his first church meeting before the church is actually built. He has only his friends in the congregation; nervous and tongue-tied, he fiddles endlessly with the sermons which were written by his predecessor. Sensing his nervousness, Maddy starts singing "Abide with Me" and eventually

Lissy, sitting in a tree, shouts out, "Why don't you tell us about Hell? You raised enough when you were here." Everyone laughs and the tension is relieved, but Luke is annoyed. His embarrassment registers in his face allied to his sense of shame and feeling that he will never escape his past.

His second dedication of the church is interrupted by Yancey and his men. The whole thing ends up in a raucous brawl at the center of which is Luke in his new preacher's outfit. Selma arrives with her girls, a whole made-to-order congregation all dressed to the nines. Luke and the towns-folk are aghast as the girls pile out of the carriage. At this the fighting stops; the pious citizens vacate the church and go home. The unanimous feeling is that Luke will never change. During this scene, Heflin has few lines. He has to display all his conflicting emotions in his face: He starts with hope; dismay when the ruckus starts; shame at his feelings of anger; fury as he takes his coat off, rolls his sleeves up and goes outside to slay a few; and finally defeat at what he sees as his failure.

Made with a great spirit, *Count Three and Pray* is lively, touching and humorous by turns. It has some of the same feeling as *Shane* at times; a similar sense of a community uniting in a common purpose. Instead of homesteaders fighting for their rights, this addresses some of the difficul-ties of adjusting to the aftermath of the Civil War. The approach is far more light-hearted than Stevens' masterpiece but the same essential integrity is present.

Joanne Woodward had fond memories of working on the film. Despite being inundated with script offers, this was the first which really appealed to her. "It was a lovely thing about a wistful waif who went bare-foot, rode a horse, and shot guns, so I did it," she said.[18] She was perfect in the role and her scenes with Heflin had an unconscious joy about them. The film was directed with assurance by Western veteran George Sher-man, who had previously worked with Heflin on *Tomahawk*. Unusually, the supporting characters were also well-defined and more integral to the plot. Writer Herb Meadow adapted his own story well.

Heflin played comedy in precisely the right vein, never for laughs. *Count Three and Pray* is a fast-paced action-packed comedy Western with elements of farce and slapstick, but he remained true to his character throughout and the center around which everything else revolves. His stillness is a perfect counterpoint to all the uproar around him and gives the movie its balance. Hence the moments of pathos are as successful as the moments of high comedy.

There is an essential truth to Luke Fargo. Ashamed of his past, and trying desperately to escape it, he agonizes constantly over his sermons and his very ability to become a preacher. He is spurred by the best of motives: from the bloodshed he witnessed at the Battle of Vicksburg, he seeks to help people rather than hurt them. Thwarted at every turn, he nonetheless struggles against the opposition of some of the townspeople and his own inner demons. His seriousness ensures the comedy works. During the hearing when his morality is being assessed by the bishop, Lissy enters in an over-the-top outfit provided by Selma, a black silk number with red feathers. As soon as he sees her, he is livid. "Take those clothes off!" he demands, as the bishop looks on. This line would not have been as funny if he had played it for laughs; it was because he was so much in character that it worked so sublimely. Heflin was offered other comedies but unfortunately declined them. He was a consummate interpreter of the genre and this is one element of his all-round ability which is consequently often overlooked.

Count Three and Pray is one of the most enjoyable and overlooked films of the era. While not in the same league as *Shane*, it is nonetheless undeserving of its obscurity. This and *The Raid* were arguably Heflin's best lesser Westerns; they had good stories with heart and life to them and their characters were conflicted individuals. The drama came from the central characters just as much as the situations in which they find themselves. They were all good ensemble pieces of inspired filmmaking far advanced from the witless Saturday afternoon B-movie horsefests which proliferated at the time. They all owe their success in no small measure to the characterizations which Heflin brought to the screen with such brilliance.

Apart from some shots of the Columbia Ranch, Delmer Daves' *3:10 to Yuma* was mostly filmed at locations in Arizona including Old Tuscan, Sedona, Elgin, Wilcox, Texas Canyon and the Triangle T Ranch in Dragoon. Cinematographer Charles Lawton Jr. made exquisite use of all these places to create a memorable atmosphere: the harsh, dry landscape dotted with old cacti and stark one-horse towns; the very stillness of the air is palpable. The scale and nature of the terrain gives a real sense of the freedom and inherent peril of the west: the hard everyday struggle to carve out a living the honest way; and the sore temptation to follow the dishonest route when the law is a five-day ride away.

Notorious outlaw Ben Wade (Glenn Ford) is unexpectedly captured in the small town of Bisbee. Several deputies are sworn in to escort him to Contention City and then on to Yuma for trial. The deputies soon melt away once it becomes clear that the mission will be fraught with danger, not least from Wade's gang. Hard-up small-time rancher Dan Evans (Heflin) agrees to stay for the $200 reward money which he sorely needs

In the superior noir Western *3:10 to Yuma* (1957), Heflin (right) rendered a per-fectly pitched portrayal as struggling farmer Dan Evans, trying to withstand the constant needling by outlaw Ben Wade (Glenn Ford) as Robert Emhardt looked on. Directed by Delmer Daves there was a spare, taut feel to the screen-play and outstanding cinematography by Charles Lawton, Jr.

for his drought-ridden farm. The only other volunteer is Alex Potter (Henry Jones), the town drunk. While Wade's gang is decoyed, Evans takes Wade to his ranch for the night prior to the ride into Contention the fol-lowing day to catch the 3:10 train to Yuma. But when they reach the hotel in Contention, the secret is soon out as one of Wade's men is already there. In the ensuing battle of wits, Evans tries desperately to hold his resolve while he is constantly undermined by Wade.

The tone of this superior noir Western is set by the distinctive voice of Frankie Laine, "old leather lungs," with the rousing title song which sub-limely evokes the 1950s and creates a distinctive atmosphere. Based on a 1953 short story by Elmore Leonard, the taut screenplay by Halsted Welles held audiences in rapt attention throughout. There was a spare feel to the whole scenario and a telling script riddled with feeling, menace, dry humor and a sharp eye for character and motivation. While the obvious compar-ison is to *High Noon* of five years before, the approach here is somewhat different, the action more contained and the characterizations more concentrated.

Ford's character holds all the aces throughout. He knows he will escape and is ultra-cool; he constantly needles Evans about his hard life and how he could earn thousands of dollars by letting him go. Heflin reflects all the passing emotions in his expression and demeanor. He is sorely tempted more than once and has a sneaking admiration for Wade; this admiration is crucially reflected by Wade, who longs to have the true stability of a home life. The actors expertly handled their respective roles and worked well together. Heflin was nominated for a Golden Laurel.

3:10 to Yuma was neatly summarized by a contemporary critic as "a vivid, tense and intelligent story about probable people, enhanced by economical writing and supremely efficient direction and playing."[19]

There were several telling scenes: the opener in the Bisbee bar when Wade is arrested and Evans is suddenly left with the sole responsibility of guarding him; and the glimpse of Evans' home life when Wade is kept there overnight. There is an affecting scene between Evans and his wife Alice (Leora Dana) near the end when the situation seems almost hopeless for him. This tender moment is all the more moving because of his quiet heroism and her dignity and warmth.

Ford turned down the role of Evans in order to attempt to widen his range by playing the bad guy. The two men became good friends during the making of the movie; both were excellent and often underrated actors. According to Australian television personality Bert Newton's gossipy memoir *Bert!* they shared a friendship akin to that of John Wayne and Ward Bond:

> Van introduced Glenn to a new drink—beef extract spiked with vodka. They tried five or six of these things before shooting the final scene. Both considered they had turned in the best performances of their lives…. The director asked next morning if they would like to see the rushes. In Glenn Ford's words he saw two professional actors of some stature mumbling and smiling at each other. Glenn decided never to drink before shooting again.[20]

Ford Rainey, a supporting actor in *3:10 to Yuma*, recalled that Ford expected to be treated like a star while on set. He found Heflin more approachable. "[He] had been a stage actor," Rainey commented. "He wasn't so interested in image and the star system."[21] Heflin and Ford worked well together; Ford as the laidback, ultra-confident Ben Wade contrasted sharply with the ever-flustered, desperate Heflin. (Whenever a director asked Ford to speed up his slow and deliberate acting style, he would say "I've only got one other speed and it's slower.")

The 2007 remake of *3:10 to Yuma* starred Russell Crowe as Ben Wade and Christian Bale as Dan Evans. The movie did well at the box office and was critically acclaimed. It is technically superior as would be expected after fifty years; the story is opened out and more background is given. The storyline is also altered; in effect, it is a re-imagining for the twenty-first century. It would be a great shame if the original is eclipsed by the remake; each is a product of its time and will no doubt resonate for its generation. For all the technical brilliance and scope of the remake, the original has a unity of purpose which makes it live in the mind, and clear black and white photography which renders it timeless. The performances of Ford and Heflin, two excellent actors of their era, are comparable to their successors Crowe and Bale. Interestingly Bale has made a career out of playing what one critic called "wounded, desperate, stubborn men," a description which could easily describe Heflin.

By the time of *Gunman's Walk* Tab Hunter was becoming one of the hottest young stars; he had come a long way since *Battle Cry* of three years earlier. A fable of generational conflict, *Gunman's Walk* fitted into the same subgenre as *Rebel Without a Cause* but also had some of the timelessness of *East of Eden*. Filmed at Patagonia in Arizona and directed with intent by the excellent and underrated Phil Karlson, the screenplay by Frank S. Nugent utilized an original idea by Ric Hardman.

Lee Hackett (Heflin) has two sons, both of whom call him by his Christian name. He seems to compete with them as though he is "one of the boys." Having lost his wife, he has raised his sons alone; his favorite is Ed (Hunter), who is very much in his own mold—ebullient and rebellious. The other, Davy (James Darren), is more thoughtful; Lee doesn't understand him. Davy indulges Ed and allows him to do whatever he wants. There is a horse drive during which Ed is antagonistic towards half–Indian scout Paul Chouard. After the drive, Ed sees a white mare and chases after it; Chouard is also in pursuit. Ed rides past Chouard on a narrow ledge on top of a cliff; Chouard is pushed over and falls to his death. From a distance, two Indians have witnessed everything. The case comes to trial; the witnesses are believed until a stranger, Jensen Sieverts (Ray Teal), appears and says he saw the whole thing and that it was an accident. The stranger lied because he heard that Lee is wealthy and hopes Lee will make it worth his while. After Ed is freed, he spies Sieverts riding out of town with his horses, including the white mare. Ed challenges Sieverts, who pulls a gun; Sieverts is shot. Ed takes to the saloon; Lee comes to town and confronts Ed, who at first defies him. In time Ed is taken to jail by the sheriff. Lee goes to Sieverts and tells him at gunpoint to clear Ed of attempted murder. Meanwhile, impatient and angry, Ed kills the genial deputy Motely (Mickey Shaughnessy) and escapes from jail. For the people and for Lee, this is the last straw. He goes out ahead of the posse to find his son, and there is a tense confrontation. Ed is about to shoot more people so Lee instinctively shoots him. Once back in town with Ed's body, he walks up to Davy and his half–Indian fiancée and breaks down.

Millions of teenage girls went dreamy-eyed at the sight of Tab with tight shirts and skinny jeans adorning his all–American college footballer physique; he provided a ready-made audience for *Gunman's Walk.* Although he was not a trained singer, the all-pervasive "pop" influence saw him warbling the catchy soundtrack song "I'm a Runaway." However, this was not just another 1950s teen movie. The presence of Heflin ensured that here was a film of which to take note. The familiar themes of generational conflict were underscored by a quietly devastating exposition of the unintentional damage of excessive love. Hunter especially did well as the wayward son. Although a relative newcomer, he relished his co-star status with Heflin: "The intense one-on-one scenes with Van Heflin were my biggest thrill making *Gunman's Walk.* To me, Van was the ultimate actor. He completely disappeared into character, and everything he did was totally believable."

Tab gave an insight into working with Van and the way in which he influenced and improved the performances of the other cast members:

> The climax of the picture, in which father and son square off in a final confrontation, was the most powerful and emotional scene I'd had to that point of my career. All his long-simmering resentment released, Ed Hackett goads his father into a duel, and the old man, tears in his eyes, guns down his own flesh and blood.
>
> Van had already figured out how to play it for maximum effect. Wanting to make sure I was up to snuff, I asked him to take some extra rehearsal time with me. He was so committed to the play, to *everyone* being good, he'd have taken as long as I wanted to get it right. Believe me, not all actors are like that.[22]

The movie had great momentum and proved popular with audiences and critics alike. The *Los Angeles Times* commented; "Heflin and Hunter generate so much emotional power that the build-up becomes a terrific thing." Studio boss Harry Cohn reportedly cried at the end of his screening and promised the director better assignments. Unfortunately for Karlson, Cohn died three weeks later.[23]

Set in Mexico but filmed at Saint George, Utah, Columbia's *They Came to Cordura* was Heflin's final American film for some time; he played another heel among a cast of heels. Produced by William Goetz and written by Ivan Moffat, this was a tense Western which tackled questions of courage and cowardice over its two-hour running time. The morality of the film was brought into question in some quarters; Bob Thomas described it thus: "Rita Hayworth is almost raped by Van Heflin and Richard Conte and later gives herself to Heflin for the night in order to save Gary Cooper."[24]

The story begins as a U.S. Expeditionary Force enters Mexico in 1916 in pursuit of Pancho Villa and his men. Major Thomas Thorn (Cooper) believes himself to be a coward; he hid in a ditch during a fight at Columbus, Ohio. He only escaped a court martial for cowardice through the intercession of Colonel Rogers (Robert Keith), a friend of his father who was a famous general. He is relieved of his command and as a further punishment is made a field officer and assigned with recommending decorations for bravery. During an action against Pancho Villa in which the objective is to take a fort, Thorn watches all elements of the fight from a distance. He observes many acts of bravery and identifies five outstanding individuals whom he selects as potential Congressional Medal of Honor winners: Lieutenant William Fowler (Tab Hunter), Private Andrew Hetherington (Michael Callan), Sergeant John Chawk (Heflin), Corporal Milo Trubee (Richard Conte) and Private Renziehausen (Dick York).

Colonel Rogers leads the cavalry charge for the fort and he is bitterly disappointed that he is not also considered for a medal after all he had done to help Thorn in the past. As a result he orders Thorn to escort the five Congressional Medal nominees to the rear base at Cordura, along with Adelaide Geary (Rita Hayworth), who is accused of treason for sheltering the enemy. Far from being the great heroes he envisaged, the five are deeply flawed human beings. During the long and arduous march back to base, the true natures of all seven in the party are laid bare. The journey is made all the harder by the rough terrain. Attacked by some of Pancho Villa's men, they give them their horses in return for their lives.

During the course of their difficult journey Thorn tries to find out about each man and discover why he acted in the courageous way he did. He aims to define the true nature of courage and examine his own motivations in the process. The results of his endeavors leave him disappointed. Hetherington rediscovered the "hellfire" religion of his childhood when he was cornered and acted from that. Fowler does not want the medal as he feels he cannot live up to it. Trubee is a ne'er-do-well, and Renziehausen only wanted to make his mark. Chawk acted out of self-preservation and reveals that he does not want the medal because of the publicity: He is wanted for murder.

Heflin gives an interesting, nuanced performance in which he reveals a violent and unpredictable character with little moral sense. The actor hints at some of the reasons for his torment when he tells of his harsh upbringing and how his father beat him regularly. At times he appears almost affable but his ire is raised very quickly, particularly by Adelaide, who in addition to being the only female on the trip also has the last few cigarettes and a bottle of tequila which she jealously guards. There is a sense of menace from the beginning, even while he smiles as he sings "Wandering" as they ride along; he is already taunting Thorn. When he starts to goad Thorn further about how long the major can stay awake, he is quite vicious and sneering. The tension builds and he seems coiled up like a cobra ready to strike. Once Adelaide gives herself to Chawk so that the exhausted Thorn can sleep, Chawk is more certain of himself and taunts both Adelaide and Thorn. When he finally gets to read what Thorn has written about him in the little black book, he is shocked into silence. By the end Chawk is a reformed character and ready to take his punishment. Heflin does not make this change appear forced; he makes it seem natural and, indeed, necessary.

Heflin relished the chance to work with Gary Cooper. "There's a man who likes to hunt and fish and make a picture now and again," he once observed. He always rated him highly as an actor. "Coop playing within his range, no one could touch him, not Henry Fonda, not Jimmy Stewart, no one," he said, "I had the opportunity to work with him in *They Came to Cordura*. We had been great friends for years. We met at so many social functions. He didn't care for parties too much. I don't either and we would seek each other out."

Cooper was looking and feeling his age by now. "My back hurts every time I look at a horse," he commented dryly but with feeling. He was much relieved when told he would not to have to participate in too many action scenes.[25] He appeared tired at times and his character certainly suffered in this. It was not an easy movie for any of the participants who were glad of home-cooked meals on site provided by their own outside caterers. Heflin found the movie a trial to make and said it was the toughest he had ever done. He described it as "a murderous schedule over rough country."[26]

The movie suffered some after it left the director's hands. It was "drastically cut and re-cut" (almost a half-hour was cut) and consequently made less dramatic sense, in the opinion of some. However, two hours seems ample time to explore the characters and their motivations and there is a unity of purpose to the action in line with the story. Only the ending was altered from the original. The director discussed the ending with author Moffat. In the book, Thorn is stoned to death by the others. Rossen considered this too downbeat and decided that Thorn should live and lead them towards Cordura. Although more satisfying from a dramatic sense, as the author readily agreed, there was also an element of bathos. What would have been a natural conclusion instead leaves one dissatisfied and wanting to know what happens when they actually reach their destination.

They Came to Cordura is interesting from the point of view of the development of the Western and a sign of the strides made during the 1950s in terms of psychology. Gone were the days when heroes wore white hats and villains black hats. Characters were less cut-and-dried and there was room for variance. Previously a hero was always expected to act as a hero should, with no shading. A far deeper understanding of human nature pervades the later films of the era, particularly those of Anthony Mann and *Cordura.* Each character here is deemed a hero but three of the five prove they are anything but; the other two merely seem weak. Thorn torments himself with trying to atone for his one act of cowardice and proves himself far more courageous than the rest. Adelaide Geary, although deemed a traitor, displays great integrity when it comes to her greatest test.

Tab Hunter was thrilled to be working in such vaunted company and reflected on the experience in his highly engaging and evocative memoir:

> In hindsight, making *They Came to Cordura* felt like the end of an era. Although they lived longer than Coop, Rita and Van didn't have many movies left in them, either. Starring roles for them were few and far between after this.... Old Hollywood, which I cherished, was on the way out, and I'd rarely have the chance to work with people of this caliber again. I'm glad I had the opportunity, and if I had a hundred more chances to choose between *77 Sunset Strip* and *They Came to Cordura,* I'd go with Coop, Rita and Van every time.[27]

Over the years Heflin received many offers of Westerns; he was slated to appear in *Ox Train, Distant Paths* and William Dieterle's *Texas Trail,* none of which materialized.[28] He lost to Joel McCrea for the lead in the intriguing *Stars in My Crown;* and although his great friend Alan Ladd sought him out for his own production *Guns of the Timberland,* the part went to Gilbert Roland instead.[29] Robert Bren wanted him to play the part of the rugged adventurer in *The Treasure of Pancho Villa* (1955) but his role in this forgettable Western went to Rory Calhoun.[30] In 1956 he got a call from Raymond Gary, the governor of Oklahoma, to star in *Showdown,* a movie charting the story of the state, to be produced by the evangelist Billy Graham. The project came to nothing.[31] There was also the intriguing prospect of co-starring with Sammy Davis Jr. in a post–Civil War story, *Rebel Territory*, concerning "a former slave and a Quaker from the north who desire to live peacefully in a southern community where they are surrounded by hostile neighbors." Davis was set to produce with the screenplay by Aaron Spelling but unfortunately the movie was never made.[32]

Heflin made a great impression in Westerns. He was every inch the "rugged outdoorsman" and thoughtful hero combined; he could also be an unnerving heel. He made two classics and several excellent but vastly underrated entries in the genre. The run of 1950s movies starting with the high watermark of *Shane* progressed through generational conflict in *Gunman's Walk* and ended with the moral ambiguity of *They Came to Cordura*. He had numerous other offers for Westerns and would make one more in Europe.

Soon the future shape of the Western would become fractured: comedy Westerns, Spaghetti Westerns, mere remakes. The dark and searching psychology of the age which produced *The Man from Laramie, The Searchers* and *Shane* would be lost, replaced by a more leavened form of entertainment which seldom found its way into the public consciousness in quite the same way.

Ten

Return to the Stage (1952–65)

"I would rather be better on stage than mediocre in pictures."[1]

Ever since he arrived in Hollywood, Heflin's avowed intention was to make a name for himself in the movies and return to the stage, bringing his fans with him. No sooner had he become successful during his second attempt at film stardom in 1942 than the Theater Guild and Katharine Hepburn tried to lure him back to New York with a starring role in her vehicle *Without Love,* but his contract would not allow it.[2] In 1947 he was one of a number of actors sounded out for the role of Stanley Kowalski in Tennessee Williams' *A Streetcar Named Desire,* and in 1949 he attempted to persuade Metro to give him a leave of absence to appear on Broadway but they refused.[3] The following year he was announced as the co-star of Gertrude Lawrence in his friend Noël Coward's *South Sea Bubble.*[4] The play was re-titled *Island Fling* and played in Southport, Connecticut, for a mere eight nights in 1951. The star was Claudette Colbert.[5]

Heflin had not envisaged staying away for so long. But thirteen years after his greatest stage success he finally fulfilled the next ambition in his long term career plan. The play which lured him back was a challenging one, *The Shrike,* a Pulitzer Prize winner by Joseph Kramm set in a mental ward.

When he was first offered the script two years earlier, he was unable to accept due to film commitments and the unsuitability of bringing his family with him to New York; Jose Ferrer had taken the play successfully to Broadway. However, Heflin was not content with Broadway alone, and from the first wished to tour extensively. As he said more than once, cities such as Milwaukee and Cincinnati were just as important as New York.[6]

As the curtain rises, Jim Downs (Heflin) has already attempted suicide

In 1952 Heflin made a successful return to the stage in *The Shrike* with Doris Dalton, a harrowing play set in a mental ward. He admitted it tied him in knots: "There was so much emotional intensity, it took me hours to get un-keyed."

and is incarcerated in the mental ward of a city hospital. Although he has recovered, he is being held for observation. His wife Ann (Doris Dalton) has "successfully and malevolently poisoned the minds of the doctors against" him.[7] He has come to hate Ann but realizes that he can only be released with her consent and into her care. He knows that if he stays in the hospital, he will lose his mind.

Heflin was nervous about the reaction to his return to the stage after so long away, but his fears were unfounded: The reviews were glowing. Harold Cohen was among many critics who had nothing but praise for Heflin and the difficult subject matter: "[A] fine actor and a penetrating play have come together to tap some rare treasures. The story is taut and tormenting, and its crescendos have a stormy pitch. [Heflin's] portrayal of hopelessness and agony is brilliant.... It is a performance of skill and integrity, and he has returned to the theater first class."[8]

Ferrer had played the same part for three months on Broadway; Heflin stayed for close to seven months and took The Shrike to the East and West Coast and points in between, including Chicago. As one commentator noted, he "lives the part rather than acts it."[9] Downs is a very demanding role that required him to be on stage almost continually, using up all his energy. He later admitted that the emotional strain of it "tied him in knots ... you could never relax. There was so much dramatic intensity that it took me hours to get un-keyed." He further remarked that psychiatrists had likened each performance to twelve hours of hard labor. It was both physically and emotionally demanding. As he explained:

> At the end ... the character I portray must sob, and to do that he has to dig deep into his own past experience, into all the heartbreak he has known. And he has to start with that first entrance and work up to that final scene.... I have to concentrate on every line, if I once lose out, I'm gone.[10]

All his efforts were worthwhile and this thought-provoking and controversial play was still being talked about long afterwards. Variety was glowing in its praise of Heflin, who, they said, gave "a sincere, moving and sympathetic performance that carries an authenticity that has every member of the audience living the part with him."[11]

In the end the tour was somewhat curtailed because he was required at Universal to start work on Wings of the Hawk. The Chicago run was cut to four weeks by the producer and theater owner. In the meantime Universal had bought the film rights to The Shrike with Heflin all set for the starring role.[12] However the part eventually went to Jose Ferrer.

Heflin's intention was to alternate between films and the stage, and to undertake a play every two years or so. His physically and emotionally draining experience with The Shrike led him to ask his theater agents to find him something less demanding next time. The result was Arthur Miller's A View from the Bridge along with a small role in the accompanying minor work A Memory of Two Mondays.

"You couldn't turn that one down," said Heflin of *A View from the Bridge*. Previously he had declined six good offers for plum Broadway roles, some of which had been big hits. "But," he maintained, "when I came back I wanted to be absolutely ready, and to return in as dignified a way as possible, with material I believed in."[13] However, in his phone conversation with producer Kermit Bloomgarten, he was told he couldn't be guaranteed the role because Miller had never seen him work. "I finally figured out what was wrong," he remarked, "[T]hey wanted me to read for them and were afraid I'd be insulted—so I suggested it. The next step was to meet Miller. I read my role, Miller read the part of my stage wife and we won each other over."[14]

He read for the part successfully. Rehearsals began on the roof because the city was so hot that summer, and there was nowhere else cool.

The story concerns the life of Eddie Carbone, a Brooklyn laborer. The most important thing in his world is his family. He and his wife have raised a niece as their own, and he becomes over-possessive of the niece to such an extent that he takes actions which betray his family and all the values for which he stands. His niece seeks to marry Rodolpho (Richard Davalos), an illegal immigrant. Carbone goes to great lengths to stop this romance in its tracks, even trying to prove that Rodolpho is homosexual.

Difficulties arose for Heflin in mastering the Italian accent of his character. Miller described in his memoirs:

> I had accepted the chestnut that good actors, regardless of type, can surmount anything. They can't. Van Heflin, the son of an Oklahoma dentist, was filled with doubts about his ability to portray an Italian longshoreman and asked me to introduce him to people. He studied their speech like a foreign language which was unfortunately how it sounded on his tongue, and it was his preoccupation with accents and mannerisms that kept him from feeling the part in the end.[15]

Miller was notoriously scathing about many actors, especially those who had forsaken theater for the movies. Elsewhere he acknowledged that Heflin was a "wonderful actor" and likened him to Arthur Kennedy in that he too "never fitted anywhere." Miller's future wife Marilyn Monroe went to see Heflin as Carbone on at least four occasions.[16]

One reviewer commented on the same problem "[Heflin is] so concerned with Eddie's inarticulate speech and other characteristics that he never relaxes or lets go with the familiar power until the last scene."[17]

Although Miller appeared to lay much of the blame for the play's lukewarm reception on his cast, he also acknowledged the many faults in the work as first presented. A rewritten, revised and expanded version ran in London to far greater acclaim the following year and is now accepted as the standard text. By then Miller had worked out his own internal conflicts and reached the psychological truth of Carbone that he had not delineated sufficiently well in the original production.[18]

Many critics focused on the play's inherent weaknesses, one of which was a problem with its construction. For instance, the final scene was often judged to be less dramatic than the scene before it, leading to a sense of bathos. Vance Bourjaily in *The Village Voice* was fulsome in his praise of the star: "Van Heflin's performance as a tortured, semi-articulate longshoreman is the finest male acting of the season so far."[19]

Hedda Hopper commented that he was "absolutely superb," and went on to describe his reception at a provincial theater: "On a cold Monday night half a dozen persons in the audience yelled bravos."[20]

His fellow actors all enjoyed the experience of working with him immensely. "I feel like an employee of the mint who's been told he can take home all the samples," said Jimmy Broderick, a young cast member.[21] For other critics, the most notable part of the night's proceedings appeared to be when Heflin had to kiss a young actor full on the lips—a scene which shocked many on its first night in Boston. "This is the first time I've ever had to worry about a juvenile shaving," he quipped.[22] "The kiss always got gasps from the audience," he commented, "but we got away with it. I guess because neither of us looks effeminate. We haven't even had any passionate letters from *the boys.*"[23]

In total the play ran for a relatively short run of nineteen weeks; Miller's previous play *The Crucible* had had an equally brief run. For all Heflin's problems with the role, he backed it with his own money. "If you believe in something, you might as well empty your pockets for it," he said.[24] But *A View from the Bridge* made a loss of $50,000 on an initial investment of $75,000.[25] He was keen to take the play on tour to London in mid–March, transferring the "perfect" cast with him. But the English only wanted Heflin as the star name and insisted on a British cast.[26] He had always sought to play the London stage, and many other actors in his position would have jumped at the chance to elevate their own status without a backward glance at their fellow actors. But out of loyalty to his fellow players Heflin would not hear of it, and the whole project fell through.[27]

His further belief in the play was evinced by his willingness to commit three years of his life to it if necessary, and in his eagerness to have the first say over the film rights. The intention was for Martin Ritt to again direct and for Arthur Kennedy to also appear. The film as first planned never materialized. Seven years later, renowned director Sidney Lumet made a version starring Raf Vallone and it was released under the French title *Vu du Pont* in 1962.

Most of the same cast appeared in the second minor companion play *A Memory of Two Mondays* but Heflin had only a small role this time. This play was naturally overshadowed by *A View from the Bridge* and has been described as a humdrum look at the "daily life of the men and women who work in the shipping room of a dingy, barren warehouse." Brooks Atkinson described it as being "swamped in its own flood of detail."[28]

Although Heflin had won praise for his performance in some quarters, the critics were not kind to *A View from the Bridge*; most dismissed it lightly but Heflin was crushed. He invested a great deal of himself in the project, and after taking such pains to find his way into the part during fourteen hour-long rehearsals, it was a bitter blow. He took the failure personally as he showed in some of his comments at the time: "I don't know what they want, but if what they don't want is something as fine as this, then the stage is no place for me. I'll take the movies where the heartaches aren't so heavy. I've had it on Broadway."[29]

While staying in New York, he was unexpectedly offered a leading role in the film *Patterns* (1956), also known as *Patterns of Power*. Adapted by Rod Serling from his own teleplay broadcast the previous year, it has accurately been described as "a timeless autopsy of corporate viciousness."[30] *Patterns* told the character-driven story of William Briggs (Ed Begley), a long-standing and loyal employee of a large corporation. He is being elbowed out by his ruthless boss Ramsey (Everett Sloane) in favor of an ambitious but unsuspecting new man, Fred Staples (Heflin), from out of town. Constantly undermined, Briggs is being quietly humiliated so that he would be forced to resign rather than be dismissed. The secretary assigned to Staples is rather cool with him to begin with. She has been with Briggs for seven years and has great loyalty to him; she realizes what is happening long before anyone else. However Staples and Briggs become friends and collaborate on an important report on another company. When Ramsey sees the report, he insists that Staples has done all the work and removes Briggs' name. This leads to further arguments during the board meeting and humiliation for Briggs, who is belittled. Staples sticks up for him. There is a party at Staples' house during which he is offered the vice-presidency of the company, to the great joy of his ambitious wife. On a matter of principle and loyalty to Briggs, Staples feels that he should not accept, but he is persuaded otherwise by his wife. Matters come to a head when it becomes obvious that the situation is taking its toll on Briggs' health. Staples tries desperately to persuade him to resign. Some time later, Briggs collapses at work and dies. Staples harangues Ramsey: Fired by righteous anger, he makes many demands and tells him that he wants everything his way from now on—even to the extent of wanting Ramsey's job. In the process of trying to redress the harm done to Briggs, he seems to become even more ruthless than Ramsey.

As one commentator observed, "You might believe that ... a movie would be mighty dull because it is in black and white with no background music, no comedy for relief, its characters pathetic and hateful and its theme dealing with the viciousness and cold bloodedness of big business... " but the result was utterly compelling.[31] The presentation of the story, completely unadorned with its stark black and white photography, bland interiors and the complete absence of music, lent it an unusually dramatic air. The lack of music in particular heightened the whole effect. Begley was outstanding as the desperate Briggs and Sloane was equally impressive as the hard-as-nails Ramsey.

Heflin's character Staples starts out ambitious but fair-minded. By the end he is ambitious and totally merciless. In seeking to redress the harm done to Briggs, he becomes as ruthless as Ramsey. The actor makes this transition without difficulty; Staples loses his way by degrees and Heflin takes the audience along with him as he becomes somehow less human. He remains sympathetic but the point is well made that the end result shows that ruthlessness is the only way to survive in the cutthroat but ultimately self-defeating corporate world.

While filming *Patterns*, Heflin tried commuting to the studios but soon concluded that movie stars did not belong on subways. He commented; "I was holding symposiums both mornings with people who said to me: 'You ... look like—Van Heflin!' When I said I *was* Van Heflin, some people got belligerent and asked me to prove it. But I guess it would have been a lot worse if they hadn't recognized me."[32]

Four years later he was thrilled to be announced as Rod Steiger's costar in Ernest Hemingway's *Love and Death*, to be directed by A.E. Hotchner, long-time associate of the great writer. The plans fell through.[33] Nor did a part in the mooted Gordon Douglas play *Send Me a Stranger* materialize.[34] Seven years passed before he returned to the stage; this time he played a character based on a real person in an excellent courtroom drama. In Henry Denker's *A Case of Libel* he essayed the role of Louis Nizer. It was based on the book *My Day in Court* which told the story of a well-known ex–war correspondent who pursues a "painful libel suit against a ruthless communist."[35] The first of four premieres took place on October 7, 1963, at the Longacre Theater and it ran for a total of 242 performances, finally closing six months later in May 1964. After that there was a provincial tour to Boston, Philadelphia, Chicago and Los Angeles, among other places.

A Case of Libel was a long play—some two and a half hours—and for most of that running time Heflin was on stage. The part was very hard to memorize: It was longer than *Hamlet,* he was off-stage for only 70 seconds during the entire play, and "going at it full blast."[36] But the 54-year-old actor tried his best to keep in shape, taking advantage of the gym facilities while staying in New York. "I swim half a mile a day," he said, "work out, take a steam bath, get a rub-down, really train. I'd be puffing like an old goat every performance if I didn't."[37]

This time the critics were generally impressed.[38] "Solid, beautifully-acted, well-directed," said one; Heflin gave a "strong, varied and sometimes humorous performance," said another.[39] The intense drama culminates in his summation to the jury, addressed to the audience. During one of the premieres, Heflin was distracted when "he suddenly saw Noël Coward blowing kisses, for his brilliant performance."[40] The play was made into a successful television drama in 1968 and Heflin was nominated for an Emmy. The essence of his stage performance was captured for all time.

In 1951 Heflin was invited to England by Compton Bennett to play the lead in *Sunset in the Morning.* He was upset at this time about rumors concerning his marriage so he stayed in America and worked on *My Son John* instead.[41] He was keen to play the London stage after the disappointment over the transfer of *A View from the Bridge,* and in 1958 hoped to play the lead in Arthur Penn's *Two for the Seesaw* on tour; this was abandoned. He had many other offers to return to Broadway including two musicals, but after his experience in the 1955–56 season he was in no hurry to return.[42] For the 1967 season he was set to star in Ira Wallach's comedy *Beer Island* alongside nightclub comedian Shelley Berman; he had to withdraw as his divorce trial interfered with the scheduled try-out tour. A few months before his death in 1971 he was one of the names Paul Shyre suggested for his one-man play *An Unpleasant Evening with H. L. Mencken,* based on the life of "The Sage of Baltimore"—the famously acerbic dramatic critic and playwright.[43]

Eleven

European Sojourn (1958–68)

*"Hollywood these days is making very few of the pictures
I like to do."[1]*

By the early 1950s Heflin was a highly respected and sought-after actor in Europe as much as he was in America, if not more so. There had always been something decidedly internationalist about him. As he once reflected, "I was a 'name' in Europe because the type of part I appeared in and the characters I played had a special appeal for them." His early years spent roaming the oceans of the world had given him a wider perspective than if he had never strayed further than Oklahoma and practiced law. He was entirely at home in other countries and was fascinated by their cultures. During these later years he traveled widely for films and for pleasure.

After the war, many Hollywood actors began to look at Europe as a great place to make movies, sometimes for practical and financial reasons. The fees were moderate and movie personnel had modern technical know-how. Most saw it as a chance for a tax break, something that Heflin never did.[2]

In 1954 he had a chance to make a film at the Geiselgesteig Studio in Munich, Germany, which had already played host to several Hollywood companies. *The 9:15 to Freedom* was based on the real-life story of the escape of a passenger train from behind the Iron Curtain in Czechoslovakia. The plan was for two versions, one in German and one in English, to be made by the American poet Allan Dowling. Heflin and Edward G. Robinson would co-star in the English version and a German actress would appear in both films.[3] The movies were never made.

Four years later he played the leading role in *Tempest*. His performance so impressed the bosses at Paramount that they touted him for an Academy Award that year and bolstered his reputation by re-releasing

47017-7

He gave a striking portrayal as Cossack leader Pugachov who leads a coup against Empress Catherine the Great in the exciting *Tempest* (1958), based on stories by Alexander Pushkin. Filmed in Yugoslavia and Italy, it was Heflin's first European venture. Director Alberto Lattuada was one of the leading lights of Italian cinema.

Shane.[4] *Tempest* was his first appearance in a production by Dino de Laurentiis, "the Cecil B. de Mille of Europe," whose large-scale ambition often overshot his budgets. The plot, loosely based on the novels *The History of Pugachev* and *The Captain's Daughter* by Alexander Pushkin, was brought to epic life by director Alberto Lattuada utilizing a cast of thousands. Filmed near Belgrade in what was then Yugoslavia, with interiors shot in Rome, this was a prestigious French-Yugoslav production which won the David di Donatello Award for direction and production and was nominated for a Silver Ribbon award in four categories (including cinematography and screenplay) by the Italian National Syndicate of Journalists.

In 1770 Russia, Piotr Grinov (Geoffrey Horne) is ousted from the Imperial Guard in the court of Catherine the Great (Viveca Lindfors) when he shows up for a dress review drunk. He is sent to a distant fort, but on the way there discovers someone in the snow, Emelyan Pugachov (Heflin), and insists he be saved. Pugachov is revived with vodka and given a place to stay for the night. The following morning he expresses gratitude and goes his own way, taking Grinov's winter coat with him. Grinov reaches the fort whose soldiers are mostly old men, led by Captain Miranov (Robert Keith), who takes the parade in his night robe. His formidable wife Vassilissa (Agnes Moorehead) smokes a pipe. Grinov immediately falls for their daughter Masha (Silvano Mangano). He has a rival for her affections, disgraced officer Svabrin (Helmut Dantine), and the two later duel over her. Cossacks launch an attack on the fort; their sheer force of numbers overwhelms the garrison and many are hanged, including the captain. His wife tries to resist but is hacked down. Just as Grinov is about to be hanged, Pugachov realizes he is the man who saved his life. He spares both Grinov and Masha, telling them to get married. Svabrin switches allegiance and is made a major by Pugachov.

There are a number of battles between the Cossacks and the Imperial forces which eventually prove too strong for Pugachov and his men. Pugachov is captured and condemned to death. Grinov, tried for treason, also faces execution. Pugachov saves the life of Grinov again when he tells Empress Catherine that Grinov never turned traitor.

Heflin stood out in a good cast playing a complex individual described by one reviewer as "a little bit cruel, a little bit tender, a little bit confused and a whole lot tough."[5] He looked grizzled with his bushy beard and thick coat; it was said at the time that he "picked up thirty-five pounds and the nickname Orson" while working on the film.[6] There was good support from Agnes Moorehead; Vivica Lindfors was suitably imperious as Catherine the Great.

Although Heflin had top billing, the lead was an American actor, Geoffrey Horne, chiefly remembered as the young officer in *The Bridge on the River Kwai* (1957). He made little impression here and his romance with Masha seemed to belong to a different story, as indeed was the case. The splicing of two of Pushkin's tales was a weakness. *The Captain's Daughter* was the lesser of the two, but seemed to take precedence over that of Pugachov in the mind of the director. In essence there was not enough of Heflin or Pugachov. The large-scale battle scenes, although impressive at times, tended to take attention away from the human story at its core. However, *Tempest* was a very good film and Heflin managed to make a harsh, bloodthirsty man seem likable. He entered fully into the spirit of things and gave a vivid account of an entirely human persona. Lattuada, one of Italian cinema's foremost writer-directors, won many awards across Europe for such movies as *Il Bandito* (1946) and *Variety Lights* (*Luci del Varietà*) (1950); he co-wrote and directed the latter with Federico Fellini.

The film marked something of a rapprochement between east and west at a tense time in the Cold War. *Tempest* was one of the first major Western-produced films made behind the Iron Curtain. The actors enjoyed their time in Yugoslavia and found the locals very friendly. "The people greeted us warmly," said Heflin, "and were extremely hospitable." The Hotel Metropole in Belgrade was almost like the Hilton; the food was excellent with the accent on steaks, pork and lamb. Only the price of whisky was prohibitive and vodka was unknown. When possible, Heflin and his wife preferred to rent an apartment while filming on location instead of staying at a hotel as it enabled them to meet people more readily. In Rome they stayed at a flat in the Parioli district. In Belgrade he was invited to open the Balkans' first supermarket, which had previously been the American exhibit at a trade fair.[7]

The Yugoslav authorities went all out to cooperate, even to supplying 2,500 cavalry troops, all regular soldiers, for the battle—something American producers would have balked at because of the huge cost involved.

"Nor could you pay them enough for the stunts they took," Heflin commented. "The 2,500 put on a charge right through exploding charges with horsemen falling in the front ranks so the others had to leap over them. In one day alone, thirty-seven men were sent to the hospital."[8] Conditions were not easy during filming when it was ninety degrees in the shade. Heflin sweltered under layers of heavy furs as the artificial snow began to decompose in the heat.

While staying in Italy he expressed an interest in acquiring land there; he talked of building a yacht harbor halfway between Rome and Naples on the island of Circeo. "I'm going to buy ten acres of property in from the beach and close to a small lake," he remarked. "It would make the greatest natural harbor in the world."[9] His intention was to build a summer house on the ocean side and a boathouse on the bay side. This he did with the salary from his next film, *Five Branded Women.*[10]

Heflin, a very popular star in Italy, learned the language and also made his first appearance on Italian television singing "On the Old Chisholm Trail." He was awarded the Sherriff's Gold Star previously given only to European stars.[11]

Tempest was so popular in Yugoslavia that the Tito government asked Heflin to return for a starring role in *Jovanka and the Others* by Ugo Pirro, a war story set amongst the partisans.[12] He agreed and in time *Jovanka and the Others* became *Five Branded Women* and attracted several other Hollywood stars including Shirley MacLaine and Harry Guardino. It was directed by fellow American Martin Ritt, with whom Heflin had worked on Broadway in *A View from the Bridge.*

The cast changed a few times. Shirley MacLaine turned out to be unavailable. Gina Lollobrigida and Mitzi Gaynor were announced but they too dropped out.[13] New names emerged and the final casting of the women was Jovanka (Silvana Mangano, wife of the producer), Marja (Barbara Bel Geddes), Daniza (Vera Miles), Ljuba (Jeanne Moreau) and Mira (Carla Gravina). They all performed very strongly.

Five women accused of fraternizing with a German sergeant have their heads shorn and are forced to leave the town. They wander the countryside and begin scavenging. They meet up with a group of partisans led by Velko (Heflin) and are eventually invited to join their ranks. Predictably, sexual tensions build between the men and women living in close proximity and one of the men on lookout, Branco (Guardino), spends the night with Daniza (Miles) and neglects his duty. The partisans are fighting tremendous odds and discipline is vital, so the two are shot by a firing squad. There are more raids against the Germans, sabotage of railway lines and attacks on key positions, but the partisan forces are diminishing. They concentrate their attention on a plan to assassinate a German general by planting a bomb under his dais while he is delivering a speech. Although fraught with danger, the mission is successful but the partisans lose a great many men and some of the women in the process. The remaining forces move back to safer ground and stay in a mountain position in order to delay the enemy and buy time for their side to form a rear guard action.

Unlike many war movies, there is a matter-of-fact sensibility about *Five Branded Women* which gives it a reality. The action sequences were true to life and the acting uniformly excellent. Ritt handled his subject matter well. He was a sensitive and able director who made his mark with such tense movies as *Edge of the City* (1956); ambitious adaptations of William Faulkner novels including *The Sound and the Fury* (1959); and an interesting late Western, *Hombre* (1967).

This was essentially the women's film and all of them did well; Silvano Mangano had the most prominent and difficult role. Heflin was tough and rugged as always and convincingly conveyed what the heavy burden of leadership of a band of partisans in wartime actually meant. He seems harsh, but this is not from choice, it is the result of bitter experience fighting a long and protracted campaign in hard terrain against a well-equipped, highly organized enemy. The frequent loss of comrades wears the nerves and blunts the senses so that the dehumanizing effect of real war is brought home starkly. This is a sobering movie which, unlike some of Hollywood's lesser efforts, does not glorify war. Its strength is in the way it shows the brutalizing effect of conflict on everyone. The somber ending leaves hope of redemption—if not in the generation fighting in the war, then for future generations.

Producer de Laurentiis sought Heflin again for the starring role in *Love in the North Sea*, and he was to have co-starred with Curt Jurgens in *I Aim at the Stars*, a biography of Wernher von Braun "the father of rocket science," to be made in London.[14] The first project fell through; his part in *I Aim at the Stars* went to Herbert Lom; but then attention moved to another biopic, *Under Ten Flags*. This was based on the memoir of German Commander Bernhard Rogge of the surface raider *Atlantis*, which sunk 22 ships in World War II. Rogge saved the passengers and crew of every ship he destroyed. During the tense period for the British fleet between 1940 and 1941, German U–Boats and battleships held sway. Merchant ships were often attacked and vital supplies were cut off. One vessel is blasting British ships out of the water; German intelligence intercepts signals, sending false messages in order that no details ever emerge. Admiral Russell (Charles Laughton) is intent on finding and destroying the ghost ship but Rogge (Heflin) is an intelligent and canny operator who is always one step ahead of the Royal Navy. The *Atlantis* is often camouflaged as a harmless merchant ship, painted in the colors of existing vessels with the crew dressed as Japanese women or Russian sailors. Each time, a different flag is raised to allay suspicion. When enemy ships come within firing range, the guns are revealed and the swastika hoisted. There is no escape.

The *Atlantis* continues luring ships to their doom; but always rescuing survivors and keeping casualties to a minimum. Even the admiral has a great deal of respect for his counterpart. However he is intent on stopping the continual destruction of British ships and to that end an agent is sent on a dangerous mission to reach German Naval HQ in Paris and photograph the Flower Chart with which Navy chiefs plot positions and so foil British Intelligence.

Heflin gave a calm, measured performance which suited the film's low-key style and even-handed treatment of a barely known episode of the war. Laughton had little chance to do more than bluster and pace up and down at the Admiralty building; the two great character actors never meet, but did pose for publicity shots. The main action takes place on board the *Atlantis* and in the waters of the Atlantic. There are several set-piece scenes which speak for the devastation of war and the rare humanitarianism of some individuals. At one point the *Atlantis* attacks a passenger ship and calls for it to surrender; it raises the white flag; but just as the *Atlantis* comes alongside the captain of the surrendering ship gives the order to fire. Amid the chaos, several passengers are killed. Once the situation is resolved, all the survivors are rescued and the captain is seen very much as the villain of the piece. The implication is that good or bad is down to character and individual motivation. Rogge's humanism is backed by all those rescued, both passengers and crew. He even ensures that they all reach neutral ports, at great risk to his own vessel.

Heflin met Bernhard Rogge in Rome, by which time the latter was a leading light in NATO and in charge of the Navy in the northern part of Germany. He was known as "the admiral in the bowler hat" because he often donned one in order to "pass himself off as an old square-rigger captain turned master of a steamship."[15]

Not often seen since its release, *Under Ten Flags'* director was nominated for a Golden Bear at the Berlin Film Festival. Duilio Coletti began his career in the 1930s and had worked with Vittorio de Sica on *Cuore* (1948), also known as *Heart and Soul*. He made several moody noirs such as *Il Lupe della Sila* (*Lure of the Sila*) (1949) and war films concerning interesting but little-known episodes such as *Londra Chiama Polo Nord* (1956), also known as *The House of Intrigue*. In common with his usual approach, *Under Ten Flags* is an intelligent and understated film which takes a more measured view of the war as a whole. Far from the predictable heroes and villains of many war sagas, here the lead character emerges as a compassionate man and as such shows that humanity is possible in even the most brutal of conflicts; a contention which contrasts well with the conclusion of his previous film *Five Branded Women*.

Il Relitto (*The Wastrel*) was based on the 1949 novel by Frederick

Wakeman, whose previous works had formed the basis of a number of successful Hollywood movies including *The Hucksters* and *Kiss Them for Me*. Originally this was to be shot in Bermuda where the book had been set, but Cypriot director Michael Cacoyannis decided to film it in Rome instead.

In the West Indies, wealthy adventurer Duncan Bell (Heflin) has an argument with his wife Liana (Ellie Lambetti) about her supposed infidelities and storms out. He boards his speedboat with his ten-year-old son; some way out, the boat explodes. The two remain afloat, clinging to the debris for hours. Bell takes stock of his life up to that point. In flashback he recounts his marriage to an Italian girl during the war and how it failed owing to his suspicious nature. He thinks of his motives for sailing around the world and how after his aborted attempt to achieve it he was hailed as a hero when he felt he really wasn't. He recalls his addiction to alcohol and reflects on how his one success is his relationship with his son. Should they be rescued, he vows to forgive his wife and become a changed man.

Cacoyannis was nominated for a Palme d'Or at Cannes as he had been for all his earlier films; he had his greatest success with *Zorba the Greek* three years later. He shared a co-writing credit on *The Wastrel* with Suso Cecchi D'Amico, famous for her work with all the great Italian directors including Vittorio De Sica on *Bicycle Thieves* and with Luchino Visconti on *Bellissima* and others.

Heflin described the film as his toughest assignment: "I've practically spent five weeks in and under water. Some scenes were shot in the *Ben-Hur* lake with water under 60 degrees and after a few hours I was literally frozen stiff." He returned home "all in and with laryngitis."[16]

For all his efforts the critics were not generally kind. "[An] ineffectual mawkish drama" said one, who considered the flashback scenes "thinly dramatized." However the same critic remarked that between father and son "there are real moments of shared adversity and a true sense of the deeper understanding those can bring."[17] Another noted that the film was "imaginatively shot" and concluded that it was "distinctive, and finally moving."[18]

Again Heflin had been drawn to an ambiguous character, one who is weak and self-destructive. He seemed to have a penchant in his later career for playing such broken men who feel emotionally drained and either find or lose their direction in life.

He was given a memento of the movie when he received a fifty-gallon barrel of Chianti, "his favorite liquid." His initial thought was to take it back home for the family at Thanksgiving but he was "rocked back by the price" of sending it and so "decided to crack the barrel at the end of picture party."[19] Michael Stallman, who played the boy in the film, got the part after he asked for Heflin's autograph. Heflin later promised he would help him if he wished to stay in movies.[20]

During Heflin's European sojourn he was besieged by movie offers including starring roles in *Simon Bolivar* and the French-Italian production *Taras Bulba*. The biopic of the South American revolutionary was never filmed, and his role in *Taras Bulba* went to Yul Brynner instead.[21] Another planned project was the part of a German agent in *Face in the Rain* for a British company. He also tried to interest producers in a story he had bought, *The Sea Take* by Robert Blees, which would have seen him as the heavy and concerned "the kidnapping from a yacht of five of the world's greatest industrialists, sending (global) finance markets into a tailspin." Filming was to have taken place on the French Riviera. The movie was never made.[22]

Described as "beatnik noir," *Once a Thief* (1965) was a stylish French-produced thriller set in San Francisco. Ostensibly an American film, it had the feel of a European venture. It may have been the presence of Alain Delon or the seemingly sophisticated plot and situation which contributed to this impression. It also has a distinctly modern feel due to the modish violence, stark black and white photography and the hip soundtrack by Lalo Schifrin. It could almost be where the Coen brothers found their blueprint for success.

Ex-con Eddie Pedak (Delon), living with his wife Kristine (Ann-Margret) and young daughter Kathy, is under suspicion of the murder of a storekeeper's wife in the Chinatown district of San Francisco. He is hounded by Detective Mike Vido (Heflin) who was wounded by Pedak in a previous encounter; Vido keeps the bullet in a chain around his neck. Pedak's brother Walter (Jack Palance) enlists him to participate in a heist at his former works along with a psychotic accomplice, Sargatanas (John David Chandler). The heist is successful but then comes the double-cross: Eddie finds his brother Walter dead, and his daughter is kidnapped by Sargatanas. He decides to seek the help of Vido. There is a rapprochement between the two men, Vido finally releasing the hate which has consumed him. Just when there appears to be hope of a positive outcome, everything goes wrong through a series of misunderstandings.

Delon has been aptly described as "the impossibly handsome French matinee idol, who tries hard to forget his good looks in every film in which he appears, but never manages to completely."[23] This was one of his very few Hollywood movies and is distinctly Gallic in feeling and expression.

Ralph Nelson's *Once a Thief* (1965) was an atmospheric "beatnik noir" set in San Francisco. Starring French matinee idol Alain Delon in one of his rare forays in Hollywood, it featured an effective portrait from Heflin as a vengeful cop.

Delon as always follows the Jean Gabin template. He is suited to the role of taciturn hero and the general downbeat nature of the movie makes this look like a forgotten late French noir. Heflin worked well with his fellow actors as always and created another memorable character study of a driven man. Vido comes to terms with all the hate he has carried with him and one can literally feel this fall away during the scene at the house with

Delon. He also performed well during the climax and the hopeless sense of tragedy was writ large on his always expressive face at the end.

An overlooked film of the period, *Once a Thief* would work well with a present-day audience because it seems so contemporary. The presence of two of the cast of *Shane* combined with a French star at his height lends this film a resonance that few others of the era could match. Heflin and Palance raise its status and give it the feel of a noir. Chandler's chilling villain points the way to modern inheritors of the idea of noir taken to its logical conclusion. Many of the elements of the genre are present: a doomed protagonist, several villains and a dogged policeman. It has a *femme* although she is not exactly *fatale* and a very distinctive atmosphere. The term "beatnik noir" is especially fitting. The first scene of a long drum solo in a club (as hippy chicks and spaced-out cats spout hip dialogue full of drug references) firmly place this in its era. But then the story unfolds and it feels as though 1960s counter-culture is being reflected though a 1940s noir sensibility. The screenplay was by Zekio Marko (from his novel *Scratch a Thief*) and it was skillfully directed by Ralph Nelson, who won the OCIC Award at the San Sebastian International Film Festival. Nelson started out in television and made his name with *Lilies of the Field* (1963); his style derived much from the European tradition. The main criticism that could be leveled at the film is the endemic and unnecessary use of violence and the murky weather which the director expressly waited days to achieve, but which has the tendency to cast a pall over the whole proceedings both literally and metaphorically. Ultimately the tragic ending leaves one feeling bereft.

The seldom-seen British spy thriller *The Man Outside* (1967) found Heflin as CIA agent Bill Maclean, dismissed from the service for withholding a report on a colleague which he believed to be fabricated by the Russians. In London he encounters George Venaxas (Ronnie Barker), who confirms his suspicions and tells him about the ex–Soviet agent Rafe Machek (Pinkas Braun), a defector hiding in the city. Before Venaxas can say where Machek is staying, he is shot by agents. Maclean meets a girl called Kay Sebastian (Heidelinde Weis) who runs a fashion boutique. Passing himself off as an insurance man, he goes to see Kay and tells her about the death of Venaxas, who it turns out is her brother. Another CIA agent visits her apartment and tries to force her to tell him where Machek is hiding. Maclean arrives in the nick of time and saves her. The sinister Russian Nikolai Volkov (Peter Vaughan) and a slimy British financier, Charles Griddon (Charles Gray), wish to assassinate Machek. Though no longer in the service of the CIA, Maclean goes to great lengths to protect Machek, hiding him at a run-down boarding house. Kay is kidnapped by Volkov, who seeks to exchange her for Machek. Finally a meeting is arranged at St. Margaret's Church. Maclean bluffs Volkov into thinking that Machek has had a heart attack. He entices the Russian to Kay's flat where CIA agents have planted a number of weapons. In the end the foreign agents are thwarted by quick thinking and Machek is safe.

The Man Outside made good use of a number of London locations including Charing Cross Pier for a late-night rendezvous on a boat launch and St. Margaret's Church in Westminster, where Maclean meets Volkov and his heavies to strike a deal. It's ostensibly a tale of espionage, but there were numerous elements which constitute noir; even the color seemed muted and the streets very dark and full of menace. Although there was plenty of action, car chases and double-dealing, the plot tended to obfuscate as was often the case in thrillers of this era. Even so, the overall effect was good. Michael Billington commented in *The Times* of London, "Shot by Samuel Gallu in relentless close-up, it gets by mainly because its plot is so complicated that one cannot afford to let one's attention wander."[24]

Ronnie Barker, one of the foremost British comedy actors of his generation, relished the experience of working with Heflin. He later reflected:

> It was glamorous to do that film. Van Heflin had been a big star and was still a name to be reckoned with. He was a marvelous man, I liked him. He was a real, real pro. Knew everything. He said, "Ronnie, don't ever take a drag on a cigarette in a close-up, and don't ever take a drink in a close-up." I said, "Why not?" He said, "They will never be able to edit it because you will not be doing exactly the same thing in the other shot and you will lose the close-up. If you do that, your close-up will not be in." And I used to watch him and he never did. Very clever. I loved that. That was a taste of the American movies. My only one.

For the first ten minutes of the film it was Van Heflin and me, which meant you had meaty scenes together rather than just flitting through the film.[25]

American director Gallu was a television producer who directed just a handful of movies in England including the chiller *Theatre of Death* (1967) and a comedy, *Arthur, Arthur* (1969). Shooting took place during the fall of 1966; Heflin took an apartment at 49 Hill Street in Mayfair.[26] While in Britain he also had the opportunity to play the professor in Hammer's *Quatermass and the Pit*, aka *Five Million Years to Earth*, following in the footsteps of his countryman Brian Donlevy. But then the role was assigned to a home-grown actor, Andrew Keir, instead.[27]

He was next invited back to Rome to film *Four Ruthless Men* (1968),

WALTER MANLEY ENTERPRISES, INC. presents

VAN HEFLIN · GILBERT ROLAND
KLAUS KINSKI · GEORGE HILTON

SARAH ROSS

Sam
Cooper's
Gold
Started
The
Blood
Flowing
Across
The State
Of
Nevada!

In the tradition
of
TREASURE
of SIERRA
MADRE

THE
RUTHLESS
FOUR

TECHNICOLOR
TECHNISCOPE

Directed by GIORGIO CAPITANI

A Goldstone Film Enterprises, Inc. Release

also known as *Ognuno per Se, Sam Cooper's Gold* and *Every Man for Himself*. It's a strangely absorbing, rather overlooked Spaghetti Western which follows the template of *The Treasure of the Sierra Madre*. This time there are four equally untrustworthy and reluctant partners: grizzled prospector Sam Cooper (Heflin), who knows where the gold lies; his protégé Manalo (George Hilton); an ex-partner, Mason (Gilbert Roland); and a mysterious blond called Brent (Klaus Kinski) who is dressed as a preacher. Set in a nameless, dusty southwestern border town where everyone including the storekeepers is a potential threat, this was directed with gusto by Giorgio Capitani. The only real drawback was the disconcerting tendency for the characters to lapse into German at unexpected intervals.

The film begins with Cooper discovering the gold and preparing to take it back with him, having to shoot a partner in the process ("It was either him or me"). On the way home he is attacked by bandits and knocked unconscious. When he comes to, he realizes they were only after food and did not take the gold. Now without a horse and unable to carry the gold back, he hides it with the intention of returning later with one partner only, "The only one I know I can trust," namely Manalo, who he brought up almost as his own son. He sends a wire to Manalo who soon arrives. During the night another man appears, Brent, whom Manalo insists accompany them. Cooper instinctively mistrusts the stranger and begins to have misgivings about Manalo. He enlists another reluctant ex-partner, Mason, as much for his own security from the other two as anything else.

En route to the gold they encounter a band of unnamed bandits, and there is the obligatory shoot-out at a ruined adobe-type building. A great deal of tension is built up by looks and silences and the dialogue is riddled with menace and ambiguity; the suspense is enhanced by the music of Carlo Rusticelli. As the four head back with the gold, tensions rise and the unusual interplay of their relationships is developed.

It could be argued that there is a gay subtext at work. Brent wears the costume of a preacher but there is little mention of this and he does not appear to be passing himself off as a man of the cloth; one might assume this to be a fetish. His presence is never satisfactorily explained nor why he is so essential to the expedition; "He *has* to come with us," says Manalo. "Why?" asks Cooper, to which there is no answer other than "He did everything for me after you left—*everything!*" Manalo too is an ambiguous char-

Opposite: **The cult spaghetti Western *Four Ruthless Men* (1968) gave Heflin his final starring role as a member of a gang looking for gold. Absorbing and full of tension, it had an interesting four-way dynamic that held attention throughout. Shot in Rome, it was his last European film.**

acter and must be the only cowboy in history to ride with an umbrella over him. His loyalty to Brent is somewhat more than friendship; when Brent is attacked by Mason, he is beside himself with anger and then grief.

In one rather surreal scene, it starts to rain and they suddenly become animated and laugh loudly. Giddy with pleasure; Manalo rips off his shirt and all four men come together in a bizarre ecstasy which seems homo-erotic. Cooper and Manalo have an almost father-son relationship, and although there is a lot of tension between Cooper and Mason an elusive bond develops between the two older men by which time it is too late.

This is a curious film but considered a gem by many fans of Spaghetti Westerns. Director Capitani worked with verve. He began his career with a comedy drama, *Storm* (1954), and sent up the sword and sandal epic in *Samson and the Mighty Challenge* (1964). A busy director, he later moved to television where he was still working in 2012.

Heflin's years in Europe had enhanced his reputation in the wider world and he also relished the broadening of horizons for his family. "My children are enjoying being raised in the American tradition," he observed, "but they also have the advantage of a European education."[28] However by 1963 he longed to return home and again make films in Hollywood. Returning was almost like it had been after coming back from the war; he would have to begin all over again.

Twelve

Reluctantly to Television
(1950–71)

> *"I prefer to work in the entertainment field instead of advertising. Actors should just entertain and not be pitch-men."*[1]

Rather like Chaplin's reaction to the Talkies, Heflin resisted entering the world of television for as long as possible. He often spoke about the cheapening of the actor's art and how the small screen belittled those movie actors who deigned to appear. He objected to actors doing TV commercials for similar reasons (although he did many advertisements for printed media and was quite a salesman on radio). He did not even like to watch his old films on television because "they advertise how much older you are and how bad you were in those days."[2]

By the early 1950s, television was beginning to come into its own and his agents were receiving "between four and five offers a month" for work in the medium. "I have given instructions to turn them all down," he said. "I have my reasons."[3] One of the earliest ideas he rejected was a weekly CBS series about "a tough city editor of a metropolitan newspaper."[4] "I think it's dangerous for a film actor to appear more often," he said. One of the biggest roles he turned down (along with the other Van—Johnson) was that of Eliot Ness in *The Untouchables* which made a star of the estimable Robert Stack. Heflin felt there was not enough mileage in the franchise.[5]

When he entered television on a more permanent basis, it was on his terms. Mostly he preferred to be a narrator and even then had it written into his contract that networks had to get their equipment to record his voice wherever he was in the world.[6] The majority of his work in the medium was as narrator of documentaries. Sometimes he appeared before the camera as in the travelogue *U.S. Route 1* which followed the road from

Maine all the way to Key West. It was described by Heflin as "a sentimental salute, a kind of requiem" to this historical route.

He'd made his TV debut as far back as 1950 as a guest on his friend Ken Murray's show. Comedian Murray has been described as "a large, shaggy, friendly vaudevillian whose face on a clear day can be seen for twelve miles." They had known one another for some time; Murray ran his own club, Blackouts, which featured variety acts such as George Burton and his trained birds. Heflin was persuaded to invest in *Bill and Coo*, a curious all-bird movie featuring Burton's birds. It was nominated for a special Academy Award in 1947; Heflin called it "that damn bird picture"[7] Murray's near-burlesque TV show was a mixture of "mildewed sketches" and "unabashed corn" delivered in good-natured fashion. There might be somewhat incongruous interludes such as a scene from *Death of a Salesman*, and several Hollywood star guests would appear; often they did little more than walk on and shake hands. On the first show of the series, Heflin took part in a poker-playing sketch "in which his chief task was to hold up five immense cards."[8] Some years later Murray was the host of the documentary *Hollywood My Home Town* (1965) which featured footage of the homes of many Hollywood stars since the 1920s, including John Barrymore, Mary Astor and Heflin.

Later in 1950 he made his TV acting debut reprising the title role he had essayed in the radio version of Sinclair Lewis' *Arrowsmith* for *Robert Montgomery Presents*. He played the Llano Kid in the O. Henry story *A Double-Dyed Deceiver*, sponsored by Nash Airflyte. In 1952 a filmed segment of his current play *The Shrike* ran on *The Toast of the Town*. He was the guest host of a *Lux Theater* presentation, "Meet Joe Cathcart," in 1954 and made two appearances on *What's My Line?* The following year he was surprised on *This Is Your Life*, which for a private man was something of a nightmare.

He made very few TV appearances thereafter until September 1957 when he met by chance Martin Manulis, with whom he had acted at Bar-Harold twenty years earlier. Manulis persuaded him to play the part of the Russian Colonel Stern in a Rod Serling teleplay about the Hungarian Revolt, "The Dark Side of the Earth." Directed by Arthur Penn, it was an episode of CBS's *Playhouse 90*, a series which helped nurture many future talents. Co-starring Earl Holliman and Kim Hunter, this piquant drama made an incisive comment on unfolding events in Soviet-controlled Hungary. Heflin gave a "wonderful character study ... one of the greatest performances I have ever seen," said one reviewer, who further commented that the teleplay "would have far greater impact on the American public than the preachment going on now in the United Nations."[9] The power of television was just then beginning to be acknowledged. The following year, Heflin was one of several actors considered to play Joseph Stalin in another CBS *Playhouse 90* drama, "The Plot to Kill Stalin." Laurence Olivier, Fredric March and Rod Steiger also turned down the role which went to Melvyn Douglas in a production that did nothing for U.S.–Soviet relations.[10]

Heflin was very impressed by Penn as a director and later consulted him in New York to discuss playing the lead in his play *Two for the Seesaw* on its London run.[11]

Having "turned down ten previous TV scripts," Heflin jumped at the opportunity to play the lead in *The Rank and File*, in which Rod Serling did for labor relations what he had done for corporate life in *Patterns*.[12] The story concerns a "once dedicated union leader whose insatiable greed for power eventually destroys him as an ethical human being."[13] Although set against the background of organized labor, "the conflict originates from the same source as it does in *Patterns*—the obsession with power." His character turns "from a naïve, almost idealistic man into a vicious, murder-accepting racketeer." He won wide praise for his portrayal; "Heflin's portrait of Kilcoyne, the labor leader who vaulted from the ranks into the power elite, was bull strong. It was a portrait stuffed with nuance and urgency—juicy, expansive, pushy."[14]

His third *Playhouse 90* entry was "The Cruel Day" by Reginald Rose, famous for *12 Angry Men*. Heflin played a "civilized, thinking army captain" in Algeria who is asked to order the torture of a teenage rebel boy. As one reviewer observed, "The author maintains ... that such men must remain true to their souls and refuse to use evil methods for future good. At the same time super-morality and moralists must yield to the brutish immorality of war when a showdown comes along."[15]

As it transpires, he does not order the torture. But as he makes his decision he is killed, and in the ultimate irony the boy is tortured anyway. Heflin gave an incisive portrayal of the agonized captain with excellent support from a fine cast including Cliff Robertson as his aide and Peter Lorre as a café owner.

Dick Powell had such confidence in *Ricochet* that he wanted it to start CBS's 1961 season but he was overruled by the network. Written by Aaron Spies, this starred Heflin as platoon sergeant Paul Maxon, who "lets himself be blackmailed by a couple of slimy recruits Kelso and Marner (the sneering psychotic John David Chandler and John Alderman) because of a training accident (in which a recruit was killed accidentally), and is almost railroaded out of the service."[16]

In 1967 Heflin was to have played Black MacDonald in a CBS adaptation of *Johnny Belinda* starring Mia Farrow and David Carradine. When he had to pull out, the role went to Barry Sullivan instead. Three years earlier he was due to appear in an episode of the popular series *Dr. Kildare* but withdrew.[17]

A Case of Libel was a straightforward television adaptation of the successful stage play in which he reprised his role. This was essentially a filmed record of the play. He was nominated for an Emmy as Best Actor in a Leading Role.

In "Fear Is the Chain" for *Danny Thomas Theater Hour* he gave an insightful portrayal of ex–Nazi General Kreitzer, "who defects and tries to escape through a mountain pass with (Horst) Buchholz as a guide and May Britt as a tormentor accusing him of war atrocities."

In Rod Serling's "Certain Honorable Men" for Prudential's NBC *On Stage* series, Heflin played Champ Donohue, "powerful leader of the House of Representatives," an old-time political enforcer who uses kickbacks and the "politics of personal contacts and private deals" to maintain power. His nemesis is his ambitious young protégé Robert Conroy (Peter Fonda), who "uncovers his dishonest dealings and exposes him."[18] Conroy persuades an ex-girlfriend who works in Donohue's office to steal documents from his personal file; he "brings this evidence before (an) ethical committee and the result is censure" for Donohue. Heflin and Fonda were praised for their performances in a timely and prescient drama screened shortly after the chaotic Democratic Convention of 1968 and just a few years before Watergate. The drama was based on the story of Senator Thomas Dodd of Connecticut, who was censured by the Senate.[19]

"Neither Are We Enemies," an episode of NBC's *Hallmark Hall of Fame*, was shown at Easter 1970. Written by Henry Denker, this drama centered on the generation gap between a group of youths in Judea at the time of Christ and the conflicts with their parents. Heflin appeared as Joseph of Arimathea with Kate Reid as his wife and 18-year-old Kristoffer Tabori as his son Jonathon. Also in the cast was Ed Begley as Annas; it was one of his final roles as he died later the same year.

The Last Child (1971) was set in a futureworld (twenty-three years hence) in which there are strict population rules and only one child is allowed per family. Alan (Michael Cole) and Karen (Janet Margolin) lost their first child at a few days old. Karen is pregnant again but the authorities find out about it and rule that she is in violation of the law. She avoids prison through the intervention of her brother. Alan and Karen flee the country with a government agent (Ed Asner) in pursuit. When all seems lost they meet a sympathetic retired Senator, Quincy George (Heflin); a firm believer in the rights of the individual, he vows to help them all he can. The Bureau of Population Control also forbids medication to those over 65; George is 72 and only "kept alive by insulin bootlegged to him by a friendly doctor." This drama turned out to be Heflin's final performance in any medium and was shown posthumously. "He has a rather superficial role," wrote one reviewer, "but the actor managed to invest the platitudes with dignity and persuasion so that they sounded like noble philosophy."[20]

Part of *The Last Child* was shot in Pasadena, and the veteran actor was surprised to be "told to drive his own car to the location" hundreds of miles away. It was a far cry from the days of the big Hollywood studios. "I've never been to Pasadena," he told his employers. "If I get lost ... it will cost you a lot more money than it will to send a car and driver." They sent a car and driver.

For all his reluctance to initially enter television, he nonetheless realized its significance. As early as 1949 he had talked about how the four mediums would become increasingly interwoven to form a new pattern of entertainment.[21] He considered television to be the most exacting medium of the lot because it combined all the requirements of radio, stage and cinema and fully tested an actor's talents.

Ultimately, television represented something of a lost opportunity for Heflin. By the late 1960s, after his divorce, he began to appear more frequently and would surely have gone on to make the province his own given time. He never had his own show as did many other stars of the day, although he was the host of *Telephone Hour* in 1964, joining the West Point Glee Club to narrate Morton Gould's tone poem "They Dared to Be Free."[22] In July 1969 he was one of a number of big names who presented live coverage of the moon landings along with Julie Harris and James Earl Jones.[23]

The evidence of a handful of fine performances in some intense and memorable teleplays suggests that he would have been far more suited to the medium of television than he imagined. He might also have made up for some of the disappointment he must have felt at the desultory nature of much of his later film career. Had he given himself more chance, he could have come to realize that far from belittling an actor of his stature, it would more likely have enhanced his reputation in the long run.

Thirteen

The Final Years (1963–71)

"When I get too old for the movies I don't want to wind up loafing around a movie set as an extra or a bit player."[1]

By the early 1960s Heflin sought to return to making films in the United States, having been highly successful in consolidating his reputation in Europe. He declared he was "tired of travelling" and talked longingly of returning home for good. He did not consider Oklahoma home, but California, where he had spent so many years working.

However, he had been so long associated with Europe that U.S. producers seldom called him when they had a part.[2] He was still careful choosing scripts and rejected many with which he was bombarded while in Europe. In 1961 alone he was offered thirteen American scripts and turned them all down.[3] "If it comes to a choice between a good European script and a bad American one, I take the European," he once asserted. His choices were often surprising. *Cry of Battle* was dismissed by its author as "a stinker."[4] However this judgment is hasty; the passage of time and the effects of American foreign policy since the Second World War can now be viewed in proper perspective, which makes such a movie worthy of reappraisal.

Cry of Battle is now chiefly remembered for its association with the assassination of President John F. Kennedy on November 22, 1963. Lee Harvey Oswald, arrested at the Texas Theater in Dallas, may have caught a few minutes of the movie which was on a double bill with *War Is Hell* starring Audie Murphy.

Initially entitled *To Be a Man, Cry of Battle* was based on the novel *Fortress in the Rice* by Benjamin Appel, a journalist and former special assistant to the U.S. Commissioner for the Philippines during 1945 and '46. Dave McVeigh (James MacArthur), the spoiled son of a wealthy businessman, is visiting his father at his Manila plantation just prior to the

Japanese attack on Pearl Harbor. Stranded in the Philippines, his car is attacked by rebels; he narrowly escapes and is helped by Major Manuel Careo (Leopoldo Salcedo). He seeks to escape the advancing Japanese and return to America. He meets a fellow American, Joe Trent (Heflin), civilian captain of a steamer; and native girl Pinang (Marilu Munoz). Trent, left alone with Pinang while Dave is away in the village, rapes her. Fearing reprisals, he escapes to the hills. Dave reluctantly follows him; they meet a group of rebels led by Sisa (Rita Moreno) and Atong (Oscar Roncal). Trent bluffs his way into the stronghold of Colonel Ryker (Sidney Clute). He and Dave are reluctantly recruited by Ryker to join their ranks; soon all the rebels join forces in their common struggle against the invading Japanese. Trent is given the rank of lieutenant and leads several guerrilla raids against the enemy. Running low on supplies, Dave and Sisa go to a local village at night to bargain for some rice and provisions. While they are talking, Trent leads his rebels in an attack during which many villagers are killed. He also shoots Sisa's boyfriend, clearing the way for him to take his place. After further raids they arrive at another village where they are invited to a celebration. Dave and Sisa go away from the village and spend the night together. In the morning they are brought before the major who tries to charge Trent with rape and murder, but Dave refuses to give the testimony that will convict him. Trent, Dave and Sisa are held prisoner. When the Japanese arrive in the village, Dave successfully attacks a tank but Trent is shot and wounded. The three escape and hide out for some weeks at a beach on a remote part of the island.

Director Irving Lerner began his career making documentaries for the Ministry of Information during the war; *Cry of Battle* has at times a semi-documentary style. A rather convoluted plot is in keeping with the confusion which surrounds the politics and history of East-West relations, to say nothing of the dubious morality of war. The nature of the uncomfortable alliances brought by conflict is the focus of a somewhat fractured screenplay. We see how war changes all the rules so that it is not certain what the truth is or what all the protagonists are fighting for; everyone has their own agenda. Ultimately, despite the high-minded talk of morality and a "clean war," the cause of the wider fight is often lost and the battle is reduced to one of self-preservation at all costs.

Joe Trent is the nastiest of all the screen characters Heflin ever portrayed. He is amoral, racist, unscrupulous, dishonest and brutal. That somehow the actor makes us feel anything for this man says everything one needs to know about his talent. The shifting alliances between the main players invoke the audience's similarly changing feelings concerning each character. Dave is totally naïve and guileless, but by the end when he has become "a man" he is almost a pale copy of Trent and equally unscrupulous in his own way. With Trent's help he loses his virginity both literally and politically, but the change is rather too abrupt from naïve moralist to self-seeking immoralist. The major at first accepts Dave's money "reluctantly" and insists on giving him a receipt for it; his quest to prosecute Trent and rid the country of the evil he represents implicitly condones any executions and other savage acts carried out in the name of respectability. Sisa, who is indifferent, merely bends with the prevailing wind and as such represents the survivors of conflicts everywhere.

The movie was made on location in and around Manila. The Philippines government threatened at one stage to rescind the visas given to the lead American actors because, vice-president Emmanuel Peleaz claimed, the film "insults the morals and dignity of the Philippines people because the script calls for Philippine women to be shown bathing without suits."[5] After a meeting between producer Joe Steinberg and the vice-president, some changes were made to accommodate the government.[6]

According to a photographer who was on hand during the making of the movie, Heflin "unsettled everyone on the production" because he was rather too convincing. He added, "He was a method actor, who had to enter the personality of the character he played, which made it difficult for everyone involved in the production. He was playing a bastard."[7]

In the U.S. the movie was not too well received, but at Cannes it was nominated for a Palme D'Or. *New York Times* critic Bosley Crowther called it "acerbic and action-packed."[8] The sight of the normally jovial Heflin as a grizzled soldier of fortune was not one to which audiences naturally warmed. One critic asserted that he "gets stuck with the very worst scenes" and that he played the part "sharply and aggressively," a rather facile comment considering the nature of the role. Trent is a third mate on a merchant ship, the same rank Heflin had when he ended his maritime career thirty years before. An actor of imagination, he might well have envisaged just what his own life could have been like if he had stayed at sea and become a nihilist fifty-year-old bum who lived by his wits. Although Trent is a brute, Heflin keeps the character entirely real throughout and makes him true to himself.

The movie was recently released on DVD but is still not well known. It is seldom seen on television and is consequently obscure, but deserves to be viewed again and re-evaluated. The true value of a film like *Cry of Battle* is to focus on a part of the psychology of an invading force; it feels more like a comment on the Vietnam War which was then ongoing (and which still divides opinion) than on the Second World War which it ostensibly purports to depict.

Heflin had high hopes for *The Greatest Story Ever Told* and did not mind that his part in the Biblical epic was limited to eight lines of dialogue. He also relished the chance to work again with *Shane* director George Stevens. "It's worth doing anything with that guy Stevens," he commented.[9]

Heflin's Bar-Amand witnesses the miracle of Lazarus being raised from the dead by Jesus and runs to tell the townspeople. He has three scenes which took about five weeks to shoot, some in the studios at Hollywood and others on location in Nevada and along the Arizona-Utah border at the Arches National Park in Moab. Many other famous names signed up to play equally small roles including Claude Rains as King Herod, Telly Savalas as Pontius Pilate and Dorothy McGuire as the Virgin Mary. John Wayne as a Roman Centurion looks up at Jesus on the cross and intones, "This truly is the son of God," as only he could. The all-star cast seemed to share Heflin's sincere appreciation of the cause. He felt that it would dwarf all previous attempts at telling the story of Jesus and would stand the test of time. "They may bury all the other films or wear them out," he remarked, "but this one will be looked at by our grandchildren."

The original running time of three hours forty minutes might have seemed daunting even for devoted Christians but the cinematography and art direction were notable and Oscar-nominated. There was clever casting of the renowned Swedish actor Max von Sydow as Jesus. The use of so many Hollywood stars in cameo roles has divided opinion; some feel it detracted from the proceedings. All in all this is an earnest presentation of the story of Jesus but it has little of the life of, say, Pasolini's *The Gospel According to St. Matthew* which was made around the same time with a cast of unknowns.

Gordon Douglas' *Stagecoach* was, according to one reviewer, "an unnecessary use of celluloid."[10] Almost thirty years after John Ford created his timeless classic, producer Martin Rackin and Twentieth Century–Fox decided in their wisdom to make a new version. The film that made John Wayne a star and set the standard for Westerns was redone in glorious Eastman Color among the mountains of Colorado. The all-too-familiar Ernest Haycox tale followed the assorted travelers from Dryford to (in this case) Cheyenne and their encounters with the Apaches and each other. Characters include the absconding banker Gatewood (Robert Cummings), Peacock, a whisky salesman (Red Buttons), Hadfield, a gambler (Mike Connors), and an Army captain's pregnant wife (Stefanie Powers). Although Wayne wanted his son Patrick to take his role as Ringo, the part went to ex-rodeo rider-cum-Shakespearean actor Alex Cord. Bing Crosby played Doc Boone and Ann-Margret tackled the role of the prostitute Dallas that Claire Trevor brought to life so vividly in the original. Heflin played the underpaid Marshall Curly Wilcox who rides shotgun; he has known Ringo since he was a kid but is the one who has to bring him to justice.

Filming at Nederland, Colorado, was held up considerably by torrential rains that interrupted the schedule every afternoon for three weeks. "It is not just ordinary rain," an eyewitness commented. "This is mountain weather—electric storms which shake the building, hail stones which dump billiard ball–sized missiles on the ground, even traces of snow."[11]

"That's the price you pay for a mountain location," remarked Heflin wryly. Director George Douglas was asked if he would choose such a location ever again; "Damn right I would," he answered. "The scenery is so magnificent. It's worth all the trouble." Unfortunately, few others agreed. The result was "bombed by the critics and failed at the box office."[12]

No one in the cast was especially memorable. Heflin tried his best with the material. So infrequent were his film appearances at this stage of his career that some thought he had come out of retirement for the occasion. Most agreed he was "much more like the real thing" and he took his usual pains with the role, even watching a number of times how George Bancroft had approached the part in the original. He commented on his comparison in height with Bancroft: "George was actually shorter than I, but heavier. But I photograph shorter. I'm 6'1". I don't know why I photograph shorter. Maybe because I have an Oklahoma slouch. They call it a cotton-patch walk."[13]

As Ringo, Alex Cord made a "monotonously melancholy cowboy." There was far too much talk which stopped the flow of the action and the pace was "consequently torpid."[14] The script used parts of the original verbatim and where it strayed made less sense. The beginning and end were altered and opened out slightly, but not to any beneficial effect. Curly is shot in a tense saloon encounter which was one of the few interesting departures from the 1939 version. The lack of music was a distinct drawback. Although it may have been better made technically than the original, it had no humor or spark of life, and a sterile feeling pervaded. One reviewer said the experience was "like listening to an impersonator describing a movie." Another remarked, "Heflin is his noble self," and *The Times of London*'s opined that he was "one of the few redeeming features" of the film.[15] Some twenty years later yet another version of *Stagecoach* rode to the screen, again proving the law of diminishing returns and delineating in sharp relief how good Ford's original really was.

The cast members were invited to an Academy Award dinner where Prince Philip, the Duke of Edinburgh, the guest of honor, "engaged in sprightly conversation with Rosalind Russell at his left and Glynis Johns at his right." Heflin presented him with a Winchester rifle on behalf of the cast of *Stagecoach*.[16] One of the few good things to emerge from the experience was a set of illustrations of the cast by the prolific artist Norman Rockwell, whose iconic *Saturday Evening Post* covers became such a part of the national consciousness. Although often maligned in that period, he was later awarded the Presidential Medal of Honor for his "vivid and affectionate portraits of (the) country."[17] Rockwell also traveled to Hollywood at the time of the *Stagecoach* premiere to promote the movie, and his paintings of the cast were used on the poster. A set of signed prints fetched over $1000 in a sale at Bonham's Auction House in 2006.[18] In 2011 a set of six negatives shot by Pete Todd as reference for the artist were sold in the Hollywood Legends Auction for $512.[19] As for the film, it is now largely forgotten. Such a soulless piece of work deserves to remain so.

Divorce

"My goodness, I don't know what to do with myself." [20]

Heflin was suffering around this time in his personal life; after a long and, to outsiders, seemingly idyllic marriage, he was being sued for divorce and charged with "twenty-five years of mental cruelty." He countered with an equal charge.[21] She said he was subject to "violent tempers," had become "sullen, moody and indifferent" and that he "struck her on two occasions."[22] According to their eldest daughter Vana, her mother "had been having an affair with the best friend of the family.... It was all terribly ugly."[23] They separated on February 2 and the interlocutory divorce was granted in July 1967. His ex-wife was awarded the family home in Brentwood and 15 percent of his gross income for the next ten years.[24] He was also required to provide $3,500 a month for his son Tracy, then 13, whose custody went to Frances. The whole thing appeared to come as a complete shock to him, and arguably one from which he never recovered. He later told friends that he was "shaken by the breakup." Less than a year earlier the couple had attended Glenn Ford's marriage and Dorothy Manners had reported about their plans for celebrating their wedding anniversary: "Van ... gave his wife Frances a signed blank check for their 24th wedding anniversary. Now there's a husband for you! "She filled it in for a trip to Europe—without me," grins Van, "but I'm catching up with her later."[25]

But headlines seldom reflect the true nature of things. As far back as 1947 there had been talk of trouble in their marriage; in 1951 such rumors led him to abandon the notion of doing a play in Britain.[26] In 1964 when he was playing on Broadway in *A Case of Libel,* he met "and fell in love" with Maureen O'Sullivan, who was appearing in *Never Too Late* at the Playhouse. As reported by Alex Freeman at the time: "His marriage to Frances has been travelling a rocky road for several years and it only took someone like Maureen to make him move. The holdup on the divorce was caused by Van's concern for his children, but that has been worked out."[27]

He always wanted his children to have as normal an upbringing as possible and refused to send them to private schools where they might have had special treatment. "Someday they'll have to make the adjustment and the earlier the better," he observed. "I don't want them to grow up expecting anything special because their father is an actor.... We're a pretty close-knit family, and Frances and I always consider them in everything we do."[28]

Vana and Kate later followed in their father's footsteps and became actresses who have made occasional films. Vana appeared in *My Own Private Idaho* (1991) and Kate in *The Killer Elite* (1977). Vana's son Ben O'Brien, born in 1970, continues the family tradition and acted in *Game of Swords* (2005) and *Monte Carlo* (2011).

According to his son Tracy there was an "ongoing decline" in his parents' "explosive and dysfunctional marriage." Tracy once expressed a desire to be an actor and was to have accompanied his father to Mexico to see him work on *The Revengers* with William Holden. But while his sisters followed the acting route, he decided against it. He worked in the sound department at Universal before pursuing a career as a physiotherapist. He grew closer to his father in later years, after the divorce, and had nothing but praise for him as a dad. "He was a wonderful father," he once reflected; however, he added, "He could be an amazing actor and [at] home have a totally different kind of life."[29]

The public image seemed complete in the 1950s but even then there were hints of underlying tensions: "He is a Scotch and soda man—but doesn't particularly like nightclubs. He prefers 'discussions' (his wife calls them arguments). Clad in his old red flannel robe sitting in front of the fireplace."

Elsewhere he was described as "moody to the point of forgetting who's in the room; argumentative for the delight of mental conflict," and they both admitted to having huge rows.[30]

He was not a stranger at parties. In 1947 he was spotted at one of Tallulah Bankhead's soirees, and in the early 1950s he often socialized. In

1954 he was one of many Hollywood stars at a fancy dress party, costumed as a dancing Indian. It was still an era of style and larger-than-life personalities. In June 1955 he was one of a number of friends invited to a cocktail party given by Frank Sennes to welcome Noël Coward. "It was a gala occasion, with hundreds of roses and gardenias in the kidney-shaped swimming pool."[31]

By the late 1950s his drinking must have been a problem and three years before his divorce he was seen "walking all a-lonely into the Blue Fox, there to find another actor (John Payne) looking for company."[32] Many of his good friends and colleagues, including Robert Taylor, Alan Ladd and John Wayne, were all famous drinkers. Something that seemed to come with the territory in Hollywood.

He prided himself on being financially comfortable and by the mid–1960s was conservatively estimated to be worth at least $1,000,000. His investments in land alone often brought him greater remuneration than acting.[33] Ever since he was a young actor he "invested every cent he ever made [for] radio work in stocks and bonds."[34] He was always keen to use his money wisely; for instance, with his salary for *3:10 to Yuma* he bought a large ranch in Northern California; and the paychecks from *Gunman's Walk* he invested in another on the Arizona-California border. He was also "many times a millionaire from his oil wells in Oklahoma alone," and in the early 1950s made "a steady $2,800 a month from a Texas oil well which Ava Gardner had turned down."[35]

His divorce coming when it did made it seem as though the rug had been pulled from under him. On the one hand he expressed a wish not to work so hard; maybe a couple of movies a year and a television special. But on the other hand he needed to keep busy. "Apart from a little trout fishing I spend most of my spare time reading," he once said.[36] Most of his other interests were also largely solitary pursuits: sailing, swimming and collecting photographs of old Hollywood stars. He enjoyed cooking and hearing the music of Chopin, according to Liberace.[37]

While he was away during the war, he financed a millinery business which his wife ran in Beverly Hills; when she became pregnant, he insisted she quit the business "until after the baby is born and maybe permanently."[38] They had also suffered personal tragedies such as the loss of a baby in 1952. At that time he was on Broadway but flew back home the moment he heard his wife was in the hospital. They were overjoyed when their son Tracy Neal was born in April 1954.[39]

Generally they seemed to have had very few shared interests and he was often absent for long periods filming. In 1958 at the time of *They*

Came to Cordura Frances complained that her husband had not had a birthday at home in five years. The director attempted to finish filming early that day but even then they only had an hour together. However they had many European holidays as a family; for instance, in 1962 they took a vacation trip around the world lasting five months. With their 16-year-old daughter Katie they visited Manila, Hong Kong, Saigon, Bangkok, Delhi, Beirut, Cairo, Rome and Greece.[40] Frances appeared to take little interest in his work and seldom visited him on film sets. The one time she did, during the making of *Till the Clouds Roll By*, he blew all his lines.[41]

He rarely socialized and, beyond premieres, appeared to shun the limelight. But he was friendly with many in the acting fraternity. "All my friends are actors," he once remarked. Chief among them were Alan Ladd, Robert Taylor, Gary Cooper, Dick Powell, Ava Gardner, James Mason, Kirk Douglas, Glenn Ford, Peter Lind Hayes and his wife Mary Healy. Clark Gable he said was "a fine actor and what a personality!" (Like Heflin, he too was a keen outdoorsman.) There was one memorable night in 1954 when Van and Frances were among the guests of Dick Powell and his wife June Allyson at their Mandeville Canyon home. This was on the eve of the Directors banquet, and among the guests were Judy Garland, who started giving an impromptu concert. All the guests were spellbound watching her. Just a few couples remained after midnight; it got to 2:00 a.m. then 3:00 a.m. At 4:00 a.m. Frances whispered to her husband that he ought to get some sleep because he was due on location at 6:30. "Sleep I can always get," he replied. "Something like this comes along only once in a lifetime." A little after six Judy suddenly stopped singing, and everyone drifted home. Harold Cohen was reminded of that memorable night when Garland died in 1969, recalling the ride home afterwards: "Coming down through Mandeville Canyon, Van's eyes stayed glued to the winding highway with its glaze of early morning dew and he repeated over and over again 'once in a lifetime, only once in a lifetime, do you ever get to hear anything like that.'"[42]

Heflin was sometimes active politically for the Democratic cause. In October 1947 he was one of some thirty prominent Hollywood personalities who flew to Washington to support the "hostile witnesses" named as Communists by the House Un-American Committee. Also in the group were Humphrey Bogart, Lauren Bacall, John Ford, Evelyn Keyes and John Garfield. He quoted what these so-called witnesses had actually said when naming individuals.[43]

In 1948 he was one of the Hollywood stars at the annual Jackson Day dinner and tribute to Franklin D. Roosevelt organized by the Democratic

Party. This dinner was given every year on the anniversary of Roosevelt's death and Heflin was invited to read the tribute to the much-missed president. He also spoke about Roosevelt at the Democratic Party Convention that year. "When this man died," he said, "people of the world lost a friend and champion."[44] He was unable to accept President Truman's invitation to the 1949 inaugural ball "because Metro couldn't shoot around him in *Madame Bovary.*"[45] In 1950 he was recruited by Senator Elmer Thomas "to put whoof into his campaign for the Democratic senatorial nomination." His home state of Oklahoma was described as "a rough and ready state politically full of frolic and brawl, never lagging in political novelty."[46] In March 1960 he was one of a number of public supporters of the Civil Rights Movement who lent their names to a full-page piece in the *New York Times.* This took the form of a letter from Dr. Martin Luther King incorporating an informal "bill of rights" with the title "Heed Their Rising Voices." Other signers included Hope Lange, Shelley Winters and Harry Belafonte.[47]

In a candid interview with Dorothy Manners he reflected on his divorce. He said he remembered his marriage as a happy one, and thought that he, Frances and the three children had many years of happiness and only a few years of unhappiness. He tried to keep busy but he was still not accustomed to being unmarried. "Every working day around six p.m. I get that old tug of realizing with surprise that no one is waiting for me at home.... During the year since our divorce I've thought, 'My goodness, I don't know what to do with myself.'"[48]

He said that divorce was not "carefree bachelorhood." He was grateful for work and just glad the phone kept ringing, especially if it was his agent with another interesting job.

After his divorce his name was linked for some time with a Miss O'Shea (with whom he was seen at the Hollywood Beachcombers) and especially with Maureen O'Sullivan, a relationship which some observers predicted might result in marriage.[49] There was further speculation that he was planning to marry when he began construction of a $100,000 waterfront home. "I am in the market for a boat," he quipped. "Not a wife." Since his wife had the house in Tigertail Avenue, he had lived in a series of apartments or sometimes with friends.[50]

Heflin's health suffered after his divorce. Throughout most of his life he had been reasonably healthy; apart from an attack of hives in childhood he was relatively free of problems. From the mid–1960s he began to have chronic pains in his left leg which he first noticed when taking short walks. He complained of general fatigue, loss of energy and nervousness brought on by the emotional turmoil of his divorce. In 1969 he told the doctor during a medical examination at the Scripps Clinic that he used "about one pint of alcohol a day" and that he smoked a pack of cigarettes a day. He also suffered from insomnia for which he took seconal, equinal or doriden. The previous year he had been diagnosed with diabetes. He was known to be allergic to penicillin.[51]

During these latter years he lost some of his friends including Clark Gable in 1960, Gary Cooper the following year, Dick Powell two years later, and Robert Taylor in 1968. In 1965 he was one of the 300 mourners at the funeral of Michael Charles Boyer, son of his friend Charles Boyer; Michael had shot himself. In January 1964 he lost perhaps his greatest friend, Alan Ladd, who may or may not have intended to take an overdose. Ladd was certainly suffering acutely at that time with his personal demons which Heflin knew about only too well. When Ladd reached out to Van and his other great friend William Bendix, they were working in the east, Heflin on Broadway and Bendix on tour with *Never Too Late*. The desperate Ladd pleaded with Bendix to come home; he even offered to buy out his contract. But both men had commitments and a company relying on them. His insomnia worse than ever, Ladd called Van and Bendix nightly. "They tried to help. But nothing was helping."[52] Frances phoned Van in New York with news of Alan's death. "It was only the second time I heard Van cry," she said. That night he met Robert Preston for dinner; naturally they spoke about Alan. "I'm terribly saddened," said Van. "But I'm not really surprised. He tried it before, you know."[53]

His next movie *The Big Bounce*, derived from a story by Elmore Leonard, marked the film debut of Ryan O'Neal playing a character described by one reviewer as being "halfway between a janitor and a gigolo."[54] Modishly directed by Alex March who later moved exclusively to television, it was largely reviled by the critics. One dismissed it as "a rancid piece of trash."

Vietnam veteran and drifter Jack Ryan (O'Neal) is fired from his job at a vegetable farm run by manager Bob Rodgers (Robert Webber). He is offered a job as a cleaner at the motel operated by local ex–justice of the peace Sam Mirakian (Heflin). He then meets the seductive Nancy Barker (Barbara Leigh-Taylor), mistress and secretary of corrupt farm owner Ray Ritchie. Nancy persuades a reluctant Jack to take part in a heist, robbing the farm safe which she says contains a $50,000 payroll. Jack becomes increasingly wary of Nancy who he thinks will double-cross him. Her erratic behavior eventually leads to mayhem and murder.

Few critics had anything kind to say about *The Big Bounce*, which "hovers fitfully between *Pretty Poison* and *Peyton Place.*" It begins, said one, with Ryan "bashing out someone's teeth with a baseball bat" and "gets more dismal as it goes on."[55] Even the best review concluded that its chief asset was its "casual acceptance of the total corruption of our society."[56] Elmore Leonard, whose novel formed the basis of the Robert Dozier screenplay, called it a bad movie; "That's all I can say about it."[57] Central character Nancy was a psychotic girl who ends up killing for pleasure. *New York Times* critic A.H. Weiler, especially trenchant, said it was "composed largely of ersatz thrills, explicit and often amateurish dialogue, and a hedonistic attitude toward practically everything."[58]

Even when mired in such dross, Heflin managed to create a vivid and likable character with a rugged but philosophical nature; he is the human heart of an otherwise rudderless enterprise. Sam Mirakian helps and advises Ryan. He is a father figure who tries to steer him away from the baleful influence of Nancy. At one point Nancy tries to get farm manager Rodgers to fight Ryan in a bar, but Sam intervenes. His character has been variously described as a "jaded curmudgeon who doesn't believe in anything" and a "trash-talking old dude"; his dialogue is peppered with crudities and coarse humor.[59] He was funny and touching by turns; the emotionally burned-out Sam seemed to be invested with some of Heflin's own sense of world-weariness. The movie may have been "a hothouse item about swinging sex and crime junior division," and the product of "tiny-minded individuals," but Heflin salvaged something from it.[60] He was "casually ruminative as the cynical motel owner," in what was a curiously valedictory performance that hinted at his possible future direction had he been granted the years he deserved.[61] Interestingly, when the movie was remade in 2004, the Heflin role was played by Morgan Freeman, a contemporary player of comparable integrity who many critics felt was, like his predecessor, far too good an actor to waste his talents in such a forgettable venture.

The Big Bounce was shot at Carmel and Monterey, California. During filming Heflin rented a bachelor apartment of the kind which later featured in *Atlantic City.* The entertainer Tiny Tim, staying in the same building at the time, became a frequent visitor of the veteran actor. Tiny Tim was a rather bizarre singer and ukulele player who specialized in slightly surreal versions of old songs sung in a distinctive tremulous falsetto. During that year (1968) he was on the cusp of his brief fame and released a record on Sinatra's Reprise label, "God Bless Tiny Tim." He was also a "wild-eyed movie fan" and the two struck up an unlikely friendship, said Heflin: "Tiny doesn't drink—but he doesn't mind me hoisting one. The other night when

Playing wily curmudgeon Sam Mirakian, Heflin was one of the few to emerge unscathed from *The Big Bounce* (1969).

I said I'd never been fortunate to catch his nightclub act, he fetched his ukulele and gave me a run-through of 'Tiptoe Through the Tulips.' You see there are compensations."[62]

Around this time he was also visited by his youngest daughter Kate, who was starting out as an actress and had made a few TV appearances. "[S]he went to see him one day at his apartment hotel when he had been drinking. She was wearing a minidress ... and as soon as he saw her he began raving. He chased her down the corridor shouting obscenities at her."[63]

Her sister Vana's chief recollection of her father was that he was "stern ... he had a temper. [He] once objected to a date she was going to have—

didn't think the boyfriend was right for her or something. He came out of the house after her when she was leaving for the evening, walked down to the car she had just gotten into, and ordered her back into the house."[64]

Heflin was away from his family for long periods, filming. It's likely that when he was there, he appeared to play the heavy father in an effort to compensate.

He was still receiving interesting film offers including one from Federico Fellini asking him to come to Rome to play Eumolpo in *Satyricon*, his "fairy tale for adults." The renowned director wanted to assemble a divine cast including "Mickey Mouse, Mae West.... Terence Stamp, Van Heflin and The Beatles" as well as Boris Karloff, who turned it down because he was too ill at the time. Heflin was keen on the idea. "I'd have accepted it sight unseen to work with him," Heflin said of Fellini.[65] He was all set to fly to Rome in January 1969 but severe financial problems led to delays in the production and finally Fellini was forced to settle for a largely unknown cast. In the meantime, Heflin was offered *Airport* by Universal and accepted.

Heflin loved to read, especially biographies, and once said that his favorite sport was "sitting around with a group of cronies gabbing." He was described as "a colorful conversationalist, a good storyteller, [who] enjoys philosophizing at great length whether it concerns the future of mankind or the best way to plant cantaloupes." An avid gardener, he tended his extensive orange and lime groves and his two acres of cantaloupes with care.[66] He also had a garden where he raised squashes, tomatoes, artichokes and an Oklahoma favorite, black-eyed peas. He played poker and gin rummy with Hollywood friends such as James Mason and his wife or his old friend Rex Alcorn, the "square-shooting Texan" who had been his GI roommate during the war. Heflin also enjoyed watching prize fights. He was a lifelong sailor and an enthusiastic swimmer; he spent his spare time hunting, and especially fishing, often with his son Tracy in later years. He fished in the Oxnard waters of California, off Cabo Blanco near Talara in northern Peru, and Guaymas in the Gulf of California, among other places. In flat water he fished for albacore, yellow fin and tuna, and when deep-sea fishing went for black rock fish, sea bass and halibut along with striped marlin and sailfish in the Pacific. In the Caribbean he caught a black marlin that weighed over 500 pounds. In 1969 TV's *The American Sportsman* followed him on a fishing trip in the Bahamas. He set off from Crown Colony Club in Chub Cay in search of blue marlin, the "largest and toughest of marlin in [the] Atlantic" in water approximately 600 feet deep, with "rewarding results."[67]

Mostly he was motivated by pure love of the sport. As he explained between takes on the set of *Airport*, he never ate the fish but immediately released them or gave them away. If the fish had swallowed the hook and it was obviously going to die, he would give them to aquariums which welcomed fish for feeding to dolphins and whales.

He even tried ice fishing, and hoped to be allowed time off during the making of *Airport* to pursue that hobby but that proved impossible. He described the people of Minneapolis as the greatest in the world; someone offered to fly him up to the Dakota lakes but Universal would not let him have time off. Fishing held a fascination for him and he found the sport calming; "I can sit on a boat or a riverbank," he observed, "and problems that seemed unsurmountable just don't seem that important any more."[68]

Fishing also brought father and son together, and he cherished the times he and Tracy shared. In December 1969 15-year-old Tracy accompanied his father to Mexico, which Heflin described as "something he's looked forward to for months."[69]

Another of his hobbies was collecting old photographs of Hollywood "royalty" from the early days of film. He amassed almost 2,000 stills since he started in the early 1940s, all kept in the den of his home.[70] The evocative images of a bygone era held a fascination for him: Rudolph Valentino in *The Sheik*, Greta Garbo and John Gilbert in *Flesh and the Devil*, Charlie Chaplin in *The Kid* and numerous others. He had a complex cross-filing system of his collection showing myriad scenes from *The Iron Horse, The Covered Wagon, Old Ironsides, The Sea Hawk*, etc., and all the famous stars of those heady days such as Douglas Fairbanks, Lillian Gish, and Tom Mix. As he explained, "It's developed into a kind of second job that I don't get paid for. Someday, though, I hope to have the world's largest collection of still pictures." (One of the most inimitable artists of the twentieth century, Andy Warhol had a collection of 222 photographs of Hollywood stars from the golden era, among which was one of Heflin.[71])

Arthur Hailey declared himself pleased with the all-star cast of *Airport* which has been described as "*Grand Hotel* with wings." Burt Lancaster, Dean Martin, Jean Seberg and Jacqueline Bisset were the top actors involved. Two jetliners are in trouble during a Chicago blizzard. A passenger aboard one bound for Rome, Guerrero (Heflin), is a disturbed man; he aims to blow himself up so that his desperate wife (Maureen Stapleton) can claim the flight insurance money. The lives and loves of the other characters are explored as they all come together on the plane. An elderly lady stowaway (Helen Hayes) in the seat next to Guerrero notices his odd behavior and suspects him from the first. She appears to be a busybody but her keen eye is what saves the day in the end.

The producers rented a Boeing 707 and spent $3,000 transforming it into a Trans Global Airliner. A mock-up of the complete interior was created for "the authentic deck along 110 seats to the tail section."[72] For all its modernity, there was something decidedly old-fashioned about *Airport*. The all-star cast and two veteran directors (George Seaton and Henry Hathaway) ensured that the venture harked back to the golden age of Hollywood. As one critic observed, it was "The Best Film of 1944."[73]

Airport was one of the first of a run of disaster films made during the 1970s, often with all-star casts. Those which followed included further *Airport* films and others such as *The Towering Inferno, The Hindenburg* and *The Poseidon Adventure*. There appeared to be a preoccupation at the time with the idea that the world was about to end or at the very least

Heflin won wide praise as the disturbed passenger D.O. Guerrero in *Airport* (1970). Although cliché-ridden, the all-star blockbuster put him back in the public eye and may have led to more prominent roles; unfortunately, he died the following year. Pictured: Whit Bissell, Helen Hayes, Heflin.

was on the edge of disaster. *Airport* encapsulates many of the clichés of the genre apt for later mockery in the *Airplane!* movies. But there is also a thread of angst which links it to other films including *The Prisoner of Second Avenue* (1974) that culminated in *Network* (1977) in which Peter Finch has a nervous breakdown on live television and exhorts everyone to throw open their windows and shout, "I'm as mad as hell and I'm not going to take it any more!" The central characters seem ordinary, middle-ranking men but are highly disturbed and increasingly desperate. They feel powerless to change anything including their own direction in life; often they are acquisitive and may have been ambitious but are just not able to keep up and the values they once believed in seem now to make little sense. They feel they are falling behind and don't know how to get back on track; the more they try, the further back they seem to slide, and their desperation mounts. This desperation was perhaps always present but the decade tapped into the unsettling feeling that there was a serious underlying fault line in modern society which was barely being held together and which might snap unexpectedly without warning.

Airport was popular with moviegoers but not so much with the critics who found it "fogged in by film clichés." Several of the actors were praised, especially Heflin; one critic wrote that "he makes sympathetic the role of the perpetual failure whose last mad act ... also fails."[74] Another observed, "One can sense with Heflin's every movement the anxiety of Guerrero in his last attempt for success."[75]

His character is a wildly desperate man at the end of his tether and Heflin delineates him admirably. Guerrero is the ultimate failure and the epitome of despair. Something in the actor himself seemed to allow him to identify with such despair and make it understandable. He said of Guerrero, "It's an intriguing role with many dimensions. He's not a heavy, a one-dimensional character, but a desperate man. He's panic-stricken, unable to cope with life and brain-damaged in the Korean War. But he loves his family and wants to hold onto them."[76]

Accompanied by Helen Hayes, Heflin toured the world promoting *Airport*. They went to most countries in Europe including Britain, and also visited Japan and Australia (a long-haul flight he found trying). However he did manage to escape for a week of complete rest in Tahiti.[77]

He was next offered a role in a Western to be shot in Mexico, *The Revengers* with William Holden and Mary Ure. The only proviso was that he would have to lose 25 pounds in a hurry to get the part. He employed methods similar to those of his friend Clark Gable who had a special four-day diet he used during his early days if he needed to lose ten pounds in a hurry. Heflin lost the weight and was all packed and ready to travel when news came that Holden was suffering from Kenyan Jungle fever and filming had to be postponed.

Heflin loved to swim and each morning completed 25 lengths of his pool. He even used it as part of his hangover cure. He had a steam cabinet nearby and on "mornings after" used to sweat it out at 110°, then leap into his 70° pool. One morning while swimming he suffered a massive heart attack. He was not discovered until some hours later by a janitor, still alive and clinging to the bars, his head barely visible above the water.

He had been so keen to secure the role in *The Revengers* that he appeared to push himself perhaps too far for a 62-year-old man with health problems. According to the testimony of a pool attendant, "I noticed him every morning, every night, taking his long swim around that pool. He was determined. He never paused to rest."[78]

Heflin was always determined: top in Math, best student in the drama class, the best actor he could possibly be. When he suffered the heart attack he still clung on with the same determination, the same life spirit. He was still alive when taken to the Cedars of Lebanon Hospital, where he died almost a month later, on July 23, 1971.

The irony was that the role of Hoop in the forgettable Western *The Revengers* went to Ernest Borgnine. "Ironic" because Borgnine was hardly svelte and the substantial weight loss of 25 pounds which the producers demanded was not necessary after all.

Epilogue

"He was very special and there's going to be an empty spot in Hollywood that can't be filled. His talent overshadowed the rare gift he had of kindness, of gentility. He was a dedicated actor who loved his work and the people around him."[1]

In 1960 Heflin was awarded a star on the Hollywood Boulevard. It was a fitting accolade for years of hard work. Although he was not an orthodox leading man, his talent demanded more recognition than being merely in support of some bland minor "star." Whenever he was required to carry a film, he did so with ease. It was his misfortune to be trapped at an unsuitable studio and that his career momentum was stopped when he served his country in the war. But he built it back up again thereafter and created numerous memorable character studies over 35 years. He was a fine stage craftsman and his superlative acting ability added to the luster of Hollywood during its Golden Age.

He was always prepared to take risks as an actor and never sought popularity. Nevertheless he remained popular with the viewing public, who immediately picked up on his homeliness allied to a basic integrity. In one of his first breakthrough roles he was so convincing despite playing a heel that he was billed as "The man you hate to hate."

Always an internationalist, he was especially popular outside of the United States, particularly in Europe. Later he did much to enhance the reputation of his country at a time when relations between east and west were not good. At the height of the Cold War, the Communist Tito's government made a special request that he return to Yugoslavia to make another movie. He was highly regarded in Great Britain, Canada, Australia, Italy, Spain, France and Portugal, among many other countries. In 1951 a Singapore newspaper ran a competition to discover the nature of charm.

Van was a popular star in Britain where he twice made the cover of *Picturegoer*, one of the biggest-selling film magazines at the time. Cover date: April 22, 1950.

"What is charm?" the newspaper asked, "And who has it?" The winning answer was by Mrs. P. Thomas: "Charm consists of a pleasant personality combined with understanding, sincerity, tolerance and a gentle manner which puts strangers at ease." Heflin was nominated to go onto a list of people possessing this quality. The list included Winston Churchill, the Duke of Windsor and Laurence Olivier.[2]

Someone who knew Heflin personally, or at least had met him, described him rather differently; he was, she wrote, "Intense, rugged, bad-tempered, very much his own man."[3] Undoubtedly he could appear effortlessly charming on screen; "I swoon every time [he] smiles," one female reviewer recently wrote. He was well-liked and admired by his peers, and even when he played a villain he usually found some sympathetic core.[4] But he also had a quick temper which may have come from his frustration at the perception that his talent and hard work had seemed to count for little in the facile world of Hollywood. David Siff, in his unusual and intriguing memoir, perceptively described the man who might be his father: "I watched the way he moved, his laborious, passionate manner, his clumsiness, his sweetness, his buried frustration and anger, which always seemed to be an inch or so beneath a pleasant exterior."[5]

A driven man, Heflin always sought to be the best in whatever he took on. Witness his constant learning about the art of acting. Not content with his time at Yale, or his years of experience on stage and film, he went back to study his art still further at UCLA when he was in his mid-forties. He set his own standards very high and he was also his own severest critic. If, as he often perceived, he fell short of his own exacting standards, his sense of frustration increased.

He was also a naturally emotional man and was drawn to similarly emotional characters. Jeff Hartnett was an intelligent but deeply flawed individual who relied on drink to support him. He cries so easily that his well of sadness and frustration seems very close to the surface. Heflin seemed to find a direct link to Jeff; he naturally understood him so well because he might almost be describing himself. His Andrew Johnson was a misunderstood man who had a fiery temper that made him his own worst enemy. Heflin often portrayed weak characters with great insight, revealing the pain and torment of those who somehow fail. Wilson was a prototype role, a drunkard who lacks resolve but finally finds redemption. Frank Enley was haunted by his past and destroyed from within; Webb Garwood had a complex criminal mind but was essentially weak. Guerrero was the ultimate failure whose pain was unbearable. But Heflin was equally adept at portraying the essence of stoic decency as Joe Starrett, the honest but sorely tempted Ben Wade, or a string of appealing, bold adventurers. Then again, he could be a comically harassed dad, a brutal soldier of fortune, a charismatic Cossack leader and a laid-back private eye.

From the beginning he was a conflicted personality, a mixture of (as Richard Boleslawski noted) "the college-bred gentleman and two-fisted sailor." Consequently he made a convincingly tough *and* thinking hero. This inner conflict was at the heart of some of his finest characterizations.

An intensely dedicated actor, he put everything into his roles and Heflin the man sometimes disappeared. "I'm absolutely an amoeba," he once remarked, "it's my survival value." He was sensitive, intelligent and impulsive, a uniquely talented actor whose versatility was second to none and who always gave a compelling performance regardless of genre.

The last word goes to the great British actor James Mason, who once cited Heflin as one of the top six actors in America. (Among the others he named Fredric March and Spencer Tracy.) Of Heflin he observed:

> [He] has the directness which is a prerequisite of good screen acting.... Having once acquired the capacity of direct contact, the screen actor finds his range conditioned only by the depth of his feeling and imagination and by his sense of humor. In Heflin's case the range is world-embracing.[6]

Appendix: Film, Stage, Radio and Television Credits

*Available on DVD (Film & TV)

During his first crack at Hollywood in 1936–37, Heflin felt he failed to make headway in one B starring picture after another. He knew hardly anyone in the movie capitol and spent most of his evenings playing cards with a companion who had driven out with him from the east.[1] But he was being noticed and the character of Mickey Borden, the cynical rebel in *Four Daughters* (Warner Brothers, 1938), was apparently written with him in mind. Unfortunately he was unavailable, having by then returned to Broadway. Errol Flynn was given the role but fell ill and it went instead to John Garfield, marking his striking debut; he was nominated for an Oscar as Best Supporting Actor.[2]

Among the other movies for which he was mooted while at MGM in the late 1940s, he was announced as Frontier surgeon Ephraim MacDowell in *Doctors on Horseback*, with Wallace Beery as a bandit.[3] He was considered, along with Robert Taylor, for the lead in *The Judas Kiss*, as "a Confederate soldier dispatched to New Mexico to hold up a gold bullion train intended for Union forces."[4] Neither film was made. He might have played the lead in *Tension* (1948), a good Noir film set in Los Angeles about a man falsely accused of murder; the part went to Richard Basehart.[5] Heflin was intended to be the fight manager in John Sturges' boxing drama, *Right Cross* (1950), but he had left Metro by then and the part went to Dick Powell.[6]

Among other abandoned projects was a starring role in Hugo Fregonese's *7 Rue Pigalle*, which was to have been filmed in Spain in November 1953.[7] Around the same time he showed an interest in Giorgio Capitani's *Orage* in Italy, which he had to decline through too many other commitments; he later appeared in the same director's spaghetti Western *Four Ruthless Men*.[8]

There was speculation at the time that he might co-star with Tyrone Power in *Miss. Sadie Thompson* (1954) as Alfred Davidson but this did not materialize.[9] He was also slated to take the lead role in *Enchanted Island* (1956), based on Herman Melville's seafaring tale, *Typee*. Instead it devolved to an inebriated Dana Andrews, who ensured that the production was anything but enchanted, by all accounts.[10]

Among the many Westerns that came his way, Heflin was considered for the role of Wyatt Earp in *Gunfight at the OK Corral* (1957) and in *Villa Rides* (1968).[11] He was a friend of Sam Peckinpah's and was one of a number of names mentioned for Deke Thornton in *The Wild Bunch* (1969).[12] He was also involved in the genesis of the Peckinpah's *The Ballad of Cable Hogue* (1968). Peckinpah "bought the story from Warren Oates and tried to get together with Van Heflin for $700,000 but couldn't do it."[13] This was shortly after Van's divorce.

As if to emphasize the decline in the later era, he was offered the co-starring role in the aptly-named *Wake Me When It's Over* (1960), a tedious army farce, directed by his old friend Mervyn Le Roy.[14] *Deadline* (1964) was another abandoned project.[15]

In the theater he was offered many leading parts, including that of *The Loud Red Patrick* by John Boruff, a charming Irish comedy based on Ruth McKinney's reminiscences of

191

her grandfather. Unfortunately, 1954 was perhaps his busiest period and he had to turn it down.[16]

On television he was offered the role of a Rabbi in Rod Serling's *In the Presence of Mine Enemies* (1960) for Playhouse 90, which instead went to Charles Laughton in one of his final appearances.[17] Heflin was also one of a score of actors considered for Marshall Matt Dillon in *Gunsmoke*.[18]

Films

A Woman Rebels (RKO, 1936)* Lord Gerald Waring Gaythorne
The Outcasts of Poker Flat (RKO, 1937) The Reverend Sam Woods
Flight from Glory (RKO, 1937) George Wilson
Annapolis Salute (RKO, 1937) Clay V. Parker
Saturday's Heroes (RKO, 1937) Val Webster
Backdoor to Heaven (Vernon Steele Productions, 1939) John Shelley
Santa Fe Trail (Warner Brothers, 1940)* Cadet Rader
The Feminine Touch (MGM, 1941) Elliott Morgan
H. M. Pulham, Esq. (MGM, 1941)* Bill King
Johnny Eager (MGM, 1941)* Jeff Hartnett
Kid Glove Killer (MGM, 1942)* Gordon McKay
Grand Central Murder (MGM, 1942)* "Rocky" Custer
Seven Sweethearts (MGM, 1942)* Henry Taggart
Tennessee Johnson (MGM, 1942) Andrew Johnson
Presenting Lily Mars (MGM, 1943) John Thornway
Land and Live in the Jungle (First Motion Picture Unit USAAF, 1943) Lt. Lyn Harrison
Land and Live in the Desert (First Motion Picture Unit USAAF, 1944) Narrator
The Strange Love of Martha Ivers (Paramount, 1946) Sam Masterson [Entered at second Cannes Film Festival, 1947]
Till the Clouds Roll By (MGM, 1946)* James I. Hessler
Possessed (Warner Bros. 1947)* David Sutton [Entered at the second Cannes Film Festival, 1947]
Green Dolphin Street (MGM, 1947)* Timothy Haslam
The Secret Land (MGM–United States Navy, 1948)* Narrator [Best Documentary Feature, 1949]
B. F.'s Daughter (MGM, 1948)* Thomas W. Brett
Tap Roots (Universal-International, 1948) Keith Alexander
The Three Musketeers (MGM, 1948)* Athos
Act of Violence (MGM, 1948)* Frank R. Enley [Entered at Cannes Film Festival, 1949]
Madame Bovary (MGM, 1949)* Charles Bovary
East Side, West Side (MGM, 1949)* Mark Dwyer
Tomahawk (Universal-International, 1951)* Jim Bridger
The Prowler (United Artists, 1951)* Webb Garwood
Week-end with Father (Universal-International, 1951) Brad Stubbs
My Son, John (Rainbow Productions–Paramount, 1952)* Stedman
Shane (Paramount, 1953)* Joe Starrett [BAFTA Nomination: Best Foreign Actor, 1954]
The Golden Mask (Mayflower Productions, 1953) Nicholas Chapman
Wings of the Hawk (Universal-International, 1953) Irish Gallager
Tanganyika (Universal-International, 1954) John Gale
The Raid (Panoramic Productions–Twentieth Century–Fox, 1954)* Major Neal Benton
Woman's World (Twentieth Century–Fox, 1954)* Jerry Talbot
Black Widow (Twentieth Century–Fox, 1954)* Peter Denver
Battle Cry (Warner Brothers, 1955)* Major Sam 'High Pockets' Huxley
Count Three and Pray (Copa Productions–Columbia, 1955) Luke Fargo
Patterns (Jed Harris-Michael Meyerberg, 1956)* Fred Staples
3:10 to Yuma (Columbia, 1957)* Dan Evans [Nominated: Golden Bear, Top Male Action Star, Berlin, 1958]

Gunman's Walk (Columbia, 1958)* Lee Hackett
Tempest (Dino de Laurentiis, 1958)* Emelyan Pugachov
They Came to Cordura (Columbia, 1959) Sgt. John Chawk
Five Branded Women (Dino de Laurentiis, 1960) Velko
Under Ten Flags (Dino de Laurentiis, 1960) Cpt. Bernhard Rogge
The Wastrel (Lux Films-Tiberia Films, 1961) Duncan Bell
Cry of Battle (Petramonte Productions, 1963) Joe Trent
The Greatest Story Ever Told (United Artists, 1965)* Bar Amand
Once a Thief (CIPRA, 1965)* Inspector Mike Vido SFPD
Stagecoach (Twentieth Century–Fox, 1966)* Marshal Curly Wilcox
The Man Outside (London Independent Films, 1967) Bill Maclean
The Ruthless Four (PCM–Richard Eichberg, 1968) Sam Cooper
The Big Bounce (Warner Brothers-Seven Arts, 1969)* Sam Mirakian
Airport (Universal, 1970)* D. O. Guerrero

Newsreel Appearances

Screen Snapshots No. 43: Hollywood in Uniform (Columbia, 1943); stars in the services
Screen Snapshots: Memories in Uniform (Columbia, 1954); stars reminisce about war
  service.
Duke in Hollywood (British Pathé: Visit of Duke of Edinburgh to Hollywood, 1966); open
  air banquet with many stars; Heflin presents the duke with a Winchester rifle.

Theater

Mr. Moneypenny, satiric drama by Channing Pollack at Liberty Theater, New York, Oct.
  17–Dec. 1928, "Junior" Jones.
Love for Love, restoration comedy by William Congreve; and *Much Ado About Nothing*
  in repertory, ca. 1930 (roles and venues unknown).
A Bill of Divorcement Hilary Fairfield, contemporary drama by Clemence Dane, Playhouse
  Theater, University of Oklahoma, 1931.
Berkeley Square, time travel drama by John L. Balderston, based on *The Sense of the Past*
  by Henry James, Playhouse Theater, University of Oklahoma, Dec. 1931, Peter Standish.
Played in stock at Cohasset Town Hall, Cape Cod, Maine; Community Theater, South
  Carolina, and at Denver, Colorado, ca. 1931–32; took part in a Weekly Revue *Sunday
  Nights at Nine* at the Brabazon-Plaza Hotel, New York, with a troupe of players includ-
  ing Shirley Booth, 1932–34.
The King's Coat, historical drama by Fred Kleibocker at Yale University Theater, Jan. 1933,
  Major Andre.
Played in summer season at Cape Playhouse, Dennis, Massachusetts, 1933.
Birds, drama by Aristophanes, ca. 1933 (role, date and venue unknown).
Sailor Beware, contemporary comedy at Liberty Theater, New York, Sept. 1933, Herb
  Marley lead role understudy.
The Bride of Torozco, historical comedy at Henry Miller's Theater, New York, Sept. 1934,
  Andreas.
The Night Remembers, mystery melodrama by Martha Madison at the Playhouse, New
  York, Nov. 27–Dec. 1934, Paul Ivins.
Beware of the Bull, satiric drama by Robert Hare Powel, ca. 1935, New York (venue
  unknown), Minor role.
Mid-West, western drama by James Hagan at the Booth Theater, New York, Jan. 1936,
  Tooteboy Zinhiser.
End of Summer, satiric comedy by S.N. Behrman at Guild Theater, New York, Feb. 17–Jun.
  1936, Dennis McCarthy.
Western Waters, drama by Richard Carlson at the Hudson Theater, New York, Dec.
  1937–Jan. 1938, Kaintuck.
Races, first role with Group Theater at Philadelphia, ca. Jan. 1938, Unknown role.

Casey Jones, drama by Robert Ardrey at the Fulton Theater, New York, Feb.– Mar. 1938, Jed Sherman.

Ned McCobb's Daughter, drama on tour: County Playhouse, Newark, New Jersey; Sing Sing Prison Theater et al., May–June 1938, Babe Callahan.

The Philadelphia Story, comedy by Philip Barry at the Shubert Theater, New York, March 28, 1939, to March 30, 1940, Macaulay Connor; Tour: (partial list) Forrest Theater, Philadelphia, PA, week of Sept. 30, 1940; Masonic Auditorium, Rochester, NY, Oct. 7–8, 1940; Royal Alexander Theater, Toronto, Canada, week of Oct. 14, 1940; Paramount Theater, Toledo, OH, Oct. 21, 1940; Hanna Theater, Cleveland, OH, Oct. 22–26, 1940; Cass Theater, Detroit, MI, week of Oct. 28, 1940; Shrine Auditorium, Fort Wayne, ID, Nov. 4, 1940; Victory Theater, Dayton, OH, Nov. 5, 1940; Hartman Theater, Columbus, OH, Nov. 6–9, 1940; Virginia Theater, Wheeling, WV, Nov. 11, 1940; Parks Theater, Youngstown, OH, Nov. 12, 1940; Colonial Theater, Akron, OH, Nov. 13, 1940; Taft Auditorium, Cincinnati, OH, Nov. 14–16, 1940; Memorial Auditorium, Louisville, KY, Nov. 18–19, 1940; English Theater, Indianapolis, IN, Nov. 20–21; 24–25, 1940; American Theater, St. Louis, MO, week of Nov. 25, 1940; Pabst Theater, Milwaukee, WI, week of Dec. 2, 1940; Parkway Theater, Madison, WI, Dec. 6, 1940; Municipal Auditorium, St. Paul, MN, Dec. 10–11, 1940; Lyceum Theater, Minneapolis, MN, Dec. 12–14, 1940; Iowa Theater, Sioux City, IA, Dec. 16, 1940; Orpheum Theater, Davenport, IA, Dec. 17, 1940; Shrine Auditorium, Des Moines, IA, Dec. 18, 1940; Orpheum Theater, Sioux City, IA, Dec. 19, 1940; Technical Theater, Omaha, NE, Dec. 20, 1940; Municipal Auditorium, Kansas City, MO, Dec. 21, 27–28, 1940; Forum, Wichita, KS, Dec. 30, 1940; Convention Hall, Tulsa, OK, Dec. 31, 1940; Shrine Theater, Oklahoma City, OK (matinee and evening), Jan. 1, 1941; City Auditorium, Fort Worth, TX, Jan. 2, 1941; Majestic Theater, Dallas, TX(matinee and evening), Jan. 3–4, 1941; Baylor University Auditorium, Waco, TX, Jan. 5, 1941; Paramount Theater, Austin, TX, Jan. 7, 1941; Texas Theater, San Antonio, TX, Jan. 8, 1941; Auditorium, Beaumont, Texas, Jan. 9, 1941; Music Hall, Huston, TX, Jan. 10–11, 1941; City Auditorium, New Orleans, LA (matinee and evening), Jan. 13, 1941; City Auditorium, Jackson, MS, Jan. 14, 1941; Auditorium, Shreveport, LA, Jan. 15, 1941; Auditorium, Little Rock, AR, Jan. 16, 1941; Concert Hall, Memphis, TN, Jan. 17–18, 1941; Memorial Coliseum, Evansville, IN, Jan. 20, 1941; Ryman Auditorium, Nashville, TN, Jan. 21, 1941; Temple Theater, Birmingham, AL, Jan. 22, 1941; City Hall Auditorium, Montgomery, AL (matinee and evening), Jan. 23; tour continued until March.

The Shrike, drama by Joseph Kramm at New Haven, Connecticut; National Theater, Washington, September 1952; and tour from November 1952 to March 1953 Nixon Theater, Pittsburgh, Pennsylvania; Davidson Theater, Milwaukee; Philadelphia, Boston, Chicago et al., Jim Downs.

Eddie Carbone in *A View from the Bridge* and Larry in *A Memory of Two Mondays* (one-act plays), drama by Arthur Miller at the Coronet Theater, New York, Sept. 29, 1955–Feb. 4, 1956: tour.

A Case of Libel, courtroom drama by Henry Denker at Longacre Theater, New York, Oct. 10, 1963–May 9, 1964; tour 1964–65, Robert Sloane.

Radio

Recordings are available on CD compilations and as mp3 downloads from various sites including www.oldtimeradiodownloads, www.radioarcana.com, www.otrcat.com, www.radioechoes.com and www.audio-classics.com.

The Court of Human Relations: My Heart Stood Still, 1934 CBS contemporary crime drama with Elizabeth Wragg [Heflin is sometimes listed in a second episode of the series], lead role.

Way Down East, 1936–37 CBS Drama serial with Agnes Moorehead, David Bartlett.

The Goldbergs, ca. 1936–38 CBS soap opera about a Jewish family in New York, Sammy.

Our Gal Sunday, Western melodrama CBS ca. 1937–39, Slim Delaney.

CBS COLUMBIA WORKSHOP RADIO SERIES

Seven Waves Away, drama by Richard Sale Apr. 2, 1938,* Mr. Holmes.
He Doubles in Pipes, Sept. 22, 1938, biographical drama: "A modern fairy tale ... about the man who invented swing music" with trumpeter Pee Wee Erwin,* Joe Swing.
Mrs. Wiggs of the Cabbage Patch, NBC 1938, supporting role.
Central City, NBC Contemporary drama serial: "An everyday story of the lives of the inhabitants of a typical American industrial city (population 50,000)" Nov. 21, 1938–Jun. 30, 1939, crime reporter Bob Shellenberger.
Meet the Dixons later Bob & Betty, CBS soap opera series of small town life in Minnesota, Jul. 1939-ca. 1943, Bob Dixon.
The Man I Married, CBS Drama serial, 1939, Adam Waring.
Seven Sweethearts, MGM Syndicated Air Trailer, 1942, Henry Taggart.
Cavalcade of America, 1944, unknown role.
Parade aka Great Day, in Arch Oboler's plays Mutual Drama tribute to the Army Air Force on its 38th birthday, Aug. 2, 1945 Jane Morgan,* Lieutenant David.
Prudential Family Hour, 1945, unknown role.
The Philo Vance Summer Program, 1945, unknown role.
The Doctor Fights: Burma Incident, CBS Medical-War drama about Merrill's Marauders, Jul. 17, 1945, Captain Henry G. Stelling.

CBS SCREEN GUILD PLAYERS/LADY ESTHER PRESENTS/ SCREEN GUILD THEATER 1945/50

Smilin' Through Mystery, melodrama Laraine Day, Sir C. Aubrey Smith, Jul. 23, 1945, Kenneth Wayne.
Night Song, mystery melodrama, Dec. 2, 1948, Dan Evans.
The Seventh Veil, mystery melodrama, Dec. 14, 1950, Nicholas.

LUX RADIO THEATER CBS 1946–55

Johnny Eager, Robert Young, Susan Peters, crime drama, Jan. 21, 1946, Jeff Hartnett.
Presenting Lily Mars, June Allyson, romantic drama, Mar. 11, 1946, John Thornway.
Tomorrow is Forever, Claudette Colbert, romantic melodrama, May 6, 1946, John Andrew MacDonald/Erik Kessler.
Vacation from Marriage, Deborah Kerr, Tom Collins Romantic drama, May 26, 1947, Robert Wilson.
Tap Roots, Susan Hayward, romantic adventure, Sept. 22, 1948, Keith Alexander.
Brief Encounter, Greer Garson, romantic drama, Nov. 29, 1948,* Dr. Alec Harvey.
Green Dolphin Street, historical romantic drama, Sept. 19, 1949, Timothy Haslam.
The High Wall, Janet Leigh, mystery drama, Nov. 14, 1949, Steven Kenet.
The Heiress, Louis Calhern, Olivia de Havilland, drama, Sept. 11, 1950,* Morris Townshend.
Once More, My Darling, Ann Blyth, romantic drama, Jan. 1, 1951,* Collier Long.
The Big Trees, Nancy Gates, adventure romance, Nov. 2, 1954, Jim Fallon.
Shane, Alan Ladd, Ruth Hussey, drama, Feb. 22, 1955,* Joe Starrett.
Come Fill the Cup, Mona Freeman, romantic drama, Apr.1955, Lew Marsh.
Suspense, CBS mystery drama serie,s 1947–59.
Three Blind Mice, Jan. 30, 1947,* Arthur Lockwood.
Wild Oranges, Dec. 1, 1947,* John Woolfolk.
Song of the Heart, Aug. 26, 1948,* Neil Wilson.
Three O'Clock, Mar. 19, 1949,* Paul.
The Murder of Aunt Delia, Nov. 10, 1949,* Dort Sharples.
The Thirteenth Apostle aka *The Lady in the Red Hat*, Nov. 30, 1950,* Mitchell.
The Mystery of the Marie Celeste, by Gil Dowd, Jun. 8, 1953,* Sam Newcombe.
The Shot, by Alexander Pushkin, Oct. 12, 1953,* Lieutenant Zachary Payton.

The Last Days of John Dillinger, May 10, 1954,* John Dillinger.
Narrator of A Long Life and a Merry One, CBS Medical documentary, Apr. 4, 1947.
The Adventures of Philip Marlowe, by Raymond Chandler NBC Series, Jun.–Sept. 1947,
   Philip Marlowe.
Who Shot Waldo?, Jun. 10, 1947.*
Red Wind, Jun. 17, 1947.*
Pit 13 or *Trouble is My Business*, Jun. 24, 1947.*
Daring Young Dame on the Flying Trapeze, Jul. 1, 1947.
King n' Yellow, Jul. 8, 1947.*
The Sandman, Jul. 15, 1947.
Gold Fish, Jul. 22, 1947.
Trouble in High Places, Aug. 5, 1947 [Six episodes, titles unknown, Aug. 12–Sept. 17, 1947].
The Bob Hope Show, NBC Variety Discussing *The Adventures of Philip Marlowe* Jun. 3,
   1947, & Sept. 16, 1947, Guest.
It Started with Eve, CBS Hollywood Star Time Comedy drama with Audrey Totter, Mar.
   1, 1947, Johnny Reynolds.
Hollywood Fights Back, ABC Live Broadcast Hollywood stars protesting the HUAC
   (House Un-American Committee) Washington, D.C., Oct. 26, 1947, Himself.
Towards the Horizon, NBC drama about an early explorer of the Colorado River and the
   Grand Canyon, Dec. 12, 1947,* John Wesley Powell.

Mutual Family Theater

I Give You Maggie, romantic family drama, Mar. 4, 1947, Tom Paget.
The Problem Child Problem, romantic family drama, Jun. 26, 1952, Alan Towney.
The Man Who Conquered Devil's Island, CBS Mystery Drama Radio, *Reader's Digest*,
   Apr. 3, 1947,* Charles Payon.
The Strange Love of Martha Ivers, CBS This Is Hollywood, drama presented by Hedda
   Hopper; co-starring Ida Lupino, Apr. 12, 1947, Sam Masterson.
Why Keep Your Heart in Cold Storage?, CBS Thanksgiving drama, Hallmark Cards, Nov.
   1947,* lead role.
Let Truth Be Known, Advertising Council documentary "The power of free information"
   Dec. 10, 1947, unnamed role.
Madame Bovary, CBS Ford Theater drama, Sept. 1948, with Marlene Dietrich, Claude
   Rains, Rodolphe Boulanger.
Martin Arrowsmith in Arrowsmith, NBC Drama University Theater, Nov. 7, 1948.*
A Day to Remember, NBC Drama for the *United Jewish Appeal*, Oct. 16, 1948, unknown
   role.
Van Heflin Presents Conrad Janis, NBC Anacin Hollywood Star Theater, drama, Nov. 20,
   1948, Himself.
The Story of Tommy Hoxie, Seals Syndicated Christmas Charity Appeal, Dec. 1948, Him-
   self.
The Sealtest Variety Theater, NBC Variety Show Mar. 17, 1949, Guest.

NBC U.S. Steel's Theater Guild of the Air

Ladies and Gentlemen, courtroom drama with Ida Lupino, May 1949, Philip Merivale
   jury foreman.
The Thunderbolt, drama with Celeste Holm, Oct. 23, 1949, unspecified role.
State Fair, romantic drama with Gene Lockhart, June Lockhart, Dec. 31, 1951, Pat Gilbert.
Over 21, romantic comedy with Ruth Gordon, May 18, 1952, Max W. Wharton.
George Washington Slept Here, romantic comedy drama, Ann Rutherford, Sept. 21, 1952,
   Bill Fuller.

CBS Hallmark Playhouse 1949–53/ Hallmark Hall of Fame 1953–55

So Well Remembered, melodrama by James Hilton, Sept. 22, 1949, George Boswell.
The Story of Tom Edison, biographical drama, Sept. 7, 1950, Tom Edison.
Valley Forge, historical drama by Maxwell Anderson, Feb. 22, 1951, General George Washington.
John Adams & the American Revolution, historical drama, Oct. 25, 1951, John Adams.
Forward the Nation, historical drama, May 29, 1952, Captain Merriweather Lewis.
The Pathfinder, novel dramatization, Sept. 14, 1952, John Charles Fremont.
The New Star, historical Navy drama, Apr. 11, 1954, Captain Thomas Catesby Jones.
The Story of Damon Runyon, biographical drama, May 16, 1954, Damon Runyon.

CBS Hollywood Star Playhouse/ NBC Baker's Theater of Stars

The Cave, mystery drama Jul. 31, 1950, Steve.
Final Entry, drama Jun. 22, 1952, lead role.
Document A/777, CBS Human rights drama-documentary broadcast on Radio Malaya (Singapore) & elsewhere, Aug. 1950, Narrator.
The Miracle of America, CBS Patriotic drama starring William Bendix, Aug. 23, 1950, unknown role.
The Hedda Hopper Show, CBS, Nov. 4, 1950, Guest.
The Charlie McCarthy Show, CBS Comedy, Nov. 12, 1950, Guest.
March of Dimes, NBC Charity appeal by Hollywood stars on behalf of the National Foundation for Infantile Paralysis, Jan. 1951, Himself.
Stars on Parade, Army & Air Force Syndication Story of a blind writer on a flying mission, Jan. 26, 1951, unnamed role.
The Hard Core, NBC United Nations Project, Oct. 16, 1949, Narrator.
Coming Attractions, United Nations Radio Syndication, 1951, unspecified role.
Turning Points (CBS 1949); *Academy Award* (CBS 1950) *Hear it Now* (CBS 1951) *The Big Show* (NBC 1951) *Anthology* (NBC 1954) *and Biography in Sound* (NBC 1955), unspecified roles.
Welcome Travelers, NBC Current Affairs/Documentary, Jan. 29, 1951, Guest.
A Man Called X Episode 33: A Man, A Girl and a Plot, mystery drama NBC, May 25, 1951; substituting for Herbert Marshall who was recovering from surgery, Jim Kendall.
Saturday at the Chase, CBS Variety, Feb. 14, 1953, Guest.
The Apple Tree, Literary drama by John Galsworthy CBS Theater of Stars, May 17, 1953, Frank Ashurst.
Blind Alley, Drama NBC Philip Morris Playhouse, Sept. 2, 1953, Hal Willis.
The Last Boat, Treasury Department Syndication "A story about liberty at the Statue of Liberty," Jul. 4, 1954, Treasury Agent.
Monitor NBC Current Affairs; with Arthur Miller, August 28, 1955; with James Stewart Oct. 16, 1955, Guest.
The Mitch Miller Show, CBS Variety, interviewed with other stars of *Tempest*, Mar. 22, 1959, Guest.
House Party, CBS Current Affairs, interviewed by host Art Linklater from West Berlin Jul. 20, 1959, Guest.

Other Appearances (Role and dates unknown)

Aunt Jenny's Real Life Stories, CBS Romance Serial Drama [Ran from 1937–56].
Big Sister, CBS Serial Drama Romance (with sister Frances) [Ran from 1936–52].

Easy Aces, CBS Sitcom [Ran from 1930–47].
Myrt & Marge, CBS/Mutual Serial Drama Romance [Ran from 1931–46].
Norman Corwin's Plays [Corwin was a prolific radio playwright and joined CBS in 1938].
True Story Hour with Mary & Bob, NBC Blue Network Drama Romance ca. 1939.

Television

ACTOR

The Double-Dyed Deceiver by O. Henry Nash (Western) Airflyte CBS, Sept. 21, 1950, The Llano Kid.
Arrowsmith by Sinclair Lewis (Melodrama) The Robert Montgomery Presents NBC, Oct. 9, 1950, Dr. Martin Arrowsmith.
Jim Downs in a scene from *The Shrike* with Isabel Bonner as Ann Downs on *Toast of the Town,* Jul. 26, 1953.
The Other Side of the Earth, drama by Rod Serling Playhouse 90 CBS, Sept. 19, 1957, Colonel Stern.
The Rank and File, drama by Rod Serling Playhouse 90 CBS, May 28, 1959, Bill Kilcoyne.
The Cruel Day, drama by Reginald Rose Playhouse 90 CBS, Feb. 24, 1960, Captain.
Ricochet, drama by Adrian Spies The Dick Powell Theater NBC, 1961, Sgt. Paul Maxon.
A Case of Libel, drama by Henry Denker ABC, Feb. 11, 1968, Robert Scone.
Fear is the Chain, drama by Eric Bercovici for The Danny Thomas Theater Hour NBC, Feb. 19, 1968, Kreutzer.
Certain Honorable Men, Drama by Rod Serling NBC, Sept. 12, 1968, Champ Donohue.
Neither Are We Enemies, Period drama by Henry Denker Hallmark Hall of Fame, Mar. 13, 1970, Joseph of Arimathea.
The Last Child, Sci-Fi drama by Peter S. Fischer ABC, Oct. 5, 1971 [Nominated Emmy Best Made for Television Movie Award 1971] (Aired posthumously), Senator Quincy George.*

NARRATOR

U.S. #1 American Profile: U.S. Route 1 Highway: Fort Kent, Maine to Key West, FL, NBC Documentary/Travelogue, Mar. 29, 1962.
The Great Adventure, CBS historical drama-documentary, 1963–64 (13 Episodes).
The Hunley, Sept. 27, 1963.
The Death of Sitting Bull, Oct. 4, 1963.
The Massacre at Wounded Knee, Oct. 11, 1963.
Six Wagons to the Sea, Oct. 18, 1963.
The Story of Nathan Hale, Oct. 25, 1963.
Go Down, Moses, Nov. 1, 1963.
The Great Diamond Mountain, Nov. 8, 1963.
The Treasure Train of Jefferson Davis, Nov. 15, 1963.
The Outlaw and the Nun, Dec. 1, 1963.
The Man Who Stole New York City, Dec. 13, 1963.
A Boy at War, Dec. 20, 1963.
Wild Bill Hickock: The Legend and the Man, Jan. 3, 1964.
The Colonel from Connecticut, Jan. 10, 1964.
The Way Out Men, documentary ABC, 1965.
The Bold Men, documentary NBC, Feb. 3, 1965.
The General, historical documentary ABC, Mar. 16, 1965.
The Teenage Revolution, documentary ABC, Oct. 19, 1965.
Pro Football: Maybe on a Sunday, sports documentary ABC, Nov. 15, 1965.
In Search of Man, documentary ABC, Dec. 13, 1965.
Revolution in the Three R's, documentary ABC, Apr. 14, 1966.
The Thin Blue Line, documentary ABC, Sept. 3, 1966.
The American Spectacle, natural history documentary NBC News, 1966.

Miscellaneous Appearances as Himself

Guest *The Ken Murray Show* NBC Variety Show, Oct. 14, 1950.
The Ed Sullivan Show CBS, Jul. 28, 1953; Mar. 8, 1959; As Robert Sloane in a scene from *A Case of Libel*, January 26, 1964,* Guest.
A Star is Born World Premiere, NBC, Sept. 29, 1954, Guest.
Lux Video Theater: Meet Jo Cathcart, 1954, Guest host.
What's My Line?, CBS, Oct. 23, 1955, Second mystery guest; Panelist, Jan. 18, 1959, Guest; Jan. 19, 1964, Mystery guest.
This is Your Life, NBC/Ralph Edwards, May 25, 1955,* Subject.
The Death of Manolette, CBS Playhouse 90, drama, Sept. 12, 1957, Guest host.
Italian television RAI singing *On the Old Chisholm Trail* and presented with an award, ca. 1959, Guest.
Writing Awards 31st Annual Academy Awards Ceremony, NBC, Apr. 6, 1959, Presenter; *Short Subjects Award 35th Annual Academy Awards*, ABC, Apr. 8, 1963, Presenter.
Here's Hollywood, with Peter Fonda NBC, documentary, Dec. 3, 1962, Guest.
The 17th Annual Tony Awards, CBS, Apr. 28, 1963, Presenter.
Hollywood without Make-Up Filmaster Incorporated/MGM 1963,* Guest.
NBC News Special Report: The Assassination of President John F. Kennedy Presented by Studs Terkel; classical music and readings; a wide-shot of the Whitehouse; Heflin off camera reads Walt Whitman's tribute to Lincoln, *O Captain! My Captain!* NBC Nov. 25, 1963, Guest narrator.
The Bell Telephone Show NBC/Henry Jaffe Productions, variety, May 5, 1964, Host.
Hollywood My Home Town Documentary inside look at homes of the stars Filmaster/TCM 1965,* Guest.
The Best Foreign Film Award at the *22nd Annual Golden Globe Awards* CBS, Feb. 8, 1965, Presenter.
Moon Landings Coverage NBC, Jul. 20, 1969, Guest speaker.
Melbourne Tonight Channel 9 Australian Talk Show/Entertainment, Apr. 16, 1970, Promoting *Airport*, Guest.
The World of Sport Fishing ABC, 1972, stars who are fishermen. Aired posthumously; Heflin footage shot in 1968, Guest.

Articles

Oklahoma is Movies' Latest Favorite: Van Heflin Tells Own Story of Adventures at Sea & on the Stage Syndicated newspaper article *The Milwaukee Journal* Aug. 22, 1942, Sailor.
Van Heflin Talks About Philip Marlowe Ottawa Citizen, Aug. 2, 1947, Actor.
Scroll National Magazine of Phi Delt Fraternity, Oklahoma University, Jan. 1948, Lead article.
Theater Arts Magazine, Oct. 1950, Article about film acting.
Heflin for Stagecoach: Remaking of Old Picture Problem, interview with Dan Alpert *Los Angeles Times* Syndicated, Oct. 23, 1965, in which he discusses the art of film acting and directing.

Chapter Notes

Preface

1. Tribute #11799 added August 16, 2000; www.findagrave.com/cgi-bin/fg.cgi ?page=gr&Grid=11799. Tribute #11799.
2. "Barrymore Backs Heflin," *The Deseret News*, March 30, 1943, 5.
3. www.searchquotes.com/search/ Van_Heflin/.
4. Mike McCrann, www.gay.net/vintag e-hunk/2011/10/24/vintage-hunk/van-heflin.
5. Hedda Hopper, "In Hollywood: All This and Heflin Too," *Miami News*, September 15, 1946, 9D.
6. Sheilah Graham, "In Hollywood," caption under picture, *Ottawa Citizen: Evening Citizen*, January 15, 1949, Section 3, p. 3.
7. Dorothy Manners, 'Snappy Shots," Chicago *Sunday* newspaper supplement, c. 1950 (from undated archive of clippings).

Chapter One

1. www.imdb.com/name/nm0001336/ bio?ref_=nm_ov_bio_sm.
2. familysearch.org/U.S. Social Security Records.
3. U.S. Census (1900), Ardmore (West and North Part), Ward 1–2, Chickasaw Nation, Indian Territory: Aron E. Adams; Salie Adams; Joyce Adams; Emerson Adams; Emmett Heflin.
4. *The War of the Rebellion: A Compilation of the Official Records of the Union and Confederate Armies*, www.ehistory. osu.edu/uscw/.
5. U.S. Census (1900).
6. familysearch.org/ (birth, death, mar- riage indexes; census returns 1890–1940, war service records and social security records).
7. Robert Francis, "Candid Close-Ups: Van Heflin—One of the Answers to Why "Philadelphia Story," Runs On and On at the Shubert," *The Brooklyn Eagle*, February 4, 1940, 30.
8. Louella Parsons, "Louella O. Parsons in Hollywood," *The Milwaukee Sentinel*, April 5, 1942, 20.
9. "Movie Star Comes Home to Reminisce," *The Daily Oklahoman*, October 10, 1949.
10. Mary Kay Leslie quoted by Robert E. Lee, "Van Heflin Held Her Down," *The Oklahoman*, February 24, 1986. newsok. com/van-held-her-down/article2138903.
11. Leonard Lyons "The Lyons Den," *Pittsburgh Post-Gazette*, January 11, 1950, 23.
12. U.S. Census (1900).
13. Sylvia Katz, "That 'Van' Is Here Again," *Modern Screen*, November 1942, 14.
14. "Sailor from Oklahoma is Movies' Latest Favorite," *Milwaukee Journal: Green Sheet Journal*, August 22, 1942, 1–2.
15. *Ibid.*
16. David Siff, *Eleanor's Rebellion* (New York: Alfred A. Knopf, 2000), 189.
17. Van Heflin, "Twenty Five Words Or Less," *Modern Screen*, October 1955, 939.
18. Diane Scott, "Voyager," *Photoplay*, January 1947, 59, 68–9.
19. *Ibid.*
20. "Maritime Timetable Images," (collected by Bjorn Larsson). www.timetable images.com/maritime/.
21. *Ibid.*

22. "Sailor from Oklahoma is Movies' Latest Favorite," *Milwaukee Journal: Green Sheet Journal*, August 22, 1942, 1.
23. Katz, "That 'Van' Is Here Again."
24. "From College to Stage Career," XIX Van Heflin by Martha Leavitt *New York Herald Tribune*, c. 1936 (Archive of clippings, by kind permission, Melven Cornish Collection, Box 5, Folder 2, Western History Collections, University of Oklahoma Libraries, Norman, Oklahoma).
25. Robert Perkins, "Young Man With A Future," *Screenland*, March 1951, 42–3, 72.
26. "Heflin Turns Author," *Milwaukee Sentinel*, 47, January 11, 1948.
27. "'Van Was No Angel,' Says Van Heflin's Former OU Drama Coach," Conley Higdon Interview, *The Oklahoman*, April 19, 1947.
28. *Ibid.*
29. Lyons, "The Lyons Den."
30. Jack Kofoed Interview, *Miami News*, May 30, 1943; Katz, "That 'Van' Is Here Again."
31. Lyons, "The Lyons Den."
32. Kofoed Interview; Katz, "That 'Van' Is Here Again."
33. Jordan R. Young, *Reel Characters* (Moonstone Press, 1986), 139–140.
34. William Grange, "Channing Pollock: The American Theatre's Forgotten Polemicist," *Zeitschrift fur Anglistik und Amerikanistik*, vol. 35, no. 2, 158–63.
35. "Mr. Moneypenny," *Variety*, October 24, 1928.
36. Grange, "Channing Pollock."
37. http://immortalephemera.com/21538/august-6-van-heflin-tcm-summer-under-the-stars/.
38. Lyons, "The Lyons Den."
39. John Keating, "Heflin at the Bar," *New York Times*, January 19, 1964.
40. *Ibid.*
41. Siff, *Eleanor's Rebellion.*

Chapter Two

1. Hal Boyle, "Van Heflin is One Actor Who Has No Ambition to be Producer or Director," *Ocala Star-Banner*, January 20, 1959, 12.
2. Diane Scott, "Voyager," *Photoplay*, January 1947, 59, 68–9; Melven Cornish Collection, Box 5, Folder 2, Western History Collections, University of Oklahoma Libraries, Norman, Oklahoma.

3. "Film Star Finds Business, Acting, Don't Always Mix," Hedda Hopper, *The Spokesman-Review*, August 15, 1954, 45.
4. *Ibid.*
5. "TV Talk," *Modern Screen*, February 1956, 6.
6. "'Van Was No Angel' Says Former OU Drama Coach," Conley Higdon interview, *The Oklahoman*, April 19, 1947.
7. *Ibid.*
8. Yale Dramatic School Archives: Letter from archivist Suzanne Noruschat, outlining the records she consulted, July 8, 2014, Manuscripts and Archives, Yale University Library.
9. "Who Doesn't Like Acting?" *The World's News*, Sydney, NSW, August 29, 1942, 16.
10. Hedda Hopper, "Jennifer's Duel Stirs Up Fury," *Miami News*, March 2, 1947.
11. William Lyon Phelps, "Drama Department to Give Single Performance Tonight," *The Yale Times* January 11, 1933.
12. "Who Doesn't Like Acting?" *The World's News.*
13. "From College to Stage Career," XIX Van Heflin, Martha Leavitt, *New York Herald Tribune*, c. 1936 (Melven Cornish Collection, Box 5, Folder 2, Western History Collections, University of Oklahoma, Norman, Oklahoma.).
14. Boyle, "Van Heflin is One Actor..."
15. "Who Doesn't Like Acting?" *The World's News.*
16. Marriage Certificate No 16549, July 20, 1934: Emmett Evan Heflin/White/60 W8 Ave/25/Actor/Oklahoma/Father: Dr. Emmett E./Mother: Fanny B. Shippey/Bride: Esther Scherr/White/60 W8 Ave/21 b May 22, 1913/Actress/Bronx, NY/Father: Adolf/Country of Birth: Austria/Mother: Jean Ausch/Austria: "There will be no dirty glances if Van Heflin runs into visiting 'ex,' Mrs. Eleanor Heflin. They parted friends...," *Modern Screen*, December 1942, 63. (*Screenland*, June 1943, 13, refers to Heflin's first wife as Eleanor Shaw "a Broadway actress," who was by then married to attorney George E. Shibley.)
17. U.S. Census; *Modern Screen*, December 1942.
18. U.S. Census; *Modern Screen*, December 1942.
19. "Heflin Gave Away Oils of Ex-Wife," Frances Heflin to Leonard Lyons, *Toledo Blade*, August 16, 1969, 11.

20. David Siff, *Eleanor's Rebellion* (New York: Alfred A. Knopf, 2000), 211–212.

21. "Jean Arthur at the Westport Country Playhouse," January 11, 2011, posted by Jacqueline T. Lynch, newenglandtravels. blogspot.co.uk/2011/01/jean-arthur-at-westport-country.html.

22. "Bride of Torozco," review, *Jewish Telegraphy Agency*, September 17, 1934.

23. John Keating, "Heflin at the Bar," *New York Times*, January 16, 1964; Margaret McManus "TV Studies A Highway," *The Milwaukee Journal*, 24, March 25, 1962.

24. }"From College to Stage Career," *New York Herald Tribune*.

25. Amnon Kabatchik, *Blood on the Stage, 1925–50: Milestone Plays of Crime, Mystery and Detection* (Scarecrow Press, 2009), 260.

26. Louis Botto, *At This Theater: 100 Years of Broadway Shows and Stars* (New York: Applause Books, 2002), 18.

27. "End of Summer," *Variety*, February 5, 1936, 56; "Casey Jones," *Variety*, February 23, 1938, 58, and March 7, 1938.

28. *End of Summer* review: snbehr man.com/bibliography/36summerran-dom.htm.

29. George Tucker "Man About Manhattan," *Prescott Evening Courier*, February 17, 17, 1938, 7.

30. Sylvia Katz "That 'Van,' is Here Again," *Modern Screen*, November 1942, 14–15.

31. Mark Barron, "Theme is Good But Unreality Spoils Action," *St. Petersburg Times*, January 2, 1938, 10.

32. Robert Perkins "Young Man with a Future," *Screenland*, March, 1951, 72.

33. Dorothy Kilgallen, "Kilgallen Brings the Gossip About Gothamites," *Miami News*, January 21, 1940, 73.

34. Internet Broadway Database https://www.ibdb.com/Production/View/10447.

35. Mark Barron, "Theme is Good But Unreality Spoils Action," *St. Petersburg Times*, January 2, 1938, 10.

36. Bill Snow interviewed by Brooksie Bergen, "All the World Was a Stage for Talented Bill Snow," *Sarasota Journal*, February 8, 1995, 32.

37. "Heflin: From Seaman to 'Oscar,' Prize Play," *Yale Daily News*, October 14, 1952, 1.

38. "Heflin; From Seaman to 'Oscar' Prize Play," *Yale Daily News*, October 18, 1952, 1.

39. Gloria Vanderbilt, & Thelma, Lady Furness, *Double Exposure: A Twin Autobiography* (David McKay, 1958), 79.

40. Gloria Vanderbilt & Thelma, Lady Furness, *Double Exposure: A Twin Autobiography* (David McKay, 1958), 79.

41. James Robert Parrish and Ronald L. Bowers, *The MGM Stock Company: The Golden Era* (London: Ian Allan Ltd, 1973), 332.

42. *Ibid.*

43. *Ibid.*

44. Tour Itinerary in Melven Cornish Collection, Box 5, Folder 2, Western History Collection, University of Oklahoma Libraries, Norman, Oklahoma.

45. *Miami News*, January 21, 1940.

46. Katz: "That Van is Here Again."

47. *Los Angeles Times*, "Van Heflin All out for Cinema."

48. Jerry Riley, "Awakened at Thirty," *Hollywood*, August, 1942, 50.

49. Middleton, "Van Heflin Was First Choice for Shrike."

50. Bob Thomas interview, February 1, 1950, Western History Center, Van Heflin Archive.

51. "Van Heflin Now All-Out For Cinema," *Los Angeles Times*.

52. Katz, "That 'Van' Is Here Again,"

53. Middleton, "Van Heflin Was First Choice For 'The Shrike.'"

Chapter Three

1. Louella Parsons, "Louella O. Parsons In Hollywood," *The Milwaukee Sentinel*, April 5, 1942, 10.

2. "Heflin Crashes Party, Sets Course For Life," *The Miami News*, 1-E, May 30, 1943.

3. Richard B. Jewel, and Vernon Harbin, *The RKO Story* (London: Octopus Books, 1983), 10.

4. "Heflin Crashes Party," *The Miami News*.

5. Jewel and Harbin, *The RKO Story*.

6. Hedda Hopper, "Film Star Finds Business, Acting Don't Always Mix," *The Spokesman Review*, August 15, 1954, 15.

7. "Purely Personal," *Motion Picture Daily*, October 24, 1936, 1; Herb Fagen, *The Encyclopedia of Westerns* (New York: Facts on File, 2001), 103.

8. Jewel and Harbin, *The RKO Story*.

9. "Purely Personal," *Motion Picture Daily*.

10. "Film Parade: 'Outcasts of Poker Flat,'" *Variety*, March 12, 1937, 51.

11. "Entertainments: Plaza Theatre," *New Zealand Herald*, November 20, 1937, 21.

12. "Amusements: Plaza Theatre," *Auckland Star*, November 17, 1937, 13.

13. "King George and Prince Edward Theatres," *Hutt News* (Wellington, New Zealand), January 26, 1938, 1.

14. "Amusements: Plaza Theatre," *Auckland Star*.

15. "Annapolis Salute at Studio," *Prescott Evening Courier*, November 25, 1937, 4.

16. *Ibid.*

17. Jewel and Harbin, *The RKO Story*.

18. J. C. Jenkins, "Private Views in Movie World," *The Australian Women's Weekly*, January 22, 1938, 6; *Motion Picture Herald*, December 4, 1937, 89.

19. J. C. Jenkins, "Private Views in Movie World"; *Motion Picture Herald*, December 4, 1937.

20. J. C. Jenkins, "Private Views in Movie World"; *Motion Picture Herald*, December 4, 1937.

21. "Theaters," *Victoria Advocate* (Texas), October 21, 1937, 1; "Saturday's Heroes," *Motion Picture Herald*, 57, February 26, 1938.

22. "Theaters," *Victoria Advocate*.

23. "Louella O. Parsons In Hollywood," *The Milwaukee Sentinel*.

24. "Head Football Film," *The Tumut and Adelong Times* (New South Wales), August 9, 1938, 1.

25. "Entertainments: Roxy and Tivoli Theatres," *New Zealand Herald*, 11, March 16, 1938.

26. "Young Man With A Future," Robert Perkins interview. *Screenland*, March 1951, 43.

27. Clive Hirschorn, *The Warner Brothers Story* (London: Octopus Books, 1979), 218.

28. "Brown Descendant Sues Over Santa Fe Trail Movie," January 16, 2010; johnbrownkin.blogspot.co.uk/2010/01/brown-descendant-sues-over-santa-fe.html.

29. "Laughs at Dictators: Wolfe Kaufman's Film Cable From Hollywood," *Sunday Times* (Perth, Western Australia), November 10, 1940, 45; Sylvia Katz "That 'Van,' is Here Again," *Modern Screen*, November 1942, 14–15.

30. "Hepburn 'Saved,' Van Heflin From Angry Texas 'Giants,'" James Bacon Interview, *Reading Eagle*, 50, December 14, 1958.

31. Hugh Dixon "Hollywood: Around the Town," *Pittsburgh Post-Gazette*, 25, March 27, 1942.

32. Hedda Hopper, "Film Star Finds Business, Acting Don't Always Mix," *Spokesman-Review*, 15, August 15, 1954.

33. "Laughs at Dictators," *Sunday Times*; Katz "That 'Van,' is Here Again."

34. Erskine Johnson, "Hollywood Today," *San Jose News*, May 31, 1941, 20.

35. Jack Kofoed, "The Night Watch: Feminine Touch is Sparkling," *The Miami Daily News*, November 19, 1941, 16.

36. "Rialto Theater," *The Daily Times*, November 4, 1941, 3.

37. "New Films in London: A Crowded Week: Warner," *The Times*, November 17, 1941, 8.

38. "Reviewing the Screen—F. J," *The Milwaukee Journal*, October 19, 1941, 23.

39. "Screen and Stage: At the Drummond," *The Drummondville Spokesman*, December 31, 1942, 2.

40. Alex Barris, *Hollywood's Other Men* (South Brunswick, NJ: A. S. Bares, 1972), 78, 80.

41. John Douglas Eames, *The MGM Story* (Octopus Books, 1979) 174.

42. "Louella O. Parsons in Hollywood," *The Milwaukee Sentinel*.

43. "Thomas Mitchell Leaves Sick List For Priest's Role," *Brooklyn Daily Eagle*, November 20, 1941, 9.

44. Kirk Douglas, *The Ragman's Son* (New York: Simon & Schuster, 1988), 135.

Chapter Four

1. Louella Parsons, "Louella O. Parsons in Hollywood," *The Milwaukee Sentinel*, April 5, 1942, 20.

2. Tony D'Ambra, *"Johnny Eager* (1941): 'Just another hood I guess,'" October 1, 2012, http://filmsnoir.net/film_noir/johnny-eager-1941-just-another-hood-i-guess.html/.

3. "Mr. 'Ideal Actor,' Has No Secret," *Singapore Free Press*, February 28, 1956, 17.

4. "Louella O. Parsons in Hollywood," *The Milwaukee Sentinel*.

5. *Spokane Daily Chronicle*, June 1, 1949.

6. "Hollywood Reports," *Werribee Shire Banner* (Victoria, Australia), June 3, 1948, 3.

7. "Mr. 'Ideal Actor,' Has No Secret," *Singapore Free Press*.

8. "Barrymore Backs Heflin," *The Deseret News*, March 30, 1943, 5.

9. "Short Role Can Be Big," *The Milwaukee Journal*, April 18, 1943, 77.

10. "Van Heflin In Series," *Motion Picture Herald*, April 25, 1942, 42; "Theater Gossip," *The Evening Independent*, May 19, 1942, 6.

11. *Ibid.*

12. Marsha Hunt 3-part interview, San Francisco, October 23, 2013, www.youtube.com/watch?v=97t7i03RAgE.

13. "State Film Not One of Best: 'Grand Central Murder,' Second Feature, Rates at One of Better 'Whodunits,'" *Schenectady Gazette*, June 27, 1942, 4.

14. "Theater Gossip," *The Evening Independent*, March 11, 1942, 8.

15. "Mystery Film at 3 Theaters Is Diverting," *The Miami News*, May 14, 1942, 5C.

16. "Heflin Plays Leading Role," *The Miami News*, May 10, 1942, 9-A.

17. Peggy Simmonds, "A Picture Review: 'Seven Sweethearts,' at Sheridan, Paramount, and Beach," *The Miami News*, September 25, 1942, 15.

18. *Ibid.*

19. "Louella O. Parsons in Hollywood," *The Milwaukee Sentinel*.

20. John Douglas Eames, *The MGM Story* (London: Octopus Books, 1979), 182.

21. "'Tennessee Johnson,' Revives Old Controversies," *Miami News*, February 1, 1943, 10-C.

22. Harold V. Cohen, "The New Film: Van Heflin Plays Andrew Johnson at The Stanley," *Pittsburgh Post-Gazette*, March 13, 1943, 7.

23. "'Tennessee Johnson,' Revives Old Controversies," *Miami News*.

24. "'Tennessee Johnson,' at the Astor," *New York Times*, January 13, 1943.

25. "Barrymore Backs Heflin," *The Deseret News*, March 30, 1943, 5.

26. "Tennessee Johnson,' Revives Old Controversies," *Miami News*.

27. Harold V. Cohen, "The New Film: 'Presenting Lily Mars,' at the Stanley with Judy Garland," *Pittsburgh Post-Gazette*, June 19, 1943, 20.

28. "'Presenting Lily Mars,' Is At Proctors," *Schenectady Gazette*, June 24, 1943, 13.

29. "'Seven Sweethearts,' Features Screen's Prettiest Starlets," *Winthrop News*, August 12, 1943, 5.

30. *Ibid.*

31. "Film Review 'Presenting Lily Mars' (1943) by Runell," August 6, 2012. theshadesofblackandwhite.co.uk/2012_08_01_archive.html.

32. Erskine Johnson, "Hollywood Today: Kim Novak Wins Complete Victory in Columbia Strike," *Times Daily*, October 20, 1957, 1.

33. Diane Scott, "Voyager," *Photoplay*, January 1947, 58, 68–9; Maude Cheatham "Romance Comes To Van Heflin," *Screenland*, August 1942, 51, 77–78.

34. "Romance Note," *The Mail*, (Adelaide, South Australia) August 1, 1942, 9.

35. Bob Thomas "Hollywood Highlights," *Spokane Daily Chronicle*, June 1, 1949, 24.

36. Louella O. Parsons "In Hollywood," *The Milwaukee Sentinel*, April 5, 1942, 20; Louella O. Parsons, "Mimi Chandler Will Play Lead In Aldrich Films," *St Petersburg Times*, December 2, 1942, 15.

37. Carl Schroeder, "Van Heflin, That Is," *Modern Screen*, June 1947, 40, 72–4.

38. Dorothy Kilgallen, "Voice of Broadway," *Toledo Blade*, August 16, 1945, 10.

39. Dorothy Manners "Snappy Shots," *Chicago Newspaper Sunday Magazine Supplement* c1950 (From archive of undated press clippings).

40. Howard Heffernan quoted in letter to Frances "Conrad Nagel, First Star of Sound Pictures, Back Again In Hollywood," *Ottawa Citizen*, August 4, 1944, 3.

41. Edwin Schallert, *Dragon Seed*, "Drama," *Los Angeles Times*, May 6, 1942, 9.

42. *Men At Sea*, "Notes From Hollywood," *Motion Picture Daily*, February 25, 1942, 8; *Big-Hearted Maisie* Louella O. Parsons, "Warner's Daughter Gets Part," *The Deseret News*, May 29, 1942, 6.

43. "Exhibitors Elect The Stars Of Tomorrow," *Motion Picture Herald*, 12, August 29, 1942.

Chapter Five

1. Sylvia Katz, "That 'Van,' is Here Again," *Modern Screen*, 14–15, November

1942; Frank Buxton, and Bill Owen, *The Big Broadcast 1920–1950* (London: Scarecrow Press, 1977), 149.

2. "Ex-Convict Story," *Pittsburgh Post-Gazette*, November 25, 1937, 13.

3. Mark Barron, "Youthful Leading Men Find Breaks," *Prescott Evening Courier*, August 26, 1939, 8.

4. "Purely Personal," *Motion Picture Daily*, October 24, 1936, 3.

5. Earl Wilson, "Virtue Triumphs! Broadway Disowns Wicked Women," *The Milwaukee Sentinel*, October 26, 1961, 21.

6. *What's My Line?* October 23, 1955.

7. Katz, "That 'Van,' is Here Again."

8. Mark Barron, "Youthful Leading Men Finds Breaks"; Will Gordon "Broadway Wings; White's 'Scandals,' Tickets on Sale; Play Opens at the Alvin, August 28," clipping from unnamed newspaper, c. 1940, Melven Cornish Collection, Box 5, Folder 2, Western History Collections, University of Oklahoma, Norman, Oklahoma.

9. Katz, "That 'Van,' is Here Again."

10. Claude Hammerston, "History of Massey Hall," *Ottawa Citizen*, September 28, 1949, 33.

11. *Ibid.*

12. "Type-Casting Ignored by Suspense Producer," *St. Petersburg Times*, March 20, 1949, 35.

13. On some sites only thirteen episodes are listed; *Who Shot Waldo?* appears to have been the pilot episode. See Jerry Haendige's Radio Logs, www.otrsite.com.

14. "Actor Van Heflin Talks About Philip Marlowe," *Ottawa Citizen*, 12, August 2, 1947.

15. Gene Handsaker, "Hollywood Sights and Sounds," *Prescott Evening Courier*, June 19, 1947, 2.

16. "Actor Van Heflin Talks About Philip Marlowe," *Ottawa Citizen*.

17. Hedda Hopper "Filmdom's Canines Are On Strike," *Toledo Blade*, June 24, 1947, 27.

18. Claude Hammerston, "Radio Column: Mid-Month Hooperating," *Ottawa Citizen*, September 22, 1949, 41.

19. Bob Thomas, "Turns Down 'Sitting Pretty,' Alice Faye Seeks Film Role Again," *The Evening Independent*, October 13, 1947, 8.

20. "Bill of Human Rights," G. N. Gomes Letter to *The Straits Times*, 1, August 12, 1950.

21. Mike McCrann, www.gay.net/vintage-hunk/2011/10/24/van-heflin.

Chapter Six

1. Bob Thomas, "Van Heflin Ready to Free Lance," *Daytona Beach Morning Journal*, February 1, 1950, 5.

2. Florence Fisher Parry, "I Dare Say—Meet a Young Man with a Plan –Van Heflin," *Pittsburgh Post-Gazette*, May 22, 1949, 66.

3. Tony Crawley, *It's A Wonderful Life*, crawleyscastingcalls.com/index/php/van-heflin.

4. *The Hoodlum Saint* Louella O. Parsons "Movie Round-Up: European Trip May Ease Foreign Cinema Problems," *St. Petersburg Times*, June 4, 1945, 7.

5. "Hollywood Goes To War with the Memphis Censors," *The Pittsburgh Press*, August 13, 1945, 6; Kaspar Monahan, "Monahan Walks Out on 'Synthetic,' Love," *The Pittsburgh Press*, July 22, 1947, 14.

6. Sheilah Graham, *The Postman Always Rings Twice*, "Skipping Around Hollywood Town," *The Milwaukee Journal*, June 17, 1945, 62.

7. Jack O'Brian, "'The Red Mill,' Is Breaking Show Records," *Herald-Tribune*, November 10, 1945, 22. 'Studio Size-Ups: Metro-Goldwyn-Mayer," *Film Bulletin*, September 17, 1945, 672.

8. *Ibid.*

9. Sheilah Graham, *Bridgit*, "In Hollywood Today," *Ottawa Citizen*, January 7, 1946, 18.

10. "Personality Parade," *The Mail* (Adelaide, South Australia) October 20, 1945, 10.

11. en.wikipedia.org/wiki/Jerome_Kern.

12. Bob Thomas, "Bogart Denies Claims of Hollywood Immorality," *Sarasota Herald-Tribune*, December 15, 1946, 22.

13. "See Work of U.S. Services In Far South," by W. M. G. *Ottawa Citizen*, January 27, 1949, 74.

14. Hedda Hopper, "Film Star Finds Business, Acting Don't Always Mix," *Spokesman-Review*, 15, August 15, 1954.

15. Sheilah Graham, "All Around Hollywood Town," *The Milwaukee Journal*, 17, December 1, 1946.

16. Herbert Whittaker, "Thunder In Hollywood," *The Montreal Gazette*, January 31, 1948, 19.

17. *Ibid.*

18. "Construction of Huge Set Is Scheduled," *The Deseret News*, November 12, 1946, 14.

19. *Ibid.*

20. James Robert Parrish, and Ronald L. Bowers, *The MGM Stock Company: The Golden Era* (London: Ian Allan Ltd., 1974), 334.

21. Gene Handsaker, "Actor Is Most Severe Critic," *Kentucky New Era*, February 14, 1947, 2.

22. Leonard Lyons, "Battling McKellar Considers Punching August Senator Taft," *Miami News*, January 17, 1949, 17.

23. Hedda Hopper, "Looking at Hollywood," *The Evening Independent*, December 30, 1947, 14.

24. "'B.F.'s Daughter,' Comes to the Screen With Barbara Stanwyck In Vivid Role," *Ellensburg Daily Record*, August 27, 1948, 8.

25. Bob Thomas, "Bob Thomas Claims Motherhood Does Wonders For Screen Star Bette Davis," *The Evening Independent*, October 2, 1947, 16.

26. TCM Review www.tcm/tcmdb/title/2758/B-F-s-Daughter/.

27. }"'B.F.'s Daughter,' Comes to the Screen," *Ellensburg Daily Record*.

28. "The Chiel's Film Review: Fine Documentary on Antarctic Exploration: Love and War," *The Age*, March 19, 1949, 4.

29. "Fine Acting is Featured In Druid Film 'Tap Roots,'" *The Tuscaloosa News*, August 12, 1956, 5.

30. Austin Cross "Boris Karloff And Other Stars Talk To Mr. Cross," *Ottawa Citizen*, July 12, 1948, 2.

31. Kaspar Monahan, "Monahan Walks Out on Synthetic Love," *Pittsburgh Press*, July 22, 1947, 14.

32. Dorothy Kilgallen "Voice of Broadway," *Schenectady Gazette*, January 30, 1948, 9.

33. Hedda Hopper "Irene Selznick Will Produce Her Big Hit On Screen," *Toledo Blade*, January 31, 1948, 17.

34. "Filmdom Chatterbox," *Toledo Blade*, 11, January 21, 1948.

35. Beaucaire, "Off-Screen Hero," *The Argus* (Melbourne), 1S, November 16, 1948.

36. Roderick Heath, "The Three Musketeers (1948)," *This Island Rod*, July 22, 2010, thisislandrod.blogspot.co.uk 2010/07/three-musketeers.1948.html.

37. Vecchiolarry, July 13, 2008, "In the Spotlight Redux," silverscreenoasis.com/oasis3/viewtopic.php/t=704&start=360.

38. Vivien Meik "Making U.S. Films A Serious Job," *The Deseret News*, April 2, 1948, 1–2.

39. Geoffrey Wagner, *The Novel and Cinema* (Cranbury, NJ: Fairleigh Dickinson University Press, 1975), 53.

40. Vincent Minnelli, *I Remember it Well* (London: Angus & Robinson, 1974), 74.

41. Kaspar Monahan, "Show Shops: Stanwyck and Mason an Unhappy Wedded Pair," *The Pittsburgh Press*, March 16, 1950, 24.

42. "All-Star Cast Brings Famous Novel to Bama," *Tuscaloosa News*, March 26, 1950, 13.

43. Penelope Houston, *Sight and Sound*, April 1949, quoted in *Halliwell's Film Guide* (London: Granada, 4th Edition, 1983), 242.

44. Harold V. Cohen, "The New Film 'East Side, West Side,' and All Around the Penn," *Pittsburgh Post-Gazette*, March 16, 1950, 12.

45. *The Skipper Surprised His Wife*: Hedda Hopper, "M-G-M Buys Magazine Story; May Be Vehicle for Heflin," *Toledo Blade*, September 30, 1948, 52; "Lana Turner Gets Promise She Will Not Have to Dye," *The Evening Independent*, July 5, 1947, 18; *The History of Rome Hanks*: Bob Thomas, "Mary Pickford Seeks Girl to Emulate Her," *The Deseret News*, April 25, 1947, 10.

46. *Alexandra*: Thomas F. Brady, "Dumas Story Set For Parks," *The Montreal Gazette*, November 19, 1947, 10; Bob Thomas "Hollywood News," *Gettysburg Times*, April 25, 1947, 3; *Lost Boundaries*: Erskine Johnson, "Strictly For Women," *Southeast Missourian*, October 18, 1948, 4.

47. Alan Gevinson, *Within Our Gates: Ethnicity in American Feature Film 1911–60* (University of California Press, 1997), 91.

48. *The Outriders*: Henry Gris, "Hollywood Report," *The Sydney Morning Herald*, April 24, 1949, 8; Hedda Hopper, "Van Heflin and Robert Taylor Teamed Again in 'Ambush,'" *Toledo Blade*, April 26, 1949, 39.

49. *The Wall Between*: Louella O. Parsons, "Hollywood," *The Milwaukee Sentinel*, March 11, 1947, 9; *Man-Eater of*

Kumaon: Hedda Hopper, "Hedda Says: Here and There In Hollywood," *The Pittsburgh Press*, July 25, 1947, 22; *Romeo and Juliet*: Dorothy Kilgallen, "On Broadway," *Pittsburgh Post-Gazette*, September 16, 1950, 19.

50. *Look Homeward, Angel*: Bob Thomas, "Hollywood News: Sinatra Row is Talk of the Town," *Sarasota Herald-Tribune*, October 16, 1946, 10.

51. Hedda Hopper, "Roz Russell in TV Spectacular?," *The Miami News*, May 19, 1956, 14.

52. Dorothy Manners, "Tracy, Heflin in Story of Famous Trial," *The Deseret News*, July 8, 1948, F-3.

53. Bob Thomas "Van Heflin Ready To Free Lance," *The Daytona Beach Morning Journal*, 1, February 1, 1950.

Chapter Seven

1. Jonathan Davies, "Round the Studios," *The News* (Adelaide, South Australia), March 16, 1946, 4.

2. Hedda Hopper, "Film Star Finds Business, Acting Don't Always Mix," *Spokesman-Review*, August 15, 1954, 45.

3. Davies, "Van Heflin is Always an Animal."

4. Quoted by F. Keith Manzie, "The New 'Adult Approach,' To Film Making," *The Argus* (Melbourne, Victoria), September 28, 1946, 4S.

5. "The New Pictures: Ivers," *Time*, July 29, 1949.

6. "New Films Reviewed: 'The Strange Love of Martha Ivers,'" *The Sydney Morning Herald*, November 4, 1946, 1.

7. "Van Heflin In Tough Love Story," *The Argus* (Melbourne), October 19, 1946, 17.

8. Harold Heffernan, "Van Heflin, Ex-Serviceman, Adjusts To Postwar Career," *Miami Daily News*, October 14, 1945, 4.

9. Quoted in Dan Callahan *Barbara Stanwyck: The Miracle Woman* (University of Mississippi Press, 2012), 125.

10. Gene Handsaker, "Actor Is Most Severe Critic: Time in Army Seen as Rusting Up Technique," *Kentucky New Era*, February 14, 1947, 3.

11. "Coming Attractions," *The Yale Daily News*, September 18, 1946, 5.

12. Lizabeth Scott interviewed by Carole Langer at Janet Leigh's home in 1996, www.youtube.com/watch?v=jjLLnXobNUc.

13. Kirk Douglas, *The Ragman's Son* (Simon & Schuster, 1988), 133.

14. Hedda Hopper, "Hedda Says— Jeanette Pulls A Smart Trick," *The Pittsburgh Press*, September 19, 1946, 19.

15. Paula Walling, "Superb Acting," *Sunday Times (Perth, Western Australia)*, May 26, 1946, 13-S.

16. Bob Thomas, "Many Film Producers Seek the Services of Joan Crawford," *Reading Eagle*, , June 24, 1946, 14.

17. Quoted in Lawrence J. Quirk, and William Schoell, *Joan Crawford: The Essential Biography* (Lexington: University Press of Kentucky, 2002), 139.

18. Bosley Crowther, *New York Times*, May 30, 1947, quoted at www.joancrawfordbest.com/filmspossessed47.htm.

19. "Just a Line From Hollywood by Beam," *The Mail* (Adelaide, South Australia), June 8, 1946, 9S.

20. Hedda Hopper, "'Fair Wind To Java,' Set As Next John Wayne Film at Republic," *Toledo Blade*, October 13, 1949, 60.

21. Louella O. Parsons, "Hollywood," *Milwaukee Sentinel*, December 1, 1947, 11.

22. Hedda Hopper, "Hedda Hopper In Hollywood: Biggest Names In Films Attend Photographer's Ball," *The Miami News*, October 27, 1947, 16.

23. *Brittania Mews*, Edwin Schallert "Andrews Stars In Mews," *Los Angeles Times*, July 8, 1948, 10.

24. *Fiddler's Green/The Raging Tide* Hedda Hopper "'Fiddler's Green,' Is a Story About a New Kind of Gangster," *The Miami News*, November 23, 1950, 7B.

25. Dorothy Kilgallen "On Broadway: Jottings in Pencil," *Pittsburgh Post-Gazette*, March 3, 1950, 23.

26. Hedda Hopper, "Heflin Sought For 'Darling Jenny,'" *Los Angeles Times*, September 24, 1954, C8.

27. A. Nolletti, *The Films of Fred Zinnemann: Critical Perspectives* (State University of New York Press, 1999), 198.

28. "Gable Squashes Elopement Talk," *Mirror* (Perth), April 10, 1948, 12.

29. Mary Astor, *A Life on Film* (W. H. Allen, 1973), 199–200.

30. "The New Pictures," *Time*, January 31, 1949.

31. Ruth Brigham, "Good Actor Tries Role As Bad Man," *Daytona Beach Morning Journal*, June 23, 1948, 4.

32. Mitch Woodbury, "Mitch Wood-

bury Reports—On Valentine's New Picture, 'Act of Violence,'" *Toledo Blade*, February 5, 1949, 14.

33. David Thomson, *The Biographical Dictionary of Film* (Little, Brown, 2003).

34. Jack Phillips, "Movie Review: Actor At Best In Drama Role," *The Spokesman-Review*, 1, August 16, 1951.

35. Harold V. Cohen, "The New Films—'The Prowler,' at the Fulton, Along With 'Hoodlum,'" *Pittsburgh Post-Gazette*, October 6, 1951, 33.

36. Phillips, "Movie Review: Actor At Best In Drama Role."

37. Cohen, "The New Films—'The Prowler,' at the Fulton, Along With 'Hoodlum.'"

38. Thomson, *The Biographical Dictionary of Film*.

39. Howard Pearson, "Van Watches Step With Law Now," *The Deseret News*, May 30, 1951, 11.

40. Robert Perkins "Young Man With A Future," *Screenland*, March 1951, 72.

41. *Ibid.*

42. "Young Man with a Future," *Screenland*, March 1951, 72.

43. Louella O. Parsons, "Van Heflin to Star in Film on Crime," *The Milwaukee Sentinel*, May 5, 1956, part 2, 1.

44. Hedda Hopper, "Heflin and Malden Set for Picture," *The Pittsburgh Press*, December 22, 1958, 22.

Chapter Eight

1. Bob Thomas Interview, "Van Heflin Ready to Free Lance," *Daytona Beach Morning Journal*, February 1, 1950, 5.

2. "Van Heflin, Actor, Dead at 60; Won Fame in Film and On Stage," *New York Times* Obituary, July 24, 1971.

3. Robert Perkins, "Young Man With A Future," *Screenland*, March 1951, 73.

4. James Bacon, "Van Heflin Still Goes To College," *Reading Eagle*, July 19, 1953, 23.

5. Hedda Hopper, "'Untamed,' Next Film For Susan Hayward," *Toledo Blade*, February 15, 1954, 31.

6. *Variety*, quoted by Herman Middleton, "Theatre," *The Sunday Star*, November 9, 1952, 16.

7. James Bacon, "Van Heflin Still Goes To College," *Reading Eagle*, July 19, 1953, 23.

8. "Close Call For Actor," *News* (Adelaide, South Australia), August 28, 1951, 21;

Gene Handsaker, "Hollywood Sights and Sounds," *Prescott Evening Courier*, November 30, 1951, 2.

9. "'Tomahawk,' Is Full Of Action," *St Petersburg Times*, April 15, 1951, 13.

10. "A Week at the Cape Theaters," *The Southeast Missourian*, March 8, 1951, 6B.

11. Drew Pearson, "The Washington Merry-Go-Round," *Spokane Daily Chronicle*, February 21, 1951, 1.

12. "George Sherman: Tomahawk," January 29 2013, by Colin, https://livius.1.wordpress.com/category/directors/george-sherman/.

13. Herb Miller, "Tomahawk," *Sunday Herald*, February 18, 1951, 15.

14. www.imdb.name/nm0802862/bio.

15. Bob Thomas, "Van Heflin Changes His Pace, Tries First Comedy In Ten Years," *Reading Eagle*, June 18, 1951, 1.

16. "'My Son, John,' To Start Today On Bama Screen," *The Tuscaloosa News*, July 20, 1952, 10.

17. "Drama Of A Doomed City And A Man With A Terrible Secret," *The Straits Times*, January 11, 1953, 11.

18. *The Golden Mask*, www.tcm.com/this-month/article/430525 percent7C445033/The-Golden-Mask.html.

19. *Ibid.*

20. "'Golden Mask,' Takes Movie Fans To Africa, by L. B.," *St. Petersburg Times*, August 2, 1954, 27; July 29, 1954, 24.

21. *Ibid.*

22. Quoted by maralyn@britmovieforum, www.britmovie.co.uk/forums/; also Andy Owens, *Our Eric: A Portrait of Eric Portman* (Ammanford, UK: Sigma Press, 2013), 130.

23. Louella O. Parsons, "Jeff Chandler's Star Is Rising Rapidly," *The Milwaukee Sentinel*, January 19, 1952, 12.

24. Hedda Hopper, "Leslie Caron May Get Ballerina Role," *Toledo Blade*, March 1952, 35.

25. Hedda Hopper, "A Little Plug For Yours Truly," *Toledo Blade*, June 21, 1952, 15.

26. "Playhouse Audience Taken On Safari In 'Tanganyika,'" *St. Petersburg Times*, July 24, 1954, 26.

27. H. H. T., "'Tanganyika,' At the Palace," *New York Times*, June 19, 1954.

28. Erskine Johnson, "Actor Judged By Play Material, Not Performance Says Van Heflin," *Quebec Chronicle Telegraph*, October 16, 1953, 6.

29. "Van Heflin Season's Busiest Star," *The Deseret News*, November 5, 1954, B7.

30. Dorothy Kilgallen, "Martha And Husband Are Living Apart," *Toledo Blade*, March 14, 1955, 16.

31. "At the Movies: Greenwich," *The Village Voice*, February 15, 1956, 5.

32. Tab Hunter with Eddie Muller, *Tab Hunter Confidential: The Making of a Movie Star* (Chapel Hill, NC: Algonquin Books, 2006), 90.

33. Tony Crawley, "Richard Hylton," http://www.crawleyscastingcalls.com/index.php/component/actors/index.php?option=com_actors&Itemid=56&id=3662&lettre=.

34. James McKay, *Dana Andrews: The Face of Noir* (McFarland, 2010), 106.

35. *White Sheep*: Sheilah Graham, "Tyrone To Pick Leading Lady," *The Spokesman-Review*, June 1, 1951, 5; *A Matter of Life and Death*: www.glamourgirlsofthesilverscreen.com/show/71/Faith+Domergue/index.html.

36. Johnson, "Actor Judged By Play Material, Not Performance Says Van Heflin."

37. "Product Need Spurs New High For Indie Production," *Independent Film Exhibitor's Bulletin*, 10, December 14, 1953.

38. Bob Thomas, *Golden Boy: The Untold Story of William Holden* (London: Weidenfeld & Nicholson, 1983) 111; Marilyn Ann Moss, *Giant: George Stevens, a Life on Film* (Madison: University of Wisconsin Press, 2004), 215.

39. Hedda Hopper "Miss Bennett Seeks Talent For Shows In Germany," *The Miami News*, January 26, 1950, 8B.

40. "Howard Hughes To Get $100,000," *The Spokesman-Review*, August 12, 1952, 17.

41. Tony Crawley, http://crawleyscastingcalls.com/index.php?option=com_actors&Itemid=56&id=1383&lettre=H; Hedda Hopper, "Heflin Covets Artist Role," *The Miami News*, June 25, 1954, 5-B.

42. Hedda Hopper "Bogart, Heflin, Ray Cited for Brazil Duty," *Los Angeles Times*, June 28, 1954, B7.

43. Hedda Hopper "'Written On The Wind' A Sleeper," *The Miami News*, October 1, 1956, 4B.

44. *Los Angeles Examiner*, March 1947, quoted by TCM review notes; www.tcm.com/tcmdb/title/640/The-Brothers-Karamazov/notes.html.

45. Dorothy Manners, "In Hollywood," *The Milwaukee Sentinel*, August 22, 1950, part 2, 3.

46. Hedda Hopper, "Heflin, Peppard Paged as Co-Stars," *Los Angeles Times*, December 12, 1960, C12.

47. "Heflin, Heilweil Set," *Motion Picture Daily*, April 20, 1959, 5.

Chapter Nine

1. Ben Johnson, quoted Leslie Halliwell, *Halliwell's Filmgoer's Companion* (New York: HarperCollins, 1983), 733.

2. Louella O. Parsons, "Hollywood," *The Milwaukee Sentinel*, July 26, 1951, 4.

3. Hedda Hopper, "Ann Sheridan Cast Opposite Chandler," *Toledo Blade*, July 28, 1951, 15.

4. *Ibid.*

5. Interview with R. Quilter Vincent, *ABC Film Review*, c. 1953, 5 (no date, from archive of cuttings).

6. *Ibid.*

7. Beverly Linet, *Ladd: A Hollywood Tragedy* (New York: Berkley Books, 1980), 148–49.

8. Johna Blinn, "Ben Johnson: Just a Cowboy," *The Palm Beach Post*, October 28, 1971, 89.

9. Jerry Vermilye, *Jean Arthur: A Biofilmography* (Bloomington, IN: AuthorHouse, 2012), 212.

10. Linet, *Ladd: A Hollywood Tragedy*.

11. Rick Lyman, "Watching Movies With: Woody Allen; Coming Back To 'Shane,'" *New York Times*, August 3, 2001, www.nytimes.com/2001/08/03/movies/watching-movies-with-woody-allen-coming-back-to-shane.html.

12. Andre Soares, "Shane: Alan Ladd 'Subversive' Western Gets Special Academy Screening," *Alt Film Guide*, www.altfg.com/film/shane-alan-ladd/.

13. Linet, *Ladd: A Hollywood Tragedy*.

14. Louella O. Parsons, "In Hollywood," *Rome News-Tribune*, April 16, 1953, 18.

15. Louella O. Parsons, "In Hollywood: Suzie Signs," *The Milwaukee Sentinel*, December 21, 1959, 12; "Gary Gets Western," *The Milwaukee Sentinel*, December 27, 1957, 13.

16. Herb Fagen, *The Encyclopedia of Westerns* (New York: Facts On File, 2001), 231.

17. Dorothy Manners, "George Mont-

gomery Signs New Film Pact," *The Milwaukee Sentinel*, July 26, 1955, 1.

18. Hedda Hopper, "Georgia Girl Tells Secret of Success: Joanne Woodward Gets To Top As Actress Without Glamor Role," *The Miami Times*, February 2, 1955, 18; December 22, 1958, 22.

19. *The Guardian*, 1957 review, quoted in *Halliwell's Film Guide* (London: Guild Publishing, 1983), 828.

20. Bert Newton, *Bert!* (Toorak, Victoria: Gary Sparkes & Associates, 1977) 61.

21. Ed Black, "Ford Rainey Shares a Wealth of Stage and Film Tales," *The Pittsburgh Press*, November 21, 1984, C3.

22. Tab Hunter with Eddie Muller, *Tab Hunter Confidential: The Making of a Movie Star* (Algonquin Books of Chapel Hill, 2006) 192–93.

23. "Gunman's Walk (1958)," *TCM*, www.tcm.com/tcmb/title/4616/Gunmans-Walk/articles.html.

24. Bob Thomas, "Morality In Movies Is Undergoing Big Change," *Ocala Star-Banner*, September 28, 1950, 15.

25. Erskine Johnson, "Hollywood Today," *Park City Daily News*, October 27, 1958, 3; Bob Thomas, "Rita Hayworth New Person On Location For Western," *The Tuscaloosa News*, October 23, 1958, 28; Dorothy O. Rea "Film Influx Brings Money, Happiness To St. George," *The Deseret News*, October 24, 1958, 1.

26. Hedda Hopper, "Heflin and Malden Set For Picture," *The Pittsburgh Press*, December 22, 1958, 22.

27. Hunter, *Tab Hunter Confidential: The Making of a Movie Star*.

28. Edwin Schallert, "Drama: Westerns Get Featured Spot on Metro's Slate Van Heflin in 'Ox Train,'" *Los Angeles Times*, January 9, 1942, 15; *Texas Trail*: Hedda Hopper, "Dieterle Seeks Van Heflin for Western," *The Los Angeles Times*, October 1, 1957, C8; *Distant Paths*: Edwin Schallert, "'No Time To Die,' Bought for Clift," *Los Angeles Times*, July 16, 1955, 15.

29. *Stars in My Crown*, "Metro-Goldwyn-Mayer 11 Features Set," *Independent Exhibitor's Film Bulletin*, 17, March 29, 1948; *Guns of the Timberland* Dorothy Manners "Alan Ladd Seeks Van Heflin For Film," *The Milwaukee Sentinel*, 1, August 10, 1956.

30. Hedda Hopper, "Grainger Readying Two Films For RKO," *Los Angeles Times*, November 26, 1954, B6.

31. *Showdown*, Hedda Hopper, "Van Heflin Sought as 'Showdown, Star," *Los Angeles Times*, September 3, 1956, A6.

32. "Sammy Davis To Produce Movie," *The Afro-American*, August 9, 1958, 7; Earl Wilson on Broadway, "Stritch Has Him In Stitches," *The Miami News*, February 6, 1959, 8.

Chapter Ten

1. "Actor Plans to Quit Movies and Invest in Broadway Play," *Spokane Daily Chronicle*, May 16, 1955, 5.

2. "East and West," *Pittsburgh Post-Gazette*, January 29, 1942, 23.

3. Peter Manso, *Brando: The Biography* (New York: Hyperion, 1994), 672.

4. Edith Gwynn, "Van Heflin Wants Leave To Return To Broadway," *St Petersburg Times*, September 9, 1949, 21.

5. Sheilah Graham, "Hollywood: Casting Shadows," *Pittsburgh Post-Gazette*, January 1, 1950, 6.

6. "Van Heflin Has Had Varied Career," *The Milwaukee Sentinel*, January 18, 1953, 4.

7. Harold V. Cohen, "Van Heflin at the Nixon In an Absorbing Drama," *Pittsburgh Post-Gazette*, December 2, 1952, 14.

8. *Ibid.*

9. Mary Kimbrough, "Plays Heavy Role: Van Heflin Puts His Weight into 'The Shrike,'" *The Evening Oklahoman*, February 2, 1953; Melven Cornish Collection, Box 5, Folder 2, Western History Collections, University of Oklahoma Libraries, Norman, Oklahoma.

10. *Ibid.*

11. Herman Middleton, "Van Heflin Was First Choice For 'The Shrike,'" *The Sunday Star*, November 2, 1952, 18.

12. Kimbrough, "Plays Heavy Role: Van Heflin Puts His Weight into 'The Shrike.'"

13. William Glover, "Van Heflin A Success In Arthur Miller Play," *Herald-Journal*, November 27, 1955, 9.

14. Jack Gaver, "Irresistible Script Lures Van To Stage," *The Pittsburgh Press*, November 27, 1955, Section 2, 1; Joan Hanauer, "Van Heflin Has To 'Read' For Role," *The Milwaukee Sentinel*, Section 2, 1, November 27, 1955; Harold V. Cohen *Pittsburgh Post-Gazette*, December 2, 1963, 14.

15. Arthur Miller, *Timebends: A Life* (New York: Grove Press, 1987), 285.

16. Louella Parsons, "Marilyn Monroe's Marvelous Marriage," *Modern Screen*, September 1955, 96; *Sunday Herald*, November 22, 1955.

17. Brooks Atkinson, "A View from the Bridge," *New York Times*, October 9, 1955, partners.nytimes.com/books/00/11/12/specials/miller-bridge55.html.

18. "Studying Arthur Miller's *A View from the* Bridge," www.universalteacher.org.co.uk/drama/viewfromthebridge.htm.

19. Vance Bourjaily, "Theater Uptown," *The Village Voice*, November 16, 1955, 8.

20. Hedda Hopper, "Olivier Will Appear Opposite Marilyn," *Toledo Blade*, January 27, 1956, 23.

21. Leonard Lyons, "Honesty Rules On Bishop Sheen Set," *St Petersburg Times*, November 9, 1955, 17.

22. Leonard Lyons, "The Lyons Den," *Reading Eagle*, October 3, 1955, 10.

23. Robert Parrish, and Ronald L. Bowers, *The MGM Stock Company: The Golden Era* (London: Ian Allan Ltd., 1973), 334.

24. Glover, "Van Heflin A Success In Arthur Miller Play."

25. Irwin Alpert, "Night and Day in New Haven," *Sunday-Herald*, February 6, 1956, 8; "$9,000 investment": according to Martin Gottfried, *Arthur Miller: His Life and Work* (Boston: Da Capo Press, 2003), 289.

26. Hopper, "Olivier Will Appear Opposite Marilyn."

27. Hedda Hopper, "Film Freelancing Paying Off," *Toledo Blade*, April 15, 1956, Section 4, 1.

28. Atkinson, "A View from the Bridge."

29. Harold V. Cohen "An Actor's Got To Act," *Pittsburgh Post-Gazette*, February 25, 1964, 10.

30. *Patterns* (1956), www.imdb.com/title/tt0049601/reviews.

31. Herb Kelly, "'Patterns,' Fascinating; 'Hot Blood,' Is Anemic," *Miami News*, May 3, 1956, 5B.

32. Erskine Johnson, "Flashes from Filmland," *Southeast Missourian*, June 13, 1956, 3.

33. Hedda Hopper, "Steiger and Heflin Sought For Stage," *Los Angeles Times*, October 10, 1960, C12.

34. Philip K. Scheur, "Van Heflin Sending; Davis 'Golden Boy,'" *Los Angeles Times*, May 4, 1962, C13.

35. *Playbill* Vault, www.playbillvault.com/Show/Detail/6925/A-Case-Of-Libel.

36. William Glover, "Van Heflin Refuses To Be Character," *Daytona Beach Morning Journal*, November 3, 1963, 6E.

37. Harold V. Cohen, "An Actor's Got To Act."

38. Dick Kleiner, "Van Heflin Refuses To Become A Pitchman," *Ocala Star-Banner*, December 22, 1963, 39.

39. Jack Gaver, "Broadway Review: 'Case of Libel' Solid Drama," *Pittsburgh Press*, October 11, 1963, 13.

40. Leonard Lyons "The Lyons Den," *Reading Eagle*, October 18, 1963, 14.

41. *Sunset in the Morning*: Dorothy Manners, "Hayes, Heflin, Jagger And Walker In Cast," *The Deseret News*, March 2, 1951, F3; *Two For the Seesaw*: Louella O. Parsons "In Hollywood: Heflin To Rio," *The Milwaukee Sentinel*, January 28, 1958, 6.

42. Glover, "Van Heflin Refuses To Be Character."

43. *Beer Island*: Leonard Lyons "The Lyons Den," *The Pittsburgh Press*, June 25, 1967; *An Unpleasant Evening with H. L. Mencken*: Cy Rice, *The Milwaukee Sentinel*, March 29, 1971, Section 5, 16.

Chapter Eleven

1. William Glover, "There's No Such Thing as a Van Heflin Character," *Ocala Star-Banner*, November 12, 1963, 4.

2. *The MGM Stock Company: The Golden Era* (London: W. H. Allan Ltd., 1973), 331; Vernon Scott, "Van Heflin Tops In Italy," *The Pittsburgh Press*, June 8, 1961, 12.

3. J. L. Hees, "Hollywood Film Notes," *Star-News*, January 22, 1954, 10.

4. Dorothy Kilgallen, "T-Men Put Heat On Harlem Racketeers," *Daytona Morning Beach Sunday News-Journal*, February 14, 1959, 5.

5. Dick Gunderson, "Everybody Is Killing in 'Tempest,'" *Spokesman-Review*, April 22, 1959, 5.

6. Earl Wilson, "In New York: It Happened Last Night," *Sarasota Herald-Tribune*, February 1, 1959, 11.

7. "Van Heflin 'Beards Up,' For 'Tempest,' Actor Works Behind Iron Curtain," *Milwaukee Sentinel*, January 25, 1959, 5.

8. Bob Thomas, "Van Heflin Really Enjoyed Making Film in Yugoslavia," *The Tuscaloosa News*, October 1, 1958, 14.

9. L. R. Swainson, "Some Hazards of Stardom," *The Age*, September 15, 1959, 11.

10. Sheilah Graham, "Four Comedies in Row Too Much For Niven," *Salt Lake Telegram*, October 3, 1959, 8A.

11. Dorothy Kilgallen, "On Broadway: Broadway Bulletin Board," *Pittsburgh Post-Gazette*, March 20, 1959, 15.

12. Louella Parsons, "In Hollywood: Billy and Willy," *The Milwaukee Sentinel*, May 29, 1959, 12.

13. *Love in the North Sea*: Hedda Hopper "Holliman Will Do Movie in Italy," *Los Angeles Times*, June 6, 1960, D14; *I Aim at the Stars*: Erskine Johnson, "Hollywood Notes," *Lakeland Ledger*, September 8, 1959, 4.

14. Leonard Lyons, "The Lyons Den: Shah, Soraya Return to Power but Tears Fill Eyes of Queen," *Lawrence World-Journal*, December 14, 1959, 4.

15. Hedda Hopper, "In Hollywood," *News and Courier*, November 15, 1960, 20; *Miami News*, January 8, 1958.

16. Derek Prouse, "A Neurosis By Any Other Name," *The Sunday Times*, September 24, 1961, 41.

17. Derek Prouse, "Films at Cannes," *Sight and Sound*, Summer 1961, 101.

18. Sheilah Graham, "Tony Discovers Romance In Paris," *The Deseret News*, September 7, 1960, B9.

19. "De Laurentiis Plans Heflin as Bolivar," *Los Angeles Times*, April 16, 1958, A7; Hedda Hopper, "Van Heflin Named 'Taras Bulba,' Star," *Los Angeles Times*, July 21, 1961, A10.

20. *Face in the Rain*: Hedda Hopper "Another European Film Lures Heflin," *Los Angeles Times*, February 10, 1959, B6; *The Sea Take*: Hedda Hopper, "Sinatra Gets Choice Role," *The Miami News*, January 8, 1958, 8B.

21. "Violence, good looks and lots of bared torsos and curves," *The Singapore Times*, May 8, 1966, 11.

22. Michael Billington, "A Farce That Loses Its Way in the End: General Release (from June 9) The Man Outside," *The Times*, June 6, 1968, 13.

23. Ronnie Barker, *The Authorized Biography* (London: Chameleon, 1998), 53.

24. Miscellaneous Items in Melven Cornish Collection, Box 5, Folder 2, Western History Collections, University of Oklahoma, Norman, Oklahoma.

25. Tony Crawley, crawleyscastingcalls.com.

26. Miscellaneous items in Melven Cornish Collection, Box 5, Folder 2, Western History Collections, University of Oklahoma Libraries, Norman, Oklahoma.

27. *Quatermass and the Pit aka Five Million Miles to Earth*, www.imdb.com/title/tt0062168/?ref_=nv_sr_1.

28. Scott, "Van Heflin Tops in Italy," *The Pittsburgh Press*, June 8, 1961,12.

Chapter Twelve

1. Dick Kleiner, "Van Heflin Refuses To Become Pitchman," *The Times Daily*, December 14, 1963, 14.

2. *Ibid.*

3. Bob Thomas, "Van Heflin Spurns Many Video Offers," *The Deseret News*, October 5, 1953, 7.

4. Erskine Johnson, "Flicker Flashes From Filmland," *The Southeast Missourian*, July 19, 1950, 8.

5. Hal Humphrey, "Van Heflin Can't Lose," *The Pittsburgh Press*, July 15, 1963, 36.

6. Hank Grant, "Cameras Must Follow Van Heflin Around," *The Evening Independent*, June 3, 1963, 12-A.

7. Letter from Van Heflin to Ken Murray c1946, listed on eBay June 30, 2014.

8. John Crosby "Radio In Review," *Pittsburgh Post-Gazette*, January 21, 1950, 10.

9. Hedda Hopper, "'Big Bad One,' Is War Story," *The Miami News*, September 24, 1957, 7B.

10. William Ewald, "Ewald Notices Hardening Of The Arteries At Disney Studios," *The Bulletin*, August 14, 1958, 12.

11. Louella O. Parsons, "In Hollywood: Heflin To Rio," *The Milwaukee Sentinel*, January 28, 1958, 6.

12. "TV Scout Preview," *St. Petersburg Times*, May 28, 1959, 13B.

13. Howard Pearson, "All-Star Playhouse 90 Tackles Labor Theme Tonight," *The Deseret News*, June 4, 1959, B13.

14. William Ewald, "'Rank and File,' to Raise Some Hackles," *Beaer Valley Times*, 13, May 29, 1959.

15. Fred Danzig, "Tammy Grimes Stole Show In Sleeper, TV Critic Says," *Reading Eagle*, February 25, 1960, 24.

16. "Van Dyke And Cartoon Shows Debut," *The Milwaukee Sentinel*, part 2, October 3, 1961, 16.

17. "Drama: Heflin To Appear in Dr. Kildare Episode," *Los Angeles Times*, July 3, 1964, D8.

18. "TV Highlights," *The Daily Reporter*, September 12, 1968, 2.

19. "Van Heflin, Actor, Dead at 60; Won Fame in Film and on Stage," *New York Times*, July 24, 1971.

20. Cynthia Lowry, "'Ironside,' Has Acquired New Female Aide," *Gettysburg Times*, October 6, 1971, 19.

21. Florence Fisher Parry, "I Dare Say—Meet a Young Man With a Plan—Van Heflin," *Pittsburgh Post-Gazette*, May 22, 1949, 66.

22. "TV Highlights," *The Telegraph*, May 5, 1964, 17.

23. Jerry Buck, "Television In Review: Countdown To Splashdown," *Reading Eagle*, July 15, 1969, 27.

Chapter Thirteen

1. James Bacon, "Van Heflin Still Goes To College," *Reading Eagle*, July 19, 1953, 23.

2. Dick Kleiner, "Dean Martin For Lead Role," *Sarasota Journal*, December 16, 1968, 12.

3. "Van Heflin Plans Return to U.S. Films," *Star-News*, July 22, 1962, 6.

4. Don Brice, "Crucian News & Views: Author Writing Novel In St. Croix," *Virgin Islands Daily News*, November 30, 1966, 4.

5. *Ibid.*

6. "People: Philippines Bars U.S. Film Shooting," *The Pittsburgh Press*, February 11, 1962, 2.

7. Carl Kuntze, "Falling Through the Cracks," *JPG Mag*, March 28, 2008, jpg-mag.com/stories/3558.

8. Bosley Crowther, www.nytimes.com/movies/movie/11696/Cry-of-Battle/overview.

9. Joseph Finnigan, "Van Heflin Okays Small Portrayal," *Pittsburgh Press*, March 17, 1963, 41.

10. Colin Bennett, "New Film: The Stagecoach Runs Again," *The Age*, October 14, 1966, 3.

11. Don Alpert, "Remaking of Old Picture Problem," *Spokesman-Review*, 12, October 23, 1965.

12. Bennett, "New Film: The Stagecoach Runs Again."

13. Alpert, "Remaking of Old Picture Problem."

14. Bennett, "New Film: The Stagecoach Runs Again."

15. Bob Hill, "'Stagecoach,' Remake Trails First Version," *Spokane Daily Chronicle*, June 24, 1966, 49.

16. Bob Thomas, "Prince Philip Feted By Hollywood Stars," *The Free-Lance Star*, March 18, 1966, 5.

17. Rockwell received the Presidential Medal of Freedom, the United States' highest civilian honor, in 1977. en.wikipedia.wiki/Norman_Rockwell.

18. "A Group of signed Norman Rockwell photographic prints from *Stagecoach*," Bonhams Lot 1095, December 17, 2008, www.bonhams.com/auctions/14034/lot/1095.

19. Norman Rockwell Van Heflin Reference Photograph Negatives For *Stagecoach*, www.julienslivedotcom/view–auctions/catalog/id/151/lot/62818.

20. Dorothy Manners, "Heflin Rationalizes Divorce," *The News and Courier*, May 19, 1968, 21.

21. "Heflin's Wife Seeks Divorce," *The Deseret News*, February 21, 1967, 7.

22. "Milestones: Divorced," *Time*, August 11, 1967.

23. David Siff, *Eleanor's Rebellion* (New York: Alfred A. Knopf, 2000), 197–200.

24. "Heflin's Wife Seeks Divorce," *The Deseret News.*

25. Peter Ford, *Glenn Ford: A Life* (Madison: University of Wisconsin Press, 2011), 234; Dorothy Manners, "Off the Grapevine," *Toledo Blade*, May 25, 1966, 31.

26. Carl Schroeder "Van Heflin, that is," *Modern Screen*, June 1947, 74.

27. Alex Freeman, "Few Films But She's No. 1," *The Deseret News*, October 23, 1964, 11.

28. Vernon Scott "Van Heflin Tops In Italy," *The Pittsburgh Press*, June 8, 1961, 12.

29. Barry M. Grey, "Shane's Van Heflin a Respected Actor of Power, Irony, Subtlety," August 20, 2010, suite.io/barry-m-grey/42cp2be.

30. Carl Schroeder, "Van Heflin, that is," *Modern Screen*, June 1947, 74.

31. Bob Thomas, "Noel Coward Finds He's Not Too English For U.S. Audiences," *Reading Eagle*, June 4, 1955, 7.

32. Herb Caen, "It's News To Me," *The Victoria Advocate*, November 22, 1964, 17.

33. Rick Du Brow, "Bowling Alleys, Land,

Ranches, Other Investments Draw Stars,"
The Deseret News, April 29, 1960, 18.
34. "Film Stars Have Eggs In Other Baskets Too," *Milwaukee Sentinel*, October 1954, 10.
35. "Orson Welles Different Now," *The Spokesman-Review*, August 13, 1952, 29.
36. Bacon, "Van Heflin Still Goes To College."
37. Jay Dee, "Liberace in Hollywood," *The Milwaukee Journal*, September 11, 1949, 145.
38. Jimmy Fidler, "Hollywood Shots," *Reading Eagle*, March 3, 1946, 15.
39. "Milestones," *Time*, July 19, 1954.
40. "Van Heflin Plans Returns to U.S. Films," *Star-News*, July 22, 1962, 7.
41. Sheilah Graham, "In Hollywood Today," *Ottawa Citizen*, March 22, 1946, 82.
42. Harold V. Cohen, "At Random: An Old Echo," *Pittsburgh Post-Gazette*, June 24, 1968, 8.
43. "Film Figures Fight Back At Red Hunt: While One Group Flies To Washington Another Broadcasts Criticism Of Probe," *Schenectady Gazette*, October 27, 1947, 5; "Disney Says Reds Run Movie Unions," *Ellensburg Daily Record*, October 24, 1947, 1, 5.
44. "Democratic Session Pauses For Those Who Died In War," *The Milwaukee Journal*, July 14, 1948, 2.
45. Hedda Hopper, "Like Wuthering Heights: Buddy Rogers To Star In Mary Pickford Film," *The Evening Independent*, January 12, 1949, 21.
46. Thomas L. Stokes, "Political Shows Shifting," *Toledo Blade*, March 13, 1950, 12.
47. Advertisement: "Heed Their Rising Voices," *New York Times*, March 29, 1960, www.archives.gov/exhibits/documented-rights/exhibit/section4/detail/heed-rising-voice.html.
48. Manners, "Heflin Rationalizes Divorce."
49. Marilyn Beck, "Hollywood Close-Up: Maureen, Van Heflin Seem Altar-Bound," *The Milwaukee Journal*, May 20, 1969, 5.
50. Earl Wilson, "Oscar Tie Odds Are More Than A Million To One," *The Milwaukee Sentinel*, April 29, 1969, 13.
51. Scripps Medical Report, October 2–5, 1969, in Melven Cornish Collection, Box 5, Folder 2, Western History Collections,

University of Oklahoma Libraries, Norman, Oklahoma.
52. John J. Raspanti, "Alan Ladd: Escaping the Demons," itchyfish.com/alan-ladd-escaping-the-demons.
53. Beverly Linet, *Ladd: A Hollywood Tragedy* (New York: Berkley Book, 1980), 259.
54. Roger Ebert, "*The Big Bounce* Skips Along as Characters Unfold," *The Southeast Missourian*, January 30, 2004, 8.
55. Dane Lanken, "Looking at the Movies," *The Montreal Gazette*, July 4, 1969, 76.
56. Andrew Sarris, "Films: The Nihilism of Nudity," *The Village Voice*, March 20, 1969, 22.
57. Mike Householder, "Elmore Leonard Turns Novel into Film," *Luddington Daily News*, February 2, 2002, A4.
58. A. H. Weiler, "The Big Bounce (1969)," www.nytimes.com/movies/movie/84949/The-Big-Bounce/overview.
59. www.dvdtalk.com/dvdsavant/s1088/bounce.html.
60. Lanken, "Looking at the Movies."
61. A. H. Weiler, "The Big Bounce (1969)," *New York Times*, www.nytimes.com/movies/movie/84949/The-Big-Bounce/overview.
62. Manners, "Heflin Rationalizes Divorce."
63. Siff, *Eleanor's Rebellion*.
64. *Ibid.*
65. Manners, "Heflin Rationalizes Divorce."
66. "Van Heflin," *Adam & Eve* (Australian Film Magazine), February 9, 1946, 20–21.
67. "Van Heflin Fishes For Blue Marlin," *Schenectady Gazette*, 13, March 29, 1969.
68. John A. Blinn, "Peripatetic Angler: Ice Fishing Challenges Van Heflin," *The Victoria Advocate*, 15, June 26, 1969.
69. Beck, "Hollywood Close-Up: Maureen, Van Heflin Seem Altar-Bound."
70. Harold Heffernan, "Van Heflin Looks Back," *The Singapore Free Press*, August 10, 1954, 13.
71. Portrait of Van Heflin by Virgil Apger, Andy Warhol Collection of Photographs of Actors, Houghton Library, Harvard Theater Collection, Harvard College Library, Harvard University: oasis.lib.harvard.edu/oasis/deliver/~hou01571.
72. "Heflin's 'Airport,' boasts a starry cast," *The Age*, April 16, 1970, 24.

73. Judith Crist quoted in *Airport* review, *Halliwell's Film Guide*, (London: Guild Publishing, 1983), 15.

74. Norman Dresser, "Enjoyable 'Airport,' at Valentine," *Toledo Blade*, May 28, 1970, 18.

75. Margaret Futch, "New Films," *The News & Courier*, June 27, 1970, 16.

76. Heffernan, "Van Heflin Looks Back."

77. Dorothy Manners "Troubles Are Universal, Traveler Van Heflin Finds," *Toledo Blade*, May 17, 1970, G2.

78. Harold Heffernan, "Heflin's Death Shocks Dieters," *The Milwaukee Journal*, August 30, 1971, 23.

Epilogue

1. Russ Hunter quoted, "'Actor's Actor,' Van Heflin Dies," *Herald-Journal*, July 24, 1971, 1.

2. "What you thought of 'Charm,'" *The Straits Times*, June 17, 1951, 8.

3. Susan Shevey, *The Marilyn Scandal* (London: Sidgwick & Jackson, 1987), 233.

4. David Siff, *Eleanor's Rebellion* (New York: Alfred A. Knopf, 2000), 194.

5. "Musical Monday: Seven Sweethearts (1942)," by Jessica Pickens 1/20/2014 www.moviefanfare.com/seven-sweethearts -1942/.

6. James Mason, "A Villain Turns Hero Worshipper," *New York Times Sunday Magazine Supplement*, 1946, 20, (From archive of cuttings).

Appendix

1. "Fearless: The Truth About Stars' Pasts" *Photoplay*, 67, July 1942.

2. Tony Crawley, crawleyscastingcalls .com/index.php/component/actors/index. php?option=com_actors&Itemid=56id=13 83&letter=H

3. "MGM's Frontier Story" *The Brooklyn Daily Eagle*, 30, December 29, 1947.

4. Lew Sheaffer, "Paramount's Birthday Bill: Production News from the Studios," *The Brooklyn Daily Eagle*, 8, November 18, 1948.

5. "MGM's 'Tension'" *The Brooklyn Daily Eagle*, 18, October 19, 1948.

6. Sheilah Graham "Hollywood Flashes" Pittsburgh Post-Gazette, 13, May 11, 1949.

7. Edwin Schallert, "Notable Stellar Trio for 'Pigalle'" *Los Angeles Times*, B9, September 21, 1953.

8. Hedda Hopper, "Ava To Do Film in Africa, Paris" *The Miami News*, 7A, October 7, 1952.

9. Hedda Hopper, *Toledo Blade*, 28, February 9, 1953.

10. Edwin Schallert, "Van Heflin Would Star in 'Typee,'" *Los Angeles Times*, B7, March 19, 1956.

11. *Gunfight at the OK Corral*, Michael Coyne "Stagecoach to Tombstone: The Filmgoer's Guide to the Great Westerns Howard Hughes," www.cercles.com/review /r65/Hughes.html. *Villa Rides*, Harold V. Cohen "At Random: The Monday Wash: Van in Demand," *The Pittsburgh Post-Gazette*, 21, October 23, 1967.

12. *The Wild Bunch* Mell, Eila *Casting Might-Have-Beens: A Film-by-Film Directory of Actors Considered For Roles Given to Others* (McFarland & Co., Inc., 2005)

13. Parallax View Sam Peckinpah parallax-view.org/category/director/sam-peckinpah-directors/

14. "From Our Hollywood Reporter" *The Straits Times*, 13, October 9, 1959.

15. Sheilah Graham "No Room For Beatles At Hotel" *The Deseret News*, A11, June 23, 1964.

16. Harold V. Cohen "The Drama Desk: Addenda" *The Pittsburgh Post-Gazette*, 2, December 24, 1954.

17. Hedda Hopper "Laughton Gets Role Heflin Passed Up" *Los Angeles Times*, 20, November 26, 1960.

18. Yoggy, Gary A. *Back in the Saddle: Essays on Western Film & Television Actors* (McFarland & Co. Inc., 1998) 73.

Bibliography

Astor, Mary. *A Life on Film.* W. H. Allen, 1973.

Bacall, Lauren. *By Myself* Alfred A. Knopf, 1978.

Barris, Alex. *Hollywood's Other Men.* A. S. Bares, New Jersey, 1972.

Barrymore, Diana, and Gerold Frank. *Too Much Too Soon.* London: Frederick Muller, 1957.

Berg, A. Scott. *Kate Remembered: Katherine Hepburn a Personal Biography.* Simon & Schuster, 2003.

Bergan, Ronald. *The United Artists Story.* Octopus Books, 1986.

Bickford, Charles. *Bulls, Balls, Bicycles & Actors.* New York: P. S. Ericksson, 1965.

Botto, Louis. *At This Theater: 100 Years of Broadway Shows and Stars* New York: Applause, 2002.

Bronner, Edwin. *The Encyclopedia of American Theater 1900–75.* New York: A. S. Barnes, 1980.

Buxton, Frank, and Bill Owen. *The Big Broadcast 1920–50.* Latham, MD; London: Scarecrow Press, 2nd edition, 1997.

Callahan, Dan. *Barbara Stanwyck: The Miracle Woman.* Jackson: University of Mississippi Press, 2013.

Carter, David. *The Western.* Kamera Books, 2008.

Chandler, Charlotte. *The Real Kate: A Personal Biography of Katherine Hepburn.* J. R. Books, 2010.

Clurman, Harold. *The Fervent Years: The Group Theatre & the 1930's.* Boston: Da Capo Press, 1980.

Cook, Bruce. *Dalton Trumbo.* New York: Scribner, 1977.

Curtis, James. *Spencer Tracy.* London: Hutchinson, 2011.

Dewey, Donald. *James Stewart: A Biography.* Atlanta: Turner Publishing, 1996.

Dick, Bernard F. *Hal Wallis: Producer to the Stars.* Lexington: University of Kentucky Press, 2004.

Dickens, Homer. *The Films of Barbara Stanwyck.* New York: Citadel Press, 1987.

Dickens, Homer. *The Films of Gary Cooper.* New York: Citadel Press, 1972.

Douglas, Kirk. *The Ragman's Son: An Autobiography.* New York: Simon & Schuster, 1998.

Durgnat, Raymond. *King Vidor, American.* Berkeley: University of California Press, 1992.

Eames, John Douglas. *The MGM Story.* London: Octopus Books, 1979.

Eames, John Douglas. *The Paramount Story.* London: Octopus Books, 1985.

Eisenschits, Bernard. *Nicholas Ray: An American Journey.* Boston; London: Faber & Faber, 1993.

Epstein, Edward Z., and Joseph Morella. *Rita: The Life of Rita Hayworth.* London: W. H. Allen, 1983.

Eyman, Scott. *Lion: The Life & Legend of Louis B. Mayer.* New York: Simon & Schuster, 2005.

Fagen, Herb. *The Encyclopedia of Westerns.* New York: Facts on File, 2001.

Fane-Saunders, Kilmeny. *Radio Times Guide to Films.* London: BBC Worldwide, 2000.

Ford, Peter. *Glenn Ford: A Life.* Madison: University of Wisconsin Press, 2011.

Fricke, John. *Judy Garland: A Legendary Film Career.* Philadelphia; London: Running Press, 2010.

Fury, David A., *Maureen O'Sullivan: No*

Average Jane. Minneapolis: Artists Press, 2004.

Gevinson, Alan. *Within Our Gates: Ethnicity in American Feature Films, 1911–60*. Berkeley: University of California Press, 1997.

Giddins, Gary. *Warning Shadows*. New York: W. W. Norton, 2010.

Gottfried, Martin. *Arthur Miller: His Life and Works*. London: Faber & Faber, 2004.

Grange, William. *Channing Pollock: America's Forgotten Polemicist* in *Zeitschrift Fur Anglistik und Amerikanistik Vol. 35, No 2*. Lincoln: University of Nebraska, 1987.

Halliwell, Leslie. *Halliwell's Film Guide*, 4th Edition. London: Guild Publishing, 1983.

Halliwell, Leslie. *Halliwell's Filmgoers Companion*. New York: HarperCollins, 1983.

Hirschorn, Clive. *The Columbia Story*. London: Hamlyn, 1988.

Hirschorn, Clive. *The Universal Story*. London: Octopus Books, 1983.

Hirschorn, Clive. *The Warner Brothers Story*. London: Octopus Books, 1970.

Holtson, Kim R. *Susan Hayward: Her Life and Films*. Jefferson, NC: McFarland, 2009.

Hunter, Tab, with Eddie Muller. *Confidential: The Making of a Movie Star*. Chapel Hill: Algonquin Books, 2006.

Jacobs, Stephen. *Boris Karloff: More than a Monster*. Sheffield, UK: Tomahawk Press, 2011.

Jarlett, Franklin. *Robert Ryan: A Biography and Critical Filmography*. Jefferson, NC: McFarland, 1997.

Jewell, Richard B., and Vernon Harbin. *The RKO Story*. London: Octopus Books, 1982.

Kelly, Kittey. *His Way: The Unauthorized Biography of Frank Sinatra*. Toronto; New York: Bantam, 1987.

Keyes, Evelyn. *Scarlett O'Hara's Younger Sister*. London: W. H. Allen, 1978.

Kezich, Tullio, and Alessandra Levantest. *Dino: The Life and Films of Dino de Laurentiis*. New York: Mirimax Books, 2004.

Klevan, Andrew. *Barbara Stanwyck*. London: British Film Institute, Palgrave Macmillan, 2013.

Klinger, Barbara. *Melodrama & Meaning: History, Culture & the Films of Douglas Sirk*. Bloomington: Indiana University Press, 1994.

Le Roy, Mervyn, and Dick Kleiner. *Take One*. New York: Hawthorn Books, 1974.

Leaming, Barbara. *Katherine Hepburn*. New York: Crown, 1995.

Leaming, Barbara. *Marilyn Monroe*. New York: Crown, 1988.

Lindsay, Cynthia. *Dear Boris*. New York: Alfred A. Knopf, 1975.

Linet, Beverly. *Ladd: A Hollywood Tragedy*. London: Robson Books, 1980.

Macksoud, Meredith C. *Arthur Kennedy, Man of Characters*. Jefferson: McFarland, 2003.

Manso, Peter. *Brando: The Biography*. New York: Hyperion, 1994.

McKay, James. *Dana Andrew: The Face of Noir*. Jefferson, NC: McFarland, 2010.

Mell, Eila. *Casting Might-Have-Beens: A Film-by-Film Directory of Actors Considered for Roles Given to Others*. Jefferson, NC: McFarland, 2005.

Miller, Arthur. *Timebends*. New York: Grove Press, 1987.

Minnelli, Vincente. *I Remember it Well*. London: Angus & Robinson, 1974.

Moreno, Eduardo. *The Films of Susan Hayward*. New York: Citadel Press, 1979.

Morris, Edmund. *Dutch: A Memoir of Ronald Reagan*. New York: Random House, 1999.

Moss, Marilyn Ann. *Giant: George Stevens, a Life in Film*. Madison: University of Wisconsin Press, 2004.

Negulesco, Jean. *Things I Did and Things I Think I Did: A Hollywood Memoir*. New York: Linden Press/Simon & Schuster, 1984.

Newton, Bert. *Bert!* Toorak, Victoria: Gary Sparkes & Assoc., 1977.

Nolletti, Arthur, Jr. *The Films of Fred Zinnemann: Critical Perspectives*. State University of New York, 1999.

Oller, John. *Jean Arthur: The Actress Nobody Knew*. New York: Limelight Editions, 2004.

Owens, Andy. *Our Eric: A Portrait of Eric Portman*. Sigma Leisure, 2013.

Palmer, James, Michael Riley. *The Films of Joseph Losey*. Cambridge, UK; New York: Cambridge University Press, 1993.

Parrish, James Robert, and Ronald L. Bowers. *The MGM Stock Company: The Golden Era*. London: Ian Allan Ltd., 1973.

Quinlan, David. *The Illustrated Directory of Film Stars*. London: B. T. Batsford, 1982.

Quirk, Lawrence J. *The Films of Robert Taylor.* New York: Lyle Stuart, 1979.

Quirk, Lawrence J., and William Schoell. *Joan Crawford: The Essential Biography.* Lexington: University of Kentucky Press, 2012.

Robertson, Dr. James C. *The Casablanca Man: The Cinema of Michael Curtiz.* London: Routledge, 1994.

Rollyson, Carl. *Dana Andrews: Hollywood Enigma.* Jackson: University of Mississippi, 2012.

Sayre, Nora. *Running Time: Films of the Cold War.* New York: Dial Press, 1982.

Server, Lee. *Ava Gardner: Love is Nothing.* London: Faber & Faber, 2006.

Shearer, Stephen. *Patricia Neal: An Unquiet Life.* Lexington: University Press of Kentucky, 2013.

Shevey, Susan. *The Marilyn Scandal.* London: Sidgwick & Jackson, 1987.

Shipman, David. *Judy Garland.* New York: Fourth Estate, 1997.

Silver, Alan, and Elizabeth Ward. *Film Noir.* London: Secker & Warburg, 1980.

Silver, Alan, and James Ursin. *Film Noir.* Köln; London; Los Angeles: Taschen, 2004.

Sperber, A. M. *Bogart.* New York: William Morrow, 1997.

Spoto, Donald. *Possessed: The Life of Joan Crawford.* William Morrow, 2010.

Thomas, Bob. *Golden Boy: The Untold Story of William Holden.* London: Weidenfeld & Nicholson, 1983.

Thomas, Tony, and Aubrey Soloman. *The Films of Twentieth Century–Fox.* New York: Citadel Press, 1979.

Thomson, David. *The Big Screen: The Story of the Movies.* London: Allen Lane, 2012.

Thomson, David. *The Biographical Dictionary of Film*, Fourth Edition. New York: Little, Brown, 2003.

Tranberg, Charles. *Robert Taylor: A Biography.* Albany, GA: Bear Manor Media, 2011.

Tucker, David C. *Shirley Booth: A Biography and Career Record.* Jefferson, NC: McFarland, 2003.

Turner, Lana. *Lana: The Lady, The Legend, The Truth.* Sevenoaks, Kent: New English Library, 1982.

Valentino, Lou. *The Films of Lana Turner.* New York: Lyle Stuart, 1979.

Vanderbilt, Gloria, and Thelma, Lady Furness, *Double Exposure,* New York: David McKay, 1958.

Vinson, James, ed. *The International Dictionary of Films and Filmmakers: Actors and Actresses* New York: Macmillan, 1986.

Wagner, Geoffrey. *The Novel and Cinema.* Cranbury, NJ: Fairleigh Dickinson, 1975.

Walker, John, ed. *Halliwell's Who's Who in the Movies,* 14th edition. New York: HarperCollins Entertainment, 2011.

Wallis, Hal B. *Starmaker.* New York: Macmillan, 1980.

Wayne, Jane Ellen. *The Leading Men of MGM.* New York: Carroll & Graf, 2005.

Who Was Who in the Theatre, 1912–76, vol. 2. Detroit: Gale Group, 1978.

Wilson, Victoria. *A Life of Barbara Stanwyck: Steel-True, 1907–40.* New York: Simon & Schuster, 2013.

Winnington, Richard. *Film: Criticism & Caricatures 1943–53.* London: Paul, 1975.

Yoggi, Gary A., *Back in the Saddle: Essays on Western Film & Television Actors.* Jefferson, NC: McFarland, 1998.

Young, Jordan R. *Reel Characters.* Beverly Hills: Moonstone Press, 1986.

Index

Numbers in **bold italics** indicate pages with photographs.